Fork Handles

Fork Handles

The Bery Vest of Ronnie Barker

Volume One

Ronnie Barker

EBURY
PRESS

1 3 5 7 9 10 8 6 4 2

This edition published 2013 by Ebury Press, an imprint of Ebury Publishing
A Random House Group company
First published in the UK as part of *All I Ever Wrote: The Complete Works* by
Essential Books in 1999

Originally edited by Bob McCabe.
Photographs reproduced by permission of the BBC and Getty Images

The Random House Group Limited Reg. No. 954009

Addresses for companies within the Random House Group can be found at
www.randomhouse.co.uk

A CIP catalogue record for this book is available from the British Library

The Random House Group Limited supports the Forest Stewardship
Council® (FSC®), the leading international forest-certification organisation. Our
books carrying the FSC label are printed on FSC®-certified paper. FSC is the only
forest-certification scheme supported by the leading environmental organisations,
including Greenpeace. Our paper procurement policy can be found at
www.randomhouse.co.uk/environment

Printed and bound in Great Britain by Clays Ltd, St Ives PLC

ISBN 9780091951399

To buy books by your favourite authors and register for offers visit
www.randomhouse.co.uk

Contents

Foreword

I can remember, so clearly, the time in our lives when Ron revealed himself as such an elegant and funny writer ... such a funny writer.

We had always enjoyed the support of an amazingly varied and inspired team of lads ... they were in those days lads. It's curious that at that time we never bumped into lady authors, but that's all changed now, I'm pleased to say.

But to dear Ron. When we were doing *Frost on Sunday* – live each week from ATV Studios in Wembley – a mysterious writer appeared, via Peter Eade, Ron's then agent. Ron told me the texts had arrived at Peter's office from an unidentified gentleman, either a novelist, a playwright or a journalist, and Peter didn't even know the source, but the quality was amazing and all sorts of people were being credited with it all ... Tom Stoppard, Noel Coward even. But come the last night of recording for the series, I was honoured by a visit to my dressing room by Ronnie B ... and let into the secret that the clever rascal was – you've guessed it by now – Ronnie B. So the quality pervading all these words was not so surprising. He very kindly gave me the rights, among other things, to a lovely sketch, which I have performed in Summer Seasons, and I give him six crystal glasses, initialled not with RB but, awkwardly, GW, thereby telling the story, the story of the wonderful, inventive and gloriously funny writer, Gerald Wiley ... no, sorry ... I mean Ronnie Barker.

Ronnie Corbett
2013

Early Sketches

ONNIE BARKER ACTUALLY did his first writing for television back in the late 1950s, penning some episodes of *I'm Not Bothered*, a situation comedy starring his friend and early comedy mentor, Glenn Melvyn. Melvyn paid him £50 a go and took authorship credit himself:

"I remember the director, Henry Kendal, in his later years directed one of the shows I had written and in the bar afterwards I said, 'That went well, Mr Kendal, didn't it?' And he said, 'Bit of quality in the writing, old boy.' And I still couldn't tell him, but I was delighted with that. That was the first praise I'd had for my writing."

Receiving no on-screen credit suited Ronnie just fine. In fact it was something he was to maintain for the rest of his writing career, writing all his material under a series of assumed names, the most "famous" of which was a certain "Gerald Wiley".

"I remember going to David Frost at the end of one of the Frost shows, and it hadn't gone well, but David was always so optimistic, he said, 'What a wonderful show that was.' And I said, 'No, it was bloody dreadful, David. It was terrible, the scripts were awful.' I felt I had to say it, that we must somehow do better that this.

"So I went home and I thought people aren't writing stuff for us. And so I decided that I would write something. I had a couple of ideas and I decided I would write them and send them in under an assumed name. I spoke to my agent and he said, 'Well, you'll have to send them through me. I'll have to pretend I'm this man's agent as well.' So I picked this name, 'Gerald Wiley', because I thought most people when they have a pseudonym, they always have a glamorous name like 'Rock Armstrong' or something wonderful. So I picked a really ugly name that no one would dream of picking as their pseudonym. 'Gerald Wiley' – that's a really ugly name. Then I said, 'Supposing they want to see me?' And my agent said, 'I'll tell them you're a bit of a recluse, an older man I'll say, but you've seen the shows and thought you might try your hand.' So in came the scripts and the producer said, 'I've got two new scripts in from another writer, must be something to do with

David I suppose, a man named Wiley.' And we laughed, and I laughed, and we sat and read the scripts and he said, 'What do you think?' And Ronnie C said, 'Well, they're not bad. I think we ought to try them.' So we tried them. And I was very pleased, secretly. And for the next three weeks we did sketches by Gerald Wiley, as well as other sketches."

Only at the end of the series (after several more sketches had been accepted and, in fairness, some rejected) did Ronnie reveal himself as Wiley, at which point speculation was running wild, with everyone from Alan Ayckbourn to Frank Muir to Tom Stoppard being mooted as the potential author.

Wiley lived on as the staff writer for *The Two Ronnies*, although Barker continued to employ a number of other pseudonyms – the important thing for Ronnie being that the public was never aware that he was the writer.

Many of the pieces Wiley wrote for *Frost on Sunday* are collected in the following chapter. There are also some early radio sketches from *Variety Playhouse* and the like, and some from Ronnie's 1971 radio series, *Lines from My Grandfather's Forehead*.

(It should be noted that for the majority of his writing career Ronnie knew very clearly who he was writing for. Consequently character names in his scripts were substituted for "RC" and "RB" – obviously for Ronnies Corbett and Barker. The Editor has maintained the use of these initials here as they invariably provide a shorthand to characterisation in all these pieces.)

We begin, however, not with a sketch, but with a poem (itself attributed to Jonathan Cobbold, later the "author" of the *His Lordship Entertains* series) which, in its simple evocation of lost innocence and days gone by, speaks volumes about the work contained in this volume:

LITTLE FISH

Three boys were standing in the village stream:

> The old man bellowed "Oi! Come out o' there!
> You'll cut your feet to ribbons on them stones.
> They're poisonous, them weeds – or don't you care?
> Look well if you got stuck in that there mud

And someone had to come and get you free!
The water's full of tins, and broken glass."

The boys looked up, and rubbed a muddy knee
With a wet hand – but stayed there, in the stream.
The old man glared, but saw it was in vain;
And muttering "You'll catch your death of cold"
Stumped off; and wished he was a boy again.

LAW

(The Frost Report)

A court room.

A man (John Cleese) in the dock with a policeman standing at the side of him. The man appears slightly taller than the policeman. The judge on the bench, the counsel for the prosecution and the defence counsel (a lady) are all in evidence.

JUDGE: Arthur James Peterson, you are charged with being too tall in Arkwright Street on the morning of the sixteenth of May of this year. How do you plead?

PETERSON: Not guilty, your honour.

JUDGE: Mr Wigg?

WIGG (*Prosecutor*): How old are you, Mr Peterson?

PETERSON: Thirty-four.

WIGG: That's a little old to be doing this sort of thing, isn't it? Most people give up that sort of thing when they reach the age of twenty-one. Why do you persist in it?

PETERSON: I don't know what you mean – I've been this height since I was eighteen.

WIGG: Oh. So you've been getting away with it for sixteen years. Have you any previous convictions for this offence, Mr Peterson?

DEFENCE COUNSEL: Objection!

WIGG: Very well, I'll put it another way. Have you ever seen inside a prison?

PETERSON: No.

WIGG: Not even by looking over the wall?

PETERSON: Certainly not.

WIGG: Is it not possible to have entered a prison by walking under the crack in the door?

PETERSON: No.

WIGG: Why not?

PETERSON: I'm too tall.

WIGG: Thank you, Mr Peterson. Call Bernard Botley!

(Bernard Botley enters the witness box.)

WIGG: Now, Mr Botley, tell us what happened in your own words.

BOTLEY: I was walking along Arkwright Street on the sixteenth of May when I saw a man being much too tall outside the tobacconists. I went up to him and asked him what he meant by it, and he tried to cover it up by kneeling down and pretending to be a pavement artist.

WIGG: And what did you do?

BOTLEY: I put threepence in his cap. Well, he was bigger than me.

WIGG: Thank you, Mr Botley. That is the case for the prosecution.

JUDGE: I wish to discuss a point of law with "Prosecution", so there will therefore be a ten-minute recess. The accused will remain where he is.

PETERSON: Excuse me, your honour.

JUDGE: Well?

PETERSON: I wonder if I might sit down, I feel rather faint.

JUDGE: But I ordered a chair to be brought to you earlier on!

PETERSON: I know.

JUDGE: Well, what have you done with it?

PETERSON: I'm standing on it.

JUDGE: Case dismissed!

DOCTOR'S WAITING ROOM

(Frost on Sunday – first piece written and submitted by Gerald Wiley)

A doctor's waiting room in Harley Street. Eight or nine well-dressed patients are waiting, reading old copies of The Tatler and The Field. One has a bandaged foot, another an eye patch, another, a cough. Ronnie Corbett enters – a very well-cut suit, gloves and spats, and carries a newspaper (the Telegraph).

RC: Good morning! *(No response from anyone.)* I said, good morning.

(No response.) Oh, so nobody's speaking, eh? Isn't it amazing!

(He sits next to Ronnie Barker, who is a very smart, moustachioed military type of some sixty years.)

RC: Isn't it extraordinary how no one ever talks to each other in a doctor's waiting room? *(No response from Barker.)* Odd, isn't it? *(No response.)* No, of course it's not odd. *(Answering himself)* Oh, I thought it was. Well, it's not, so keep quiet. Sorry. Don't mention it.

(A pause. RC picks up the newspaper.)

RC: I see they are stopping all the tube trains tomorrow.

(There is a slight shuffling and a lowering of magazines from the patients.)

RC: To let the people get on and off.

(He smiles, encouragingly. The patients, without a flicker, return to their magazines.)

RC: *(standing up)* Simple Simon met a pie-man,
  Going to the fair.
  Said Simple Simon to the pie-man,
  Pray, what have you there?
  Said the Pie-man to Simple Simon,
  Pies, you fool.

(No response. RC sits down – then stands up again, singing, quite charmingly)

  Night and Day, you are the one –
  Only you beneath the moon and under the sun,

(He moves round the room, a sort of soft-shoe shuffle as he sings in strict tempo.)

  In the roaring traffic's boom,
  In the silence of my lonely room,
  I think of you – Night and Day –

(He begins to tap-dance, very fast.)

  Day and Night, under the hide of me,
  There's oh, such a hungry, yearning burning inside of me.
  Whether near to me or far,
  It's no matter darling where you are, I dream of you,
  Night and Day!

(He finishes the tap-dance. The patients are now staring at him. He sits.)

Well, I've done my best. I can't think of anything else.

(A pause. Ronnie Barker stands up.)

RB: John has great big water-proof boots on
  John has a great big water-proof hat
  John has a great big water-proof mackintosh.
  And that, says John, is that.

A A Milne.

(A maiden lady of forty claps politely. She is joined by two or three other patients.)

RC: Ah, that's more like it. Anyone else know anything?

(The maiden lady stands up. She begins to sing sweetly.)

LADY: If you were the only boy in the world, and I was the only girl
   Nothing else would matter in the world today
   We could go on loving in the same old way.

LADY & RC: A garden of Eden, just made for two
   With nothing to mar our joy–

LADY, RC & RB: I would say such wonderful things to you.

ALMOST EVERYONE: There would be such wonderful things to do.

ALL: If you were the only girl in the world,
   And I was the only boy!

(Everyone bursts into applause – by now they are all on their feet)

RC: Wonderful, wonderful! Right! Everybody conga!

(Singing)

   Aye, aye Conga!
   Aye, aye Conga!

(They all form into a conga line, kicking their legs, etc.)

ALL: I came I saw I conga-ed
   I came I saw I conga-ed.
   La La La Laa
   La La La Laa

(They are all going round the waiting room in a line)

RC: Come on everyone, back to my place!

(Still conga-ing, they go out of the door. A pause. The door to the doctor's room opens and a nurse enters. She speaks to the doctor inside)

NURSE: Doctor, there's no one here!

(The doctor appears round the door.)

DOCTOR: Ah, I thought as much. That bloody little Doctor Corbett has been here again and pinched all my private patients!

YOU ARE WHAT YOU EAT

(Frost on Sunday)

A restaurant, smartish, at lunch time. RB, the waiter, is seating RC, the customer.

RC: Thank you. Sorry to barge in without booking. I know it's frowned upon by the management, but I thought I'd just dodge in and sort of merge in with the background, and he might not notice.

RB: That's alright, sir. Would you like a drink, sir?

RC: Yes. I'll have a ...

RB: Gin, sir – tonic?

RC: How did you know I wanted gin?

RB: Your subconscious sir – you've already said it three times since you came in.

RC: Have I?

RB: Yessir – bar*ge in*, dod*ge in*, and mer*ge in*. Oh yes – I always know what people want – it's the same with food as well – people behave like what they eat, you know. You can tell by what they say, what they'll order.

RC: How interesting. Speaking as one who knows absolutely nothing about such things, I would hazard a guess that you're talking a load of absolute cods-roe, old chap.

RB: Not at all, sir.

RC: Pure unadulterated cabbage-water. Alright, what about this chap – what's *his* favourite meat?

PERKINS: *(Passing by.)* Shan't be a minute, waiter – just getting some cigarettes from the Baaar.

RB: From the where, sir?

PERKINS: From the Baaar.

(He goes)

RB: *(To RC)* Lamb.

WARBECK: *(Approaching.)* Waiter – could I have my bill – bit late. Got to make a mooove.

RB: A what, sir?

WARBECK: A mooove. When you've got to mooove, you've got to mooove.

RB: Yes, sir – you had the beef, sir, right? *(Gives bill to Warbeck.)*

WARBECK: Thank you.

RC: Very clever! What about him over there? *(Indicates man on open wall phone near bar.)*

PHONE MAN: Quite, quite, quite, quite, quite. *(He quacks these in a northern accent.)*

RB: Duck. Oh yes, they're all at it. Listen to her over there.

(Cut to woman. Another woman is whispering in her ear.)

MRS BROWN: Oh dear. Dear, dear. Oh, dear, dear, dear.

RB: Venison. Listen to him over there.

(Cut to George and David at table.)

GEORGE: I just cleared off for the weekend – just stuffed everything into the banger.

RB: Sausages.

DAVID: I wish I could, but I daren't – I'm too scared of her – I'm terrified, I just daren't.

RC: What about him?

RB: He's chicken.

(Cut to a German, with a girl.)

GERMAN: Oh ja, I have lived in Hamburg most of my life. I love Hamburg. It's my home.

RC: I suppose he's a Hamburger.

RB: No, Beef Stroganoff.

RC: He didn't *mention* Beef Stroganoff.

RB: I know, but it's all down the front of his tie.

MR FOX: *(talking to another man)* Oh, she was fabulous, I mean, she had big round, you know, and this low-cut dress made them, you know, and I mean she's just got absolutely wonderful, I mean, you know.

RC: And what's *his* favourite food?

RB: Dumplings.

RC: This is all absolute rubbish. Now, come on then, listen to this, and then tell me what I'm going to have.

"Oh, I must go down to the sea again,
To the lonely sea and the sky –
And all I need is a tall ship
And a star to steer her by."

… and don't say fish and chips.

RB: You're going to eat chicken liver pâté, followed by lamb chop, cauliflower and new potatoes, trifle and cream and coffee.

RC: What? How can you *possibly* know that?

RB: That's all we got left.

IMPERSONATOR SKETCH

(Frost on Sunday)

RC is at a restaurant table, being seated by the head waiter. RC is expensively and somewhat flashily dressed.

HEAD WAITER: There we are, Mr Pigeon. I'll get someone to take your order right away, sir.

RC: Thank you, Alfred. *(He speaks rather better than one would expect from his clothes.)*

HEAD WAITER: Incidentally, sir, may I say how much the wife and I enjoyed your last TV show. We didn't stop laughing all evening, thinking about it. By the time we got to bed we were helpless.

RC: Oh – not *too* helpless, I hope!

HEAD WAITER: Er, no, we – *(Then seeing the joke)* Ah, you're too quick for me, sir. I'll get Luigi to take your order now, sir.

(He goes.)

(Ronnie Barker comes and sits at RC's table.)

RC: Good morning.

RB: *(with the same inflection)* Good morning.

(Luigi, the waiter, arrives to take the order.)

RC: Ah!

RB: Ah!

(The waiter gives them each a menu.)

RC: Good morning, Luigi!

RB: Good morning, Luigi!

(Luigi stares at RB, who is obviously a stranger to him.)

RC: *(looking at menu)* Well, now ...

RB: *(ditto)* Well, now ...

RC: I think a fillet steak, very rare, you know, barely singed – er *(drums fingers on table)* and a coleslaw salad on the slide. *(He laughs)* Difficult to say that, isn't it? A coleslaw salad on the side. And have you any lobster pâté?

LUIGI: Yes, sir.

RC: Fine – lobster pâté to start with.

LUIGI: *(To RB)* And for you, sir?

RB: I think a fillet steak, very rare, you know, barely singed – er *(drums fingers on table)* and a coleslaw salad on the slide. *(He laughs)* Difficult to say that, isn't it? A coleslaw salad on the *side*. And have you any lobster pâté?

LUIGI: Yes, sir.

RB: Fine – lobster pâté to start with.

(RC stares at RB as the waiter goes. RC lights a cigarette – so does RB. RC takes off his glasses, and sucks at the side piece – so does RB. RC starts to put them on again – so does RB. RC stops – so does RB. Finally, RC settles them on his nose again – so does RB.)

RC: *(clearing his throat)* A-hem!

RB: *(ditto)* A-hem!

RC: *(rather desperate now)* Waiter!

RB: Waiter!

(The waiter arrives.)

RC: Could I have some water?

RB: Could I have some water?

(The waiter goes.)

RC: *(To RB)* It is rather warm, isn't it?

RB: *(To RC)* It *is* rather warm, isn't it?

RC: Nice place, this.

RB: Nice place, this.

RC: Yes.

RB: Yes.

RC: I'm in show business.

RB: I'm in show business.

RC: What do you *do?*

RB: What do you *do?*

RC: I'm a comedian.

RB: I'm an impersonator.

FIND THE LADY

(Frost on Sunday)

A fairly seedy bedroom. Enter RC dressed in top hat and opera cloak with red lining. He dumps a suitcase on the bed.

RC: Come on in, darlin'.

Enter a popsie – a showgirl or dancer, wearing a PVC raincoat.

GIRL: Is it alright?

RC: 'Course it's alright. I told you, the wife's staying at her mother's. By the time she comes back on Tuesday, we'll be at the Theatre Royal, Huddersfield.

GIRL: I wouldn't like anything to happen, Marvo.

RC: Oh, wouldn't you – well, you've come to the wrong place then, darling – it's all going to happen here in the next twenty-four hours, eh? *(He grabs her)* Come here, let's have a look at you.

GIRL: *(soppily)* Oh, I do love you, Marvo!

RC: Look, don't keep calling me Marvo, darling – that's just for the act, isn't it? I'm not a magician when I'm with you. I'm pretty sensational, but I'm not a magician.

GIRL: I think you're wonderful.

RC: Yes, well never mind that, you get your coat off and that, and I'll get us a drink.

(They disentangle themselves and the girl exits. RC goes to bedside cupboard and gets out bottle of gin and two tumblers. He pours out two drinks, gets out a bottle of tonic, opens it on the side of the table, and puts some into the glasses. He then takes off his cloak and top hat, and drapes them over a chair. The girl enters, wearing a shortie nightie with a short negligée over it.)

RC: (looking up) Blimey, that was quick!

GIRL: *(giggling)* I'm used to quick changes!

RC: Yes, well hop into bed and have a nice drop of gin.

(She takes off negligée and gets into bed. There is a door slam off-stage. Panic from both of them.)

RC: Oh gawd!

GIRL: What is it?

RC: The wife – quick.

GIRL: (leaping out of bed) You said she was with her mother!

RC: Get in there! *(indicating built-in wardrobe)* Her mother's probably died or something. Trust her to spoil the weekend. *(He bundles her into the wardrobe, shuts the door and just has time to sit on the bed, when in walks the wife.)*

RC: Hello, dear.

WIFE: Hello, Johnnie.

RC: I thought you were at your mother's.

WIFE: She's not feeling well.

RC: Oh good.

WIFE: What?

RC: I meant good 'cos you've come home.

WIFE: (*sniffing the air*) What's that perfume?

RC: Which perfume is that, dear?

WIFE: The perfume I can smell.

RC: Oh. Oh that perfume would be on the carnation in my button-hole. Smell it.

(*Wife does so – it squirts water at her.*)

WIFE: Oh, for heaven's sake, don't mess about, Johnnie. Stupid jokes – (*She sees two gin glasses.*) What are these two glasses here?

RC: (*quickly picking them up*) Oh, I was just practising a trick, dear – see? (*He pours one into the other and the liquid changes colour.*) Rather good, isn't it?

WIFE: I suppose so.

(*She turns away to remove her coat, and as she does so RC notices the girl's negligée on the floor. He quickly stuffs it down his trousers.*)

RC: (*As the wife goes to hang up her coat up in the wardrobe*) No, I'll do that for you, dear. (*Takes coat and stands with it for a moment, then puts it on top of his own on the chair*) I'll hang it up in a minute. No point in hanging it up just yet. You go and make some tea and when you've gone I can while away my time hanging up your coat.

WIFE: You're being very strange. (*Sees bulge in trousers*) What's that bulge in your trousers?

RC: Where? Oh that's another trick. (*He begins to pull out yards and yards of silk flags from his trousers. They go on for ever.*)

WIFE: You're up to something, Johnnie. (*She goes to him and discovers the negligée. Holds it up.*) You've got a woman here! (*She looks under the bed.*)

RC: 'Course I haven't – I use this in the act –

WIFE: You've got a woman here. *(Starts to go to wardrobe.)*

RC: *(grabbing gun from suitcase)* Keep away from that wardrobe.

WIFE: Don't point that stupid toy gun at me!

RC: Alright – I warned you!

(As the wife opens the wardrobe door, RC fires the cap pistol into the air, and a flock of pigeons fly out of the empty wardrobe.)

THREE CLASSES: LEISURE

(Frost on Sunday)

A: I am upper class.

B: I am middle class.

C: That doesn't leave me much of a choice.

A: I work hard all day and at night I live life to the full.

B: I work hard all day and at night I like to relax.

C: I work hard all day and at night I'm clapped out.

A: Leisure, to me, is nature's safety valve, releasing the pressures caused by the strains of modern living.

B: Leisure, to me, is forgetting about work, and doing as I like.

C: Leisure, to me, is getting me boots off.

A: I employ my leisure time as usefully as possible, dividing it between exercise, relaxation and informative reading.

B: I play a bit of golf, enjoy a night out with the boys, and occasionally take the wife shopping.

C: I watch the telly.

A: I find the best way of unwinding, after a very full week, is to play squash.

B: My way of switching off is to have one over the eight on a Friday night.

C: I never switch off. I watch everything.

A: My wife and I have the choice of flying to Paris for the weekend, entertaining friends at our country house – or riding to hounds.

B: My wife and I have three choices: eating too much, drinking too much or going to bed early.

C: My wife and I have two choices – BBC or ITV.

B: Three different attitudes to leisure; but is it, after all, the universal cure for the stresses we have to undergo?

A: My worry is that increased leisure-time will bring with it boredom and apathy.

B: My worry is that by the time it comes I shall be too old to enjoy it.

C: My worry is – what's going to happen when me tube goes?

THREE CLASSES: WORK

(Frost on Sunday)

A: I am managing director of a company with a very large export commitment.

B: I work for a hardware firm with a very large annual turnover.

C: I work for the public health department with a very large shovel.

A: I start work at 9.30 and finish when I have completed my day's schedule.

B: I start work at 9 o'clock and finish when the hooter goes.

C: I start work at 8.30 and finish when it gets too dark to see what I'm shovelling.

A: I work in a large suite of centrally heated air-conditioned offices in the West End.

B: I work in a converted warehouse in Camden Town.

C: I work in the fresh air, but only when the wind's in the right direction.

A: Although I am managing director, I must always be on my guard against a younger, ambitious man usurping my position in the organisation.

B: I, too, have to be on the look out, in case anyone's after my job.

C: I have to tread very carefully, an' all.

A: Not counting entertainment and out-of-pocket expenses, I receive an annual increment of twelve thousand pounds a year.

B: I receive an annual increment of two thousand eight hundred pounds a year.

C: I don't have anything to do with increments. Quite the reverse.

B: We all serve the community in our different ways; but at the end of the day, have we any doubts as to the value of our contribution to society?

A: No one is more conscious than I am of the need to work together for the common good.

B: No one can deny that I genuinely try to pull my weight.

C: No one will sit next to me on the bus.

THREE CLASSES: FAMILY LIFE

(Frost on Sunday)

INTRODUCTION: We have been researching, once again, into the upper, middle and lower classes, with regard to various aspects of modern living in Britain. Tonight we have representatives of the three classes in the studio to report on "family life".

A: I have three children: Jeremy, Alison and Jane. My wife and I have been married for eight years.

B: I have two children: Derek and Doreen. My wife and I have been married for six years.

C: I have eight children: Peter, Rita, Anita, Sandra, Dawn, Clint, Rock and Elvis. My wife and I are not married.

A: My wife is on several committees, runs the local opera group and is secretary of the bridge club.

B: My wife is a member of the Mothers' Union, enjoys organising coffee mornings and is a driver for Meals on Wheels.

C: My wife is pregnant again.

A: We give dinner parties two or three times a week – this enables us to keep in touch with our wide circle of friends.

B: We give a wine and cheese do once a month – this enables us to do it on the cheap.

C: Her mother comes round Saturday nights. This enables me to clear off round the pub.

A: We stopped having children when we decided we had the ideal-sized family unit.

B: We stopped having children when the school meals went up.

C: We stopped having children when we found out what was causing it.

A: We employ a housekeeper, a chauffeur, a gardener and a cleaning woman.

B: My wife has a woman who comes in three times a week and a babysitter in the evenings.

C: My wife has a babysitter, a cook, someone to clean the house at weekends and a washer-up. And I'm bleedin' exhausted.

B: Three family units, each of a different class. But are our opinions of family life really so different?

A: It's my opinion that family life, on the whole, is the anchor and cornerstone of our present civilisation.

B: It's my opinion that family life, on the whole, is the most economical way of living.

C: It's my opinion that the sooner I get out of this hole, the better.

ANTIQUE SHOP

(Frost on Sunday)

An antique shop. RC is seated in a Victorian chair. RB enters the shop.

RB: Good morning.

RC: Good morning, sir.

RB: Er – do you have a rather nice coffee table? I want to give someone a present, and I thought a coffee table.

RC: Coffee table. Now, let's have a look. *(He looks round)* That's a nice one, sir. *(Going over to a Victorian oval table)* How about that one, sir?

RB: *(looking at it)* Yes, that's awfully sweet. She'd like that.

RC: I take it it's for a lady, sir?

RB: Yes.

RC: I thought as much. Yes, that's a beauty, that one.

RB: How much would that one be?

RC: That one is three shillings, sir.

RB: Three shillings?

RC: Well, half-a-crown, then.

RB: *(mystified)* Oh, well I'll have that. Oh, and *(catching sight of a rather dainty chair)* that little chair is rather nice. That would go with it rather nicely.

RC: Oh, it would, sir. That's a Ming.

RB: Ming? That chair's a Ming?

RC: That's right, sir.

RB: How much?

RC: One and nine.

RB: Oh, right, I'll have it. *(RC writes on a notepad.)* Er – what else have you got?

RC: I beg your pardon?

RB: I mean, what else have you got that I might like?

RC: Well, it depends what you're looking for, sir.

RB: Oh, anything. You know, anything that might suit me – anything at all.

RC: Well now, let's see. That's nice. *(He picks up a Staffordshire.)*

RB: Oh, yes! How much?

RC: Threepence.

RB: (*excited*) I'll have it! Now then, what else – that paperweight?

RC: Ah, that's beautiful. That is actually prehistoric. Made by French craftsmen in the 18th century, when London was all fields.

RB: And what will you take for that?

RC: I'm prepared to accept tenpence for that, sir.

RB: Done. That grandfather clock?

RC: Ah, now you're going into money with that, sir.

RB: Never mind – how much is it?

RC: Seven and eleven.

RB: Right! These silver spoons? (*in a frenzy by now*)

RC: Ninepence a dozen.

RB: Right! This pair of oil lamps?

RC: A shilling.

RB: This plate?

RC: Four thousand pounds!

RB: Right. No! Four thousand?

RC: Yes, sir – that's new stock.

RB: Oh, well I won't have that then.

RC: No, sir.

RB: Well, what else –

RC: I think you've bought enough, sir.

RB: Oh, no, I've got plenty of room at home.

RC: I would rather not sell you anything more, sir.

RB: What? Oh. Yes. Well, perhaps so. Mustn't be greedy.

RC: No, sir. I've got the list here (*Refers to the list he has been writing.*) Let's see – coffee table, chair, Staffordshire figure, paperweight, Grandfather clock, silver spoons and the two oil lamps. That comes to (*a quick addition*) fifteen shillings altogether, sir.

RB: (*fumbles in his pocket*) Here you are. Fifteen shillings.

RC: Thank you, sir. Now, where would you like these delivered to?

RB: Oh. Er – my card. *(Hands him a visiting card)*

RC: Esher. That will be alright, sir. Some time on Monday?

RB: Er – yes, fine.

RC: Right. Thank you, sir. Good day.

RB: Good day. And thank you.

RC: Thank you, sir.

(RB leaves the shop. RC sits down in the chair. A man appears through the door to the back of the shop.)

MAN: There we are, Mr Hibberd. Sorry I took so long to find it. I'm in a terrible muddle at the moment in there. *(He hands RC a wrist-watch.)* It just needed cleaning again.

RC: Thank you. How much do I owe you?

MAN: Same as usual, sir, fifteen shillings.

RC: Oh yes. *(Hands him the fifteen shillings)* It's always fifteen shillings, isn't it?

PARTY POOPER

(Frost on Sunday)

SHE: George!

HE: Yes, Margaret?

SHE: I found this in your coat pocket last night.

HE: What, dear?

SHE: *(showing him)* This picture of a girl with nothing on but a pair of knee-length boots.

HE: Good heavens! Penelope!

SHE: What!

HE: I mean. Good heavens, Penelope, how could that have got there?

SHE: Why did you call me Penelope?

HE: Isn't that your name, Margaret? Your middle name?

SHE: No.

HE: No, of course not. I called you Penelope because I thought I'd call you Penelope. I thought I'd start calling you Penelope. For short.

SHE: Penelope is one syllable longer than Margaret.

HE: Well, it's not much, is it? One measly syllable. I don't know what all the fuss is about.

SHE: You know her, don't you?

HE: Who?

SHE: Penelope.

HE: Never heard of her. I've never seen her before. There's nothing about her that I recognise. She's a complete stranger to me. I'll have a word with her husband about this.

SHE: Oh, you know her husband, do you?

HE: Er – vaguely, yes. By sight. Not to speak to.

SHE: If you've never seen her, how do you know she's his wife?

HE: He told me. When he slipped her into my pocket.

SHE: I thought you said you'd never spoken to him.

HE: I haven't. When he said that it was his wife, I didn't reply.

SHE: Why not?

HE: I had my mouth full.

SHE: Of what?

HE: Christmas pudding.

SHE: Ah, now we're getting somewhere. Christmas pudding. Yesterday?

HE: Yes.

HE & SHE: The office party.

HE: Yes. I was just sitting there, minding my own Christmas pudding, and he slipped her into my inside pocket, with the words, "That's my wife". And then they both went out of the office.

SHE: I thought you said you'd never seen her before?

HE: Well, she had her back to me.

SHE: With no clothes on?

HE: Certainly not. She was fully clothed as always.

SHE: She's not fully clothed here.

HE: No – well, she's got to take them off sometime.

SHE: But not, I would have thought, perched on your desk at the office party.

HE: That's not my desk.

SHE: Oh yes it is. There's the blotter and the desk pen Mummy gave you for your birthday.

HE: Trust her.

SHE: What?

HE: Trust her to pick a lovely blotter and desk pen like that. Wonderful taste, your mother.

SHE: Look, are you going to own up about all this?

HE: Yes.

SHE: What?

HE: Yes. Her name is Penelope Vickers, and she works in the office, and she had her photograph taken sitting on my desk. At the office party, yesterday. And we all had a good laugh, and I bought a copy for three and six. And that's it. What are you going to do about it?

SHE: Have you got her 'phone number?

HE: Yes.

SHE: I'm going to ring her up.

HE: Whatever for?

SHE: I want to find out where she got those super knee-length boots.

A WEDDING SERVICE

(Frost on Sunday)

The bridegroom waits. The Wedding March is playing as the bride approaches on the arm of her father, followed by little girl bridesmaids. The vicar stands facing them. The bride arrives, the music stops and she lifts her veil, eyes downcast.

VICAR: Dearly beloved, we are gathered here, in the face of this congregation, to join together this man and this woman ...

MAN: *(staring at woman, then addressing vicar in whisper)* Er ... Excuse me ...

VICAR: *(whispering)* What's the matter?

MAN: This isn't the one.

VICAR: Which one?

MAN: This one isn't. She's not the one I'm marrying.

VICAR: Not the one you're marrying?

MAN: No. *(To girl)* Are you? I've never seen her before. Have I?

GIRL: *(shaking head nervously)* No.

VICAR: Are you sure?

MAN: 'Course I'm sure.

GIRL: Oh dear, everyone's looking at us.

VICAR: Well – what's gone wrong?

GIRL: Could you carry on with the service? Everyone's listening.

VICAR: Well, I can hardly ...

MAN: Yes, look, carry on for a minute while we have a think.

VICAR: Oh, alright ... which estate is not by any to be enterprised, not taken in hand, inadvisedly, lightly, or wantonly; but reverently, discreetly, advisedly and soberly – duly considering the causes for which matrimony was ordained *(This is spoken under the following dialogue)* etc. etc.

GIRL: What are we going to do?

MAN: Well, it's obvious. We've got to stop it, haven't we? I mean ...

GIRL: Oh, I can't. I can't. I've waited for months for this moment. I've been working up to it.

MAN: Well, so have I. I mean – well, we both have, but we've been working up to it with different people, haven't we?

GIRL: Yes, but my mum will go mad if we cancel it – she's got all the sandwiches and sausage rolls ready and everything – and she's doing little things in vol-au-vent cases as well.

MAN: Yes, but marriage is not just a question of little things in vol-au-vent cases, is it?

GIRL: She sat up all night in an armchair so she wouldn't spoil her new hair-do.

MAN: But I don't know anything about you. I mean, I don't know what you're like.

GIRL: How do you mean?

MAN: Well, what you're – like. You know, what you're like.

GIRL: What I'm like?

MAN: Well, I can't put it any plainer in front of the vicar, can I? What you're like.

GIRL: Oh – well, I haven't had any complaints up to now. Anyway, I don't know what you're like, do I?

MAN: Well, I'm just like anybody else, aren't I?

GIRL: You're very little.

MAN: I'm not little. It's you that's big.

VICAR: *(who has come to the end of his words)* Er – have you decided anything yet? Because I've come to the part where the whole thing tends to become a tiny bit irrevocable.

GIRL: Oh – it's just that we don't know whether we are suited. It's a question of size.

VICAR: May I remind you both that a marriage partner is usually taken on account of their quality, not quantity.

MAN: Well, you'll have to give us another minute somehow.

VICAR: Tell you what – I'll give them a hymn to be going on with. *(Aloud)* The congregation will now sing hymn number 798: "A Stranger Is Amongst Us, O Shall We Let Him In".

(The congregation start to sing.)

GIRL: Look – I don't mind short men.

MAN: Really? Matter of fact, I love tall girls.

GIRL: Do you? I'm not really tall, you know.

MAN: You are to me.

GIRL: Yes. *(A pause)* What do you think then? Shall we make a go of it?

MAN: Where would we live?

GIRL: Oh, my dad's bought me a new bungalow.

MAN: Oh, well, that settles it, you're on. *(To vicar)* OK, Reverend, you can carry on.

VICAR: Ah. *(Sings)* We'll just wait until the hymn finishes.

MAN: Oh, alright then.

GIRL: *(After a pause)* We have met before, actually.

MAN: Have we?

GIRL: Do you remember Bobby Upton's party the Christmas before last, and we all played sardines?

MAN: Were you there?

GIRL: Yeah. You crawled under the bed I was hiding under. We were the last to be found.

MAN: Good Lord, I didn't recognise you.

GIRL: Ah, well, I had my hair dark then. And I was lying on my stomach.

MAN: *(remembering)* Oh yes! Was that you?

GIRL: Yeah.

MAN: Oh good. *(He looks pleased – the hymn finishes.)* I knew you before that, and all. At school.

GIRL: Go on! Were you at the same school?

MAN: We were in the same class.

VICAR: *(declaring)* Do you, er?

MAN: Robin Cyril.

VICAR: Robin Cyril.

GIRL: Robin Bates!

VICAR: Do you, Robin Bates …

MAN: Robin Cyril.

VICAR: Robin Cyril, take …

GIRL: Old Mother Thompson!

VICAR: Take Old Mother Thompson.

GIRL: Mavis Jean.

VICAR: Take Mavis Jean to be your lawful wedded wife – to have and to hold *(etc. under dialogue.)*

MAN: I always swore I'd marry you – ever since I was nine. I never thought it would turn out like this. *(In response to the vicar)* I do.

VICAR: And do you, Mavis Jean, take Robin Cyril *(etc.)*

MAN: Here – what about the bloke you were supposed to marry?

GIRL: Oh – I never liked him much. Anyway, he was only marrying me out of sympathy, really. *(To vicar)* I do.

VICAR: For as much as Robin Cyril and Mavis Jean have consented together *(etc.)*

MAN: What do you mean, sympathy?

GIRL: Well, he took advantage of me.

MAN: Oh. Oh well, that can't be helped – doesn't mean to say you've got to marry him, does it?

GIRL: Well, I thought it only right – I mean …

VICAR: I pronounce that they be man and wife together.

GIRL: *(indicating six bridesmaids)* I've got to give this lot a father, haven't I?

(The man faints flat on his back.)

POISONING

(Frost on Sunday)

An office at the London County Council. RC is at a desk; enter RB.

RB: Good afternoon.

RC: Good afternoon.

RB: Er – I want to enrol for one of your night classes.

RC: Certainly. What sort of course are you interested in?

RB: Poisoning.

RC: Pardon?

RB: Poisoning. I want to learn how to poison things.

RC: Ah. Well, I don't think we have any poisoning classes at the moment.

RB: Well, chemistry then.

RC: Chemistry?

RB: Yes, chemistry, with access to the poison cupboard.

RC: Oh, I see. No, I don't think our chemistry course gets as far as the poison cupboard. Look, how about something else? How about metal-work?

RB: Would that include knife-sharpening?

RC: It might. It might well.

RB: And axe-grinding?

RC: Well, not really. I think, if I were you, I would keep away from that sort of thing.

RB: Why?

RC: Well, it's not normal.

RB: I'm perfectly normal. I'm a normal human being who simply wants to learn how to sharpen an old meat axe until its cutting edge is like a razor, the blade glinting in the sunlight, as I bring it down swiftly on – on whatever I bring it down on.

RC: *(desperately)* First Aid?

RB: What?

RC: First Aid's nice.

RB: Yes – how to remove blood stains from clothing.

RC: No, perhaps not. Knots and hitches?

RB: Slip-knots?

RC: No! Needlework?

RB: Hypodermic needle work?

RC: No, no! Learning an instrument?

RB: A blunt instrument?

RC: Now look here! Why do you want to learn all these dreadful things?

RB: I'm writing a book on it.

RC: A book?

RB: Yes, it's called "How to murder the woman at 49 Ashley Gardens, and other stories".

RC: 49 Ashley Gardens?

RB: Yes, do you know it?

RC: I – er – know the road.

RB: Well I live at 49 – and my wife is being unfaithful. A little chap, with glasses.

RC: Really! *(RC takes off glasses and stands on a stool)* And what's that to do with me?

RB: Absolutely nothing. I just want to write a book on it. And you're the man who can tell me about night classes.

RC: *(Relieved)* Oh, so I am. Yes, I was forgetting who I was for the moment. I'm simply the man who tells people about classes.

RB: Yes.

RC: Yes. And my private life is my own affair.

RB: Exactly. But my wife's affairs are far from private. Her affairs are completely public. She's ultra-friendly.

RC: What?

RB: Every man in the road.

RC: What?

RB: And two in the avenue. And four in the crescent.

RC: I don't believe it! *(Furious)* The rotten, skinny, ginger-haired little tart!

RB: An accurate description.

RC: Right! Right! Look, sir. I suggest you go away for the weekend – Brighton; somewhere bracing.

RB: Do you think so?

RC: Definitely. And who knows, when you come back on Monday you may have something to write a book about.

RB: Alright, if you say so. I'll see you on Monday.

RC: That's right – call in on Monday.

RB: *(as he exits)* Right!

RC: *(Dials phone.)* Hello, Daphne darling? It's me. He's just been in. Yes. And I've persuaded him to go to Brighton for the weekend. And I'll see you tonight, my dearest. *(Puts phone down and dials again.)* Hello, gardening class? Frobisher here. I want to learn how to dig a hole ... What? ... Oh, six foot deep by about 38–24–36.

HUSBAND SWAPPING

(Lines from My Grandfather's Forehead)

SHE: Good morning, darling.

HE: *(off)* Good morning, darling.

SHE: Toast?

HE: *(off)* Two, please.

SHE: Won't be a second.

(The sound of buttering toast. Rustle of newspaper.)

SHE: *(putting the toast in front of him)* There we are.

HE: *(on)* Here! You're not my wife!

SHE: I know. *(Sitting down)*

HE: Well, what's the idea?

SHE: Husband-swapping. Your wife and I had the idea. She is, no doubt, at this very moment, making breakfast for Harold. My husband.

HE: Where?

SHE: At my house.

HE: I didn't hear her leave the house this morning.

SHE: She didn't – she left last night.

HE: But I slept with her last night.

SHE: No, you didn't.

HE: Good God! I wondered why you wouldn't put the light on.

SHE: Well, you were rather late home, weren't you? I was tired.

HE: You weren't as tired as all that. Anyway, that's not the point. I'm not sure that I want my wife making breakfast for someone else's husband.

SHE: Aren't you? You can't have your cake and eat it, you know.

HE: Perhaps not.

SHE: And you certainly proved to be quite a sweet tooth last night.

HE: Now, listen, Mrs ...

SHE: Russell.

HE: Mrs Russell, I don't want to appear ungrateful, but I think my wife should have told me. She said she was going to her mother's.

SHE: Really?

HE: So the whole of last night she was lying.

SHE: Yes – but not at her mother's.

HE: No. How long is this arrangement going on for?

SHE: Only the one night.

HE: Oh.

SHE: You're with Mrs Hartley tomorrow night.

HE: What?

SHE: Mrs Hartley.

HE: What, that enormous woman across the road?

SHE: You've got to take the rough with the smooth.

HE: Rough is right. I'll take the bulb out of the light tomorrow then. Listen, do the police know about this?

SHE: They will tomorrow night – I'm with Police Constable Vickers.

HE: You're making all this up!

SHE: *(laughing)* Yes, I am actually. No, it's just you and me, and Harold and Penelope. We just thought it would make a nice change. And it has, hasn't it?

HE: Yes, I must admit it has. Now, there's just one point we have to clear up. Who is Penelope?

SHE: Penelope – your wife Penelope.

HE: My wife's name is Judith.

SHE: What?

HE: *(chuckling in an evil manner)* You've come to the wrong house, haven't you? Last night, in the dark, you came to the wrong house. My wife's name's Judith – and she's at her mother's!

SHE: Oh, God!

HE: *(with a glint in his eye)* You haven't got any more of that delicious cake, have you?

The (almost) Silent Comedies

The "almost-silent" comedy was a popular form of supporting feature in 1960s cinema, the most famous example probably still being Eric Sykes's *The Plank*. These movies often featured the pick of Britain's comedy talent, moving through a series of sight gags, constantly mumbling inaudible mumblings, which came to be known as "rhubarb" (largely because people were often mumbling or indeed even munching "rhubarb" at the time).

Ronnie Barker had appeared in just such a movie, *A Home of Your Own*, in 1964, and back then the form had instantly appealed to him. "Having seen it," says Ronnie, "I thought, 'These silent things really work. I should do this.' You didn't think about it every day or every week, but occasionally I thought, 'I really must write one of those.'"

In 1968 Ronnie did just that and the result was *Futtock's End*. (Although the character he played was named Giles Futtock, Ronnie freely admits that Futtock was indeed another variation on his Lord Rustless character, of whom more later.)

Unlike much of his work, the screenplay for *Futtock's End* actually bears the legend "Written by Ronnie Barker" and no pseudonym. The movie was shot largely at W.S. Gilbert's former house in Stanmore, comparatively near to Pinner, where Ronnie was living at the time. The role of the butler, Hawk, was written specifically with Michael Hordern in mind. The two had met whilst appearing together in an advert for Crosse & Blackwell soup. "He said, 'I can't do it, Ronnie. I'm going to play Lear. I must prepare for Lear and I can't do any other work. But send the script, I'm sure it will be funny to read.'

"So he read it and rang me and said, 'I've got to do this.'"

Horden wasn't the only one impressed with *Futtock's End*. Prince Charles numbers it amongst his favourite movies.

FUTTOCK'S END

A film with almost no dialogue, by Ronnie Barker.

September 1968

NOTE (1): There should be accompanying background music, of a nature appropriate to the mood of the various sequences, almost continuously throughout the film.

NOTE (2): In a perfect world, the part of Hawk, the butler, would be played by Michael Hordern.

Opening shot is of a very large country house, with a long drive. A postman is cycling laboriously up the drive. Suddenly a motor cycle roars past him, causing him to disappear completely into the hedge. After a pause, he appears again out of the hedges considerably further up the drive, still cycling. We cut to the motor cyclist – it is Hawk, the butler. He looks back at the postman in the distance, and grins evilly. Then, in long shot again, we see him *(from the postman's point of view)* disappearing round the side of the house. The postman's cycle has now reached the front steps – he dismounts, and leans his cycle against a small stone balustrade at the side of the steps. This dislodges the stone ball on top of the balustrade, and it rolls heavily down the drive. We watch it. The postman turns, goes up the steps to the door, and goes to knock it, but it opens, causing the postman to lurch heavily into Hawk, who has removed his motor cycling gear and crash helmet, and is now dressed formally as a butler. Hawk disdainfully takes the letters from the postman, and closes the door on him.

Hawk now begins a long and tortuous journey to the bedroom of his master, Sir Giles Futtock. We follow him down endless corridors, round innumerable corners; the house is very obviously a positive maze. During this journey he meets (A) the cook, a truly enormously wide middle-aged lady who at first appears to be alone; it is only after she has passed by that we see there are two tiny kitchen-maids behind her, who were quite invisible when the cook was seen from the front.

(B) Hawk, who also comes up behind and eventually overtakes the parlour maid, Effie, a pert, plump, dainty morsel of a girl, who is proceeding about her business. Just as he is about to overtake her, she, realising he is there, increases her pace, but so does Hawk, and as he passes her she gives a little jump and a squeak. Neither looks at the other, and Hawk's face remains expressionless, but we all know what occurred. Hawk now puts his hand firmly on the salver of letters, as he approaches "windy corner". For some reason, there is a howling draught of air always present at this particular corner, and it causes the tails of his coat to fly upwards for two or three seconds, as he battles through the blast of air. Once round the corner, everything is calm again. On he journeys, until he reaches a door, rather like all the other doors in the house, solid and shut. He knocks and enters. He is in Sir Giles's bedroom – four-poster bed, large pictures. He minces over to a door off the bedroom, whence a terrible gurgling baritone voice is giving out with a hotted-up version of "Down in the Forest". Much gurgling, as if Sir Giles is under water at least part of the time. Also enormous splashings and crashings. Hawk applies his eye to the keyhole. There is an extra loud splash from the bathroom, and Hawk comes away from the keyhole with an eye full of soap suds. He thumps on the door. The singing stops, and the door opens. Sir Giles comes into the bedroom, clad only in soap-suds, of which, for propriety's sake, there are a great many. In fact, he looks rather like a giant snowball.

GILES: Oh, it's you, Hawk – I thought it was Mrs Puddy. If I'd known, I wouldn't have bothered to get out of the bath.

HAWK: With respect, Sir Giles, it's just as well it was me, isn't it?

GILES: No it's not. I wanted to see cook – I don't particularly want to see you.

HAWK: You could hardly see cook in that condition, sir.

GILES: What do you mean "that condition"? I haven't touched a drop since before breakfast. I can see as well as the next man. Anyway, cook's pretty difficult to miss even when you've got a skinful. What d'you want, anyhow?

HAWK: I've brought the post, sir.

GILES: Oh good – any letters?

HAWK: There are no parcels, if that's what you mean, Sir Giles.

GILES: That's not what I mean. I mean letters. Surely you know the difference between letters and parcels?

HAWK: There are three letters, Sir Giles.

GILES: Well, don't stand there, man, open them, open them!

HAWK: But they're private, sir.

GILES: Well, good God man, there's only you and me here. Couldn't be more private than that. I'm going to shower this lot off; come and read them to me.

HAWK: Very good, Sir Giles.

(Giles has disappeared into the bathroom again. We follow Hawk in after him and Hawk begins to open the first letter. Giles is showering away, washing off the soap.)

HAWK: *(reading)* To Sir Giles Futtock, Futtock's End, Malmsey ...

GILES: I don't want all that! Good heavens, man, I know where I live. Get on with it, do!

HAWK: Sir. We beg to inform you that our client, the honourable ...

GILES: Who's it from?

HAWK: Er – Hodgson, Hodgson and Skillett.

GILES: Skip it.

HAWK: No sir, Skillett. Solicitors.

GILES: I mean, scrap it.

HAWK: No, no, sir – Hodgson, Hodgson and ...

GILES: Ignore it – destroy it! I want nothing to do with it. I don't want to know about it. What are the others?

HAWK: *(reading the next letter)* "My darling chubby old puss-puss ..."

GILES: *(grabbing it)* How dare you!

(He glares at Hawk, and then stares at the letter. We see that the ink, having been subjected to the stream of water from the shower, is running all over the paper – indeed the writing disappears altogether as we watch it in close-up.)

GILES: I wonder who that was from. *(He peers at the now blank piece of paper.)*

HAWK: *(looking at the envelope)* There appears to have been an error, sir – it's addressed to Boots.

GILES: Boots the chemist?

HAWK: Your Boots, Sir Giles.

GILES: My Boots?

HAWK: The boy as does your boots, Sir Giles.

GILES: Oh, poor old Arthur. Well, I hope he knows who it's from. He's obviously on to a good thing there. You know you really shouldn't open other people's letters, Hawk.

HAWK: *(sullenly)* Perhaps you would like to open the other one yourself, sir.

GILES: Are you mad? And have it all run down the plug-hole again. Come on, look sharp, man!

HAWK: *(reading)* "Dear Gilly – a hasty note to say we will be arriving for the week-end after all. Have persuaded Lord Twist to come down with a view to buying the place from you. Let's hope he gets there before it falls down. He's bringing his current attraction, Carol Singer. Of course, that's not her real name. Also old Jack. Is that too many? My niece, Lesley, may turn up as well. Yours Fern. P.S. Arriving on the Friday train. Please meet. F."

GILES: Beautifully read, Hawk.

HAWK: *(with a somewhat glazed expression)* Is that *the* Carol Singer, sir?

GILES: I've no idea, Hawk. How many Carol Singers are there? I don't even know the woman. But if Lord Twist is lugging her around, she's bound to be a cut above the ordinary.

HAWK: She is indeed, she is indeed. She's a model.

GILES: Oh, you've come across her, have you?

HAWK: I caught the under-gardener looking at a picture of her without any clothes on, sir. In the conservatory.

GILES: Did you, by George? I'll have to speak to young Godfrey. He'll catch his death of cold, the young idiot.

HAWK: Miss Singer had no clothes on, Sir Giles.

GILES: What, in the conservatory? All this has got to stop, you know, Hawk. I'm holding you entirely responsible for the future conduct of the staff, both in the conservatory, and out of it.

HAWK: Very good, sir. Do I take it there will be six for dinner?

GILES: I don't know. You're the mathematician. Well, step on it, man. Move about, move about! We meet the train at 6.30. Good Lord, I must get out of this shower, quick.

HAWK: It's only 10.30, sir, there's no hurry.

GILES: There is, you know – the bally water's gone cold.

(Now a shot of the railway station. A little country halt. Hens on the line. Bindweed on the porter's trolley. A train approaching in the distance. Warm country noises. Outside the picket fence, Sir Giles and Hawk are waiting; the latter in his motor cycle gear.)

GILES: Here it comes, and *(looking down the road)* here comes Albert. *(Calls out)* Go on, Albert, you'll make it!

(We see a little old railway official on a bicycle, steaming towards the station. He arrives just before the train does.)

ALBERT: *(exhausted and sweating)* I'll have to give this up. I can't run two stations at once, it's no good. I'm half killing meself.

(He has opened the gate and let them onto the platform.)

GILES: But you're always doing this, Albert. Why don't you get here a bit earlier?

ALBERT: I can't. I have to take the tickets up at Mickleham, then try and get here before the train. It's ridiculous.

GILES: Well, why don't you come on the train?

ALBERT: Then how would I get back? It's nearly six miles.

(Before this conversation can proceed further, we see that the passengers have alighted and are drifting towards the barrier. Giles totters off to meet them, while into shot comes a small, thin, oriental gentleman. He is sad. He approaches Albert.)

ALBERT: Oh gawd, here we go again.

O. GENT: Prease. Is Matery Halt?

ALBERT: No sir, this is Malmsey.

O. GENT: Oh. Man at rast station say – next station.

ALBERT: I know he did.

O. GENT: Prease?

ALBERT: You want next station. *(The train is pulling out.)*

O. GENT: Oh. This is not next station?

ALBERT: *(suddenly exasperated)* Look, go on the coach. *(He pushes him towards the road.)*

O. GENT: Coach? That is coach?

ALBERT: Coach. Wait. There. *(Points to road.)* Get in coach. Soon!

O. GENT: Oh. Thank you, prease.

(He stares at Albert, then turns, and walks away from the barrier, towards camera.)

O. GENT: All rook arike. *(Translation: "All look alike")*

He sees Sir Giles's large ancient Rolls-Royce parked on the bus and coach stop, and gets into it. By this time, Giles and guests are coming through the barrier. They consist of:

FERN BRASSETT. *A county lady of some 68 years, doddery, fluttery, and a constant knitter. She is knitting now, as she walks along with Sir Giles.*

OLD JACK. *A lantern-jawed, balding man in his late fifties; he wears a deaf-aid, and carries a fold-up artist's easel and collapsible stool, as well as his week-end case.*

LORD TWIST. *A tall twit in his late thirties, with a stupid smile and a Savile Row suit.*

CAROL SINGER. *The photographic model: ravishing, large (top and bottom) and always rather uncomfortable. At the moment she is uncomfortable about her dress, which is too tight, much too short and much, much too low-cut.*

LESLEY. *Mrs Brassett's niece, 23 years old, a pretty flat-chested girl. This means she is pretty, and pretty flat-chested. A sympathetic figure, a romantic. Why she is here, unescorted, we shall never know. She is worthy of better things.*

The whole party wander down towards the Rolls-Royce, chattering *(we never quite hear what they say)* and begin to get in, ushered in by Hawk, who has a glint in his eye. Inside the car, we see the oriental gentleman smiling uncomfortably as the people pile in. Giles is driving, and Lord Twist sits beside him in the front seat. Mrs Brassett is next to the oriental gent, Lesley squashes in beside her, and Old Jack has to try and perch on the tip-up seat opposite, with his easel. There isn't really room. They are all chattering at once.

We then cut back to outside the car, where Carol is looking uncomfortable about getting in. This is just what Hawk had planned for. He squeezes the car door shut, over-balancing Old Jack, and signals to Sir Giles to drive off, which he does. Hawk then smiles evilly at Carol, and pats the pillion of his motor cycle. He then mounts it and waits. Carol realises that she has to go through with it and, pulling up her skirt so that it is almost round her waist, revealing a large expanse of suspender and stocking-top, she clambers astride the pillion and clasps Hawk round the waist. Hawk, delighted, his eyes bursting at the seams, kicks the machine into action, and roars away down the road.

We cut to the Rolls-Royce, tootling along. Old Jack's easel is half sticking out of the window. Inside the car they are crushed together, grunting and trying to get comfortable. From behind, we see Hawk approaching at speed. He roars round the car, and away. Then we see Giles driving. As Hawk overtakes, the back view of Carol Singer is such an astounding sight that the car swerves wildly, going completely the wrong side of a "keep left" bollard, back again to the left-hand side of the road, up the grass verge, and back onto the road again.

Hawk and his passenger arrive at the house. He dismounts very quickly, in order to see Carol struggle off the pillion – much leg in evidence. Hawk is grinning like a demented ape at all this. Carol straightens herself out and goes with Hawk up the steps and in. The car arrives. Giles gets out, opens the rear door, and Old Jack falls onto the drive. The rest of the party emerge, breathless and awry, and proceed, chattering, towards the house. The last of these is, of course, the oriental gentleman, who follows them into the house, bewildered, but afraid to be left alone.

Inside the house, they begin to walk down corridors, round corners and upstairs, with Giles leading the way. At one point they all seem to be lost, including Giles (who gets lost very frequently in this rambling house). However, he suddenly hastens round a corner, to where, on the wall, is a large map of the building, which he consults. They set off again, chattering. Carol is now being escorted by Giles, much to Hawk's disgust, and Mrs Brassett is still knitting. They approach "windy corner" and get pretty badly blown about. Up some stairs and, round the corner, a long corridor with bedrooms off it. A general sigh of relief, and they begin to peel off into various rooms. Hawk is carrying Old Jack's easel, and the two of them go into the first room. Then Mrs Brassett into the next; Lesley the next; Lord Twist the next; and finally, Giles goes into the last room with Carol. As each door closes, the oriental gent looks more worried, trying to stay with the crowd, but to no avail – as Carol's door shuts with a bang, he is left alone in the silent corridor. He hesitates sadly and, muttering to himself, wanders back the way he had come, disappearing round the corner into the maze.

Hawk emerges from Old Jack's room, and proceeds to go down the corridor, placing his eye to each keyhole in turn. We see, from his point of view: Mrs Brassett, opening a suitcase, and tipping the contents onto the bed. It consists of a plastic bag with a toothbrush and soap, and about sixty-five ounces of knitting-wool, along with a pile of knitting patterns. She sits on the bed, and continues to knit.

Lesley, looking out of the window, rather wistfully.

Lord Twist, in shirt, but no trousers, is lighting his pipe, and changing.

Carol is bending over.

Hawk's eyes light up, but the moment is short-lived, as Sir Giles suddenly moves across the line of vision and helps Carol undo the suitcase she is struggling with. We see Hawk's expressions – annoyance, jealousy, frustration – flit across his face. He applies his eye once again to the keyhole, when suddenly round the corner, some three feet away, comes cook with a laden trolley. The trolley hits Hawk, and he falls, covered with lovely things for tea. Out from behind cook come the two tiny tweenies, looking aghast. Through the door comes Giles. A moment. The tweenies start to clear up the mess, and Hawk scuttles off in confusion. Giles grunts, and disappears into a small room the other side of Carol's bedroom, marked W.C.

In Carol's bedroom, she is putting away clothes into drawers. After a moment, there is a weird and deafening assortment of noises, indicating a lavatory chain being pulled and a cistern flushing. Carol jumps in alarm, and a large portrait in oils falls off the wall, and lands, still upright, against the skirting board. The face in the portrait stares blankly at us, with a surprised expression.

Dinner. The large dining room, the long table, everything just so. The table, for some reason, is set for ten. The maids and Hawk stand at the ready. The first to enter is Carol Singer, with a dress cut down to the navel, but with a lacy kerchief tucked into the bosom, so that, while quite a lot of Carol is showing, there would be a lot more, were the kerchief not there. Lord Twist follows in her wake, in a Savile Row dinner jacket, chattering in his stupid way to Mrs Brassett, who is knitting. Hawk seats Carol, Twist sits beside her. Giles enters and sits, as does Lesley, who has come in on her own, and Mrs Brassett.

Giles then indicates to Carol, with a wink, that she should come and sit next to him, which she does. The maid, Effie, has already begun to serve soup from a large tureen on a trolley. Twist, seeing that Carol has moved up, moves up himself, taking his soup with him. This leaves Lesley rather on her own, so Giles beckons her up. She goes. While she is moving, Old Jack enters, wearing an old-fashioned dinner jacket and his white panama hat, which is constantly on his head. He sits and Mrs Brassett moves over to him with her soup. *(During this first general move, described above, the "Paul Jones" music is played, as in musical chairs.)*

The reason Mrs Brassett moved over was to inform Old Jack that he still had his hat on. Incidentally, Old Jack has relinquished his hearing-aid for a beautifully worked silver and ebony *(or ivory)* ear trumpet, which he obviously thinks goes better with his evening-dress. Anyway, he removes his panama hat, and places it on the table in front of him. Mrs Brassett is already knitting again. The maid, who keeps going to fill a soup plate, only to find it already full *(because of the general change round that has been going on),* comes round to between Old Jack and Mrs Brassett. She is staring at Mrs Brassett's wool, which is trailing through her soup, making a brown line across the table. Still staring, she carefully pours a ladle-full of soup into Old Jack's hat. Jack looks at it. Consternation; it is seeping through onto the tablecloth. Everyone notices it at once – they stand up and sit down, chattering. The maid removes it, Mrs Brassett stands up and tells Jack to move to the next seat. Meanwhile, Lord Twist has got up and come round to Jack's old seat to place his dinner-napkin over the wet patch on the tablecloth *(more "Paul Jones" music)*. As soon as Hawk sees this, he takes away Twist's chair *(as in Musical Chairs)*, so that Twist cannot sit next to Carol. Twist returns to his place, only to find his chair gone, and then hurries round the table, where he sits next to Lesley.

Jack is given more soup by a flummoxed Effie, and the chattering, which has been continuous, suddenly dies down to silence as everyone eats soup. Not a slurp or a swallow is heard. Not a scrape of a spoon. The English are eating their soup quietly. Bread rolls are accepted and refused with nods and shakes of the head. They all finish their soup, and the chatter begins to start again.

Hawk, handing round bread rolls, drops one from the basket. He looks down, looks around, and furtively kicks it under the table. Under the table, we see six pairs of legs, and the roll shooting in. The chattering begins to swell, and the twelve feet, all shuffling under the table, begin to kick the roll backwards and forwards. After a few journeys up and down the carpet, it is passed along from foot to foot, until suddenly, with an extra strong kick, it flies straight between the legs of Mrs Brassett, which legs, clad as they are in white stockings, and positioned wide apart, uncannily resemble a set of goal-posts. As the roll hits the back of her black net skirt, the chattering is mixed with the sound of a Cup Tie crowd cheering a goal. We see the table from above again, all the guests, including Mrs Brassett, quite oblivious of what has happened. Giles gets up to carve the roast, as the soup is cleared away.

Meanwhile, in the dim corridors of the house, the oriental gentleman is wandering up and down, trying to find his way out.

Back in the dining room, Giles is carving the roast beef. Already most people have been served, and Giles is standing at the side-table, which is situated behind his chair.

As he carves, his eyes are popping out of his head at the sight of Carol's thighs – her skirt, as usual, is far too short. Giles, who hasn't changed for dinner, is wearing a brown suede tie, which, at this point, manages to drape itself onto the joint of beef, with the result that he carves a good 1 1/2 inches off it, and, still ogling Carol, puts it onto a plate with more meat, covers it with gravy, and hands it to the maid, who places it before Old Jack. The vegetables are on the table and everyone helps themselves. Hawk is carrying a dish of roast potatoes round to Mrs Brassett. They are beautifully brown and crisp, and Hawk cannot resist them. As he is about to place them on the table, he pops one into his mouth without anyone seeing, and then places the dish down on the table. Unfortunately, the potatoes are red-hot, and Hawk is in agony, has face and lips contorted into a pouting gargoyle as he tries to pretend nothing has happened. Finally, it is too much for him – he whisks a vase of flowers from the table, turns his back, and spits out the red-hot potato into the vase. As he replaces it on the table, a cloud of steam rises from it, hissing. He backs away, amid the stares of the onlookers.

Old Jack is about to eat the piece of necktie – he stabs it with his fork, covers it with horseradish sauce, and puts it in his mouth. He chews. His eyes glaze. He chews on. He keeps on chewing, but doesn't swallow.

Effie, meanwhile, has been to the kitchen, and is returning along the corridor with an enormous bowl of fruit salad. She approaches "windy corner", and as she rounds it her skirt blows over her head. Having her hands full, she can do nothing about it, anyway she is used to it. As she walks away, we are aware of a brief pair of gingham check knickers. *(More of these anon.)*

The dining room again. Old Jack is still chewing. Hawk is at the side-table, being furtive. We see that there are three bottles of brandy, unopened, on the table. Hawk appraises the labels and we gather he fancies some of that, by jingo. He furtively opens a bottle, and is just about to sample some, when Effie comes in with the fruit salad. Caught in the act, he quickly plonks the bottle down on top of a couple of boxes of cigars. Effie, giving him an old-fashioned look, places the fruit salad on the side-table next to the bottle, and goes away. Hawk, meanwhile, has to go and attend to Mrs Brassett, in response to a wave from that good lady.

One of the tweenies is pushing the trolley, collecting the meat course empties. The trolley has a bent wheel, or is stiff, and the little tweeny has great difficulty in steering it – it keeps weaving from side to side. She eventually bumps into the side-table, which is sufficient to topple the brandy bottle off the cigar boxes, and into the fruit salad.

The brandy runs, unnoticed, into the bowl. The other tweeny comes up to the side-table, and sees that pepper-pots, sugar sifters, and the now empty brandy bottle have fallen over *(due to the bump)*. She stands them all up again, wiping the bottle dry with her napkin. Hawk comes back, and sees, to his dismay, an empty bottle. He looks up, sees the tweeny maid swerving about with the trolley. He can hardly believe it.

Effie now takes the fruit salad and starts to serve it, with cream. Plenty of "juice" with each helping. As the guests start to eat, a silence falls for a moment, then they all murmur their approval. They all tuck in like mad, gobbling it up and ladling the brandy "juice" into their mouths. Old Jack is still chewing, his jaw beginning to ache by this time. We presume he still has the piece of tie in his mouth as well as the fruit salad.

Second helpings are asked for. The atmosphere is definitely warming up. Carol begins to giggle. So does Mrs Brassett. The maids are now rushing round, trying to keep up with the demands for more fruit salad. Old Jack, cream round his mouth, still chewing, suddenly guffaws. Giles is merry, too. Lesley is laughing. Twist is grinning widely. Mrs Brassett, who is trying to knit, hiccoughs, and drops about fourteen stitches. Hawk, meanwhile, goes back to try another bit of brandy-smuggling. He picks up the second bottle and opens it. Then he opens the cupboard in the side-table, and takes out an empty coffee-pot, quickly pouring the contents of the bottle into it; then, placing the coffee-pot on a little silver tray, marches boldly towards the door – obviously intending to smuggle it out. As he reaches the door, however, it opens, and cook appears, looking daggers, with a large decorated jelly on a dish. She indicates that Hawk should take it. He has to put the coffee-pot down on an occasional table by the door to do so. Cook disappears. Hawk is left holding the jelly.

Giles is making a pass at Carol – leaning over and whispering in her ear. In doing so, he knocks over her glass of wine. Some of it goes into her lap and, with great presence of mind, Giles whips the kerchief out of Carol's bosom and mops her up with it. Hawk, approaching with the jelly, catches sight of Carol's now very over-exposed bosom, which is wobbling about all over the place as she brushes herself down. We see Hawk with the jelly. The jelly melts.

The oriental gentleman is standing looking at the map of the house in the corridor. He is weeping quietly.

In the dining room, everyone is in very high spirits, and quite noisy. A tweeny sees the coffee-pot *(which contains Hawk's smuggled brandy)* on the occasional table near the door. Tutting with her tongue, she takes it and puts it back on the side serving table. Effie immediately comes and picks it up, and begins to serve it. Hawk, innocent of the switch-over, follows her round with hot milk and cream. She works round the table anti-clockwise, starting with Lesley. We see the guests reactions to the "coffee". They adore it, having already been primed by the ninety per cent proof fruit salad. She reaches Old Jack. He's laughing away, and still chewing. Hawk is still driven to distraction by Carol's cleavage. Effie pours Old Jack's coffee, and asks whether he wants milk or cream. Jack puts up his ear trumpet – he didn't quite catch that. Effie repeats the question. Jack asks for cream. Effie nudges Hawk, who is ogling Carol and dreaming of conquering Everest. He recovers somewhat, and deftly pours cream into Old Jack's ear trumpet. This, of course, is all that is needed to set the table in a roar. We see everyone bellowing with laughter. Hawk rushes away in confusion to the side-table, opens the third bottle of brandy and knocks back a stiff one. Then he begins to fill everyone's glass. They are all roaring away – even Old Jack, who is now blowing cream bubbles through his ear trumpet. Hawk, too, begins to chuckle.

The outside of the house. Twilight. The lights shine out, and the laughter is plainly heard across the lawns.

Now, the outside of the house, next morning. The sun shines, birds twitter; a church clock strikes ten.

The breakfast-room. Giles sits at the table, with Lesley. Complete silence. Giles's face is a study. The previous night has taken its toll; he looks ghastly. He is staring at a poached egg, messing it about with his fork. Lesley is quietly sipping tea. She is obviously none too well either. She gives Giles a wan smile, which he tries to return, but fails miserably. Lord Twist comes in. He looks frightful. He too is very hung-over. He grunts at the company in general, and staggers over to the entrée dishes on the sideboard, which contain the breakfast. He removes a dish-cover, peers in, and replaces the cover. He does this in a normal manner, but we hear a crash like a cymbal. Giles reacts with a wince and a hand to the head. Another dish – another cymbal crash. And another. And another. He reaches the end of the line and finishes up with a bowl of cornflakes, which he pours from the packet into the bowl. This sounds to Giles *(and to us)* like a sack of coal being delivered. Twist sits down, and adds milk *(a bucket of water poured onto cement)*. During this symphony concert, Old Jack has staggered in, holding on to the furniture for support. He reacts to the frightful din in just the same way as the others. We see Giles glaring at Lord Twist pouring milk onto the cornflakes. At the same time, Giles takes a bite out of a slice of toast, which sounds like army boots on gravel as be munches, with an agonised expression. Twist, having sat down, joins in with the cornflakes *(Wellington boots in thick mud)*. Old Jack, crashing away along the entrée dishes, lifts one up and stares into it. His stare is returned by a ghastly-looking herring. Its one eye is glaring malevolently, its mouth is a twisted snarl. Close-up of Jack's face – close-up of the fish-face. Close-up of Jack's eye – close-up of the fish eye. *(Which is which?)* The dish cover crashes back. Another dish cover is lifted, and we see an arrangement of two fried eggs, a tomato and a sausage, which looks like an awful grinning face; in fact, as he stares at it, Hawk's awful grinning face appears in it, fading in, and fading out almost at once. This cover, too, is replaced. All this business has been punctuated by toast crunching, cornflakes ditto, and a new noise, like a muffin-man being drawn down into a whirlpool. It is Twist, stirring his coffee. He drinks some *(water going down a sink)*. Giles reacts again, desperately.

Old Jack has finally chosen a boiled egg. He sits at the table, lifts his spoon, and taps the egg three times. This sounds like Black Rod opening Parliament.

This last ear-splitting sound is too much for Giles. He staggers to his feet, opens the door, and ricochets along the corridor, the sounds of breakfast still echoing round the house. He enters the door marked W.C.

Carol Singer is in bed. A vision of loveliness, obviously she doesn't get hangovers. She lies there, in the flimsiest of nighties. In one hand she holds a tea cup of the most delicate china; in the other, a rose, which she is sniffing appreciatively. The ultimate in poise, obviously she is at her best in bed. The W.C. chain is pulled again – deafening. The four-poster bed collapses. Carol crawls out, looking a wreck.

Effie is marching along, with a tray containing shaving equipment, soap, hot water, razor, brush. She stops at a built-in cupboard, putting the tray down on a small table. Close-up of Effie opening the cupboard door. On the top shelf are towels – she takes one out. The camera pulls back to reveal the bottom of the cupboard. Curled up, asleep, is the oriental gent. Effie gives a little squeak, wakening the O.G., who scrambles to his feet, uttering hoarse cries. Effie makes a run for it. The O.G. makes to pursue her, but she disappears around "windy corner". More gingham knickers. The O.G. gasps at the sight, then realises he is again lost and alone. He picks up the shaving-brush from the tray that Effie has left, and begins to shave, despondently.

A picture of Carol with no clothes on. Pull back to reveal it is in the hands of Boots, a scruffy, cheery lad of seventeen. He is in the scullery.

He has a load of shoes – about six pairs, all men's, all black. They are slung in a heap on the floor. He finishes cleaning the last one. He then starts to sort them out; he has difficulty in making pairs out of them. The last pair he makes consists of one small one and one enormous one. Then he finds another enormous shoe behind him on the floor. He makes the pair. There is now one over. He looks around, nonplussed. Tries to match them up again, in the vain hope that it will come right. No luck, still thirteen shoes. He panics. He takes the odd one and stuffs it into the boiler. It burns, merrily. He puts the boiler lid back. The door opens – it is Hawk. He carries a shoe. He indicates that he found it outside the door, and gives it to Boots. Hawk sniffs the air, smells burning. Boots grabs up the rest of the shoes, and bolts from the room. Hawk picks up the discarded magazine and, recognising Carol, begins to sweat.

Mrs Brassett is in the drawing room, knitting. She is an extremely fast and vast knitter. She has just finished an enormous sweater, and is looking through a few patterns, wondering what to knit next. Effie comes in, with one of the tweenies, intending to dust. Effie is stopped by Mrs Brassett, who indicates that Effie should fetch more patterns from Mrs Brassett's room. *(She waves a pattern at Effie, indicates with her hands a pile about a foot high, and points upstairs – something like that).* Effie drops her a curtsey, and departs. The tweeny starts to dust. Mrs Brassett beckons her over; she wants to try the sweater she has knitted on the tweeny, to see the size. The tweeny puts it on. It is gigantic, with a polo-neck. The tweeny's head doesn't show at all through the neck hole. Mrs Brassett gets the tweeny to turn round, slowly, as she studies the sweater. She stands back, appraising it.

Giles is approaching the drawing room door. He half opens it, and we see, from his point of view, a headless sweater revolving slowly. Reaction from Giles. He closes the door.

In Mrs Brassett's bedroom, Effie has a bundle of paper knitting patterns about a foot high. She brings them out of the room, and down the corridor. Around "windy corner". This time, not only the now familiar gingham knickers, but patterns flying all over the place. Effie gets on her knees and attempts to retrieve them, trying at the same time to cope with her skirt. We leave her scrabbling about.

Mrs Brassett has removed the sweater from the tweeny, and is folding it up. Then she twiddles her knitting needles, obviously at a loss. Effie comes in, hair awry, with an untidy bundle of rather creased knitting patterns, gives them to Mrs Brassett, and leaves. Mrs Brassett takes the first three sheets of paper from the pile and peers at them. A hint of bewilderment.

The grounds. An open lorry drives up, containing a lot of dwarf fir trees – about six or seven feet high. They are standing in rows on the lorry. The lorry stops alongside an old garden wall. The groundsmen get out, lift off one of the trees, and begin to plant it in a ready-prepared hole.

Old Jack is in the grounds. He has set up his painting easel. We see the view he is preparing to paint – an old garden wall, and behind it a row of fir trees. He starts to sketch with charcoal on his canvas. Close-up of his hand, rapidly sketching in the fir trees. He starts to mix his paints. Behind the wall, the groundsmen are finishing planting the one tree. They throw their spades into the back of the lorry, and climb into the cab. On the other side of the wall, we see old Jack putting paint on his brush. We hear the lorry start up, and the line of fir trees moves off and disappears. Old Jack looks up and, as he goes to paint the trees, he sees they aren't there. He stares. He looks at his sketch. He looks up. He looks all around him, his jaw sagging.

The drawing room, Mrs Brassett is knitting furiously. She keeps peering at the patterns beside her. She has almost finished the garment already.

Lord Twist is fishing by the side of a lake, pond or river. Serenity. He sits in a little fold-up chair. He tips his hat over his eyes. We cut to the water. A large fin, as of a shark, is weaving its way towards us. It dives. We see Twist's line go taut, and he is pulled straight into the water.

Hawk is sounding the gong for lunch. A smallish gong on a table, with a strident note. We see Mrs Brassett put down her knitting, and head towards lunch. Carol, who has just finished getting dressed, does likewise. So does Lesley. And Giles. Hawk is now in the grounds, with an enormous gong, which is on a low trolley. He trundles it across the lawn, up to where Old Jack is painting. Stopping just behind Jack, Hawk gives the gong a tremendous swipe. It sounds like Big Ben striking one o'clock. Jack turns round, nods, and Hawk wheels the gong away.

A gloomy corridor. Cook, as vast as ever, is pushing a trolley laden with a cold collation *(for lunch)*. On her way to the dining room, she passes through the conservatory. As she approaches a clump of potted palms and rubber plants, we cut to a close-up of them. In the shadows, framed by the leafy fronds, is the oriental gentleman, waiting to pounce. He has somehow acquired a kitchen knife, which he is wearing between his teeth. Fade in jungle noises – cicadas and the occasional screech of a bird or monkey. The oriental gent is tense – it's now or never. The trolley passes, and a hand clutching a knife comes through the foliage, and stabs a chicken on the trolley, whisking it into the leafy shadows. The cook goes on her way, and we see the oriental gent devouring his spoils.

The door outside the dining room. All the guests approach in a bunch *(Lord Twist in a bath-robe, looking shaken)* and they all crowd into the dining room, chattering. They close the door.

Silence.

A loud burp.

The door opens, and out come the guests, chattering, and smoking cigars and cigarettes. They disappear down the corridor – luncheon is over.

Outside the house, Effie and Boots *(who is now much smartened up, and really looks quite presentable)* are walking, hand in hand, towards the woods. An aged gardener, with his hands in a wheel-barrow of manure, watches them go, a sad wistful look on his gnarled old face.

Giles, dressed in Norfolk jacket, and carrying a sporting gun, sets off to shoot a crow or two. With him is a young retriever dog, jumping about and getting under his feet. They head off for the woods.

On the lawn, Lesley watches them go. She is playing croquet with Lord Twist, but obviously her heart isn't in it. She plays her stroke, and Twist nods his approval, grinning inanely. Mrs Brassett is sitting, not really watching the game, knitting. Her ball of wool is on her lap. Twist plays his stroke, and his ball rolls up to Mrs Brassett's feet, unnoticed by her. An instant later, her ball of wool rolls off her lap. She leans over, gropes around without looking, picks up Twist's croquet ball and puts it in her lap. Twist comes over to look for his ball. He doesn't see it at first, but suddenly catches sight of it. He is at a loss.

Giles is in a field beside a copse. Birds fly over. He takes a pot shot at one of them. We see it fall. The retriever shoots off in the direction which the bird fell. Giles lights a cigar. We see the dog tearing back towards Giles. It rushes up to him, and drops a rabbit at his feet. Giles chokes a little over his cigar.

Hawk, in the corridor, with a silver salver, on which is a glass of frothing ale. He approaches "windy corner". As he rounds it, the head of the froth is blown straight off the beer, hitting a portrait on the wall, smack in the face. The portrait looks furious.

Old Jack is painting *(a watercolour this time)* in the garden. He is prodding away with his brush, as Hawk approaches with the beer on the tray. Old Jack nods at him as he sets it down on the ground beside Jack's paints. Hawk departs. Old Jack is just finishing the painting, and he dips his brush into the beer occasionally. He finishes the picture, drops his brush into the beer, picks up the paint water, and drinks it down in one go. He smacks his lips in appreciation, and wipes his mouth with the back of his hand.

Giles, meanwhile, is about to shoot another bird. Once again his aim is accurate, and the bird falls. The dog streaks off again. We see it racing across country, into the copse. Suddenly, we see the dog stop short, staring inquisitively. In the bushes, Effie and Boots are on the ground, necking. They both sit up at the arrival of the dog, and look embarrassed. Effie straightening her skirt and Boots straightening his tie. The dog stands there, not knowing what to do.

Giles is waiting for the dog to return – he has walked in the direction of the copse, and is just about to enter the trees when the dog runs out, clutching in its mouth the now very recognisable gingham knickers. He drops them at Giles's feet. Giles picks them up, and suddenly realising where he has seen them before, does a "well, well, well" facial expression and stuffs them into his pocket as he stalks away.

Hawk is preparing tea on the lawn. Canvas chairs with arms and little tables (or those platforms fixed to the left-hand arm of each chair) stand in a row. A large tea trolley, with sandwiches, cakes, buns and teacups. The guests are drifting towards the line of chairs – Carol is now wearing tiny, very tight shorts, and a sun-top bra. She is looking cool, and Hawk, because of her, is looking hot. Twist follows close behind her, followed in turn by Old Jack and Mrs Brassett, who is now knitting an eternal scarf, which trails along behind her on the ground. Lesley is wandering along in the rear, wistfully. In the middle distance, Giles and the dog can be seen coming across the lawns. Mrs Brassett drifts along past the seats, and sits in the end one. Her scarf has trailed across the seats, so that about a foot of it is lying on the seat that Carol is about to occupy. As she is about to sit, Hawk rushes over to help her. She sits at the same time as Hawk reaches the back of the chair. Mrs Brassett tugs the scarf away from underneath Carol, and Carol, feeling it go, jumps, and stares at Hawk, thinking he touched her. Hawk looks puzzled. Giles has by now arrived, and all the company are seating themselves. Giles sits at the opposite end of the line to Mrs Brassett, the dog crouching nearby. The cucumber sandwiches are passed and everyone is chattering, as usual. Lesley, sitting next to Giles, takes the cruet proffered by Hawk, and liberally peppers her cucumber sandwich. Giles gets some of the pepper and, about to sneeze, whips the gingham knickers out of his pocket and claps them over his nose. Lesley, in the act of apologising for the pepper, sees them and laughs. Hawk sees them, and his eyes narrow, suspicion and envy flitting across his face.

A tweeny is going round with cakes and buns, dispensing them with a pair of tongs. Giles chooses a sort of rock cake, the only one of its kind on the dish. The tweeny transfers it to Giles's plate with the tongs, and the plate is left on Giles's little table. He is busy drinking tea and chattering to Lesley, describing his shooting incidents of the afternoon. The dog ambles over, sniffs at the rock cake, and takes it off the plate, trotting away with it in its mouth. It goes off behind a hedge.

We see the dog try to bury the cake, without much success. The cake is by now pretty dirty. A gardener's boy happens along, and seeing the dog and bun, joins in the fun, throwing the bun for the dog to fetch, which it does. The next throw lands the bun in an ornamental pond *(or water butt)* from whence it is fished out, now clean again, but pretty wet. The gardener's boy squeezes most of the water from it, and drop kicks it over the hedge. It flies over the hedge, landing very near the trolley. The tweeny approaches, sees the bun on the floor, and picks it up quickly, popping it back onto the dish. Hawk comes up, picks up the dish, and goes over to Giles, who again chooses the bun, is given it by Hawk *(using tongs)* and bites into it, obviously enjoying it, completely unaware, as is everyone else, of the bun's adventures.

A long shot of the garden tea, a happy chattering group in the afternoon sun, as the church clock strikes five.

We cut to the face of the large grandfather clock in the drawing room. It says 9.30. The guests are passing a pleasant evening in various pursuits. Giles, Lord Twist and Old Jack are playing cards. Giles is smoking a cigar, Old Jack a pipe and Twist a cigarette. There are ashtrays at each corner of the card-table.

Giles puts down his cigar in the ashtray on his left. Twist puts his cigarette down in the same ashtray a little later. Giles picks it up, puffs it, and, after a moment, puts it down in the ashtray on his right. Twist picks up the cigar, puffs it, and holds it. Old Jack puts his pipe down in the ashtray with the cigarette. Giles picks up the pipe, puffs it, and puts it in the ashtray on his left. Jack picks up the cigarette, puffs it, and puts it in the ashtray on his right. Twist puts down the cigar to his right. Giles picks it up, puffs it, and puts it to his right. Twist smokes the pipe. Old Jack picks up the cigar, puffs it, and puts it to his right, where the cigarette is. Twist puts down the pipe, Giles picks it up, puffs it, and puts it to his right. Old Jack picks it up, puffs it, and puts it to his right. All three smokes are now in the same ashtray. Giles goes to smoke something, finds nothing in either of his ashtrays. An instant later, Twist does the same. They see the ashtray on Jack's side, and glare at him.

Mrs Brassett is watching television in the far corner of the room. We have already heard the strains of a symphony orchestra over the card playing scene, and now we see it on the TV screen. Mrs Brassett, as always, is knitting. The conductor is conducting. Mrs Brassett becomes very influenced by the music, vis-à-vis her knitting. As the speed and mood of the music varies, so does the speed and mood of Mrs Brassett's knitting. The conductor's movements, too, are to a large extent mirrored by Mrs Brassett's needles, as she knits – double forte, pianissimo and pizzicato.

Outside the house, Lesley is strolling in the twilight. She passes the open window of the drawing room, and the symphony concert floats out on the evening air. She walks along the side of the house, throwing a stick for the young retriever. As she moves onward, the concert begins to be mingled with the sound of a transistor radio playing beat group music. This gets louder as she approaches the window of the servants' quarters.

In the scullery, Effie and Boots are dancing in the modern, abandoned manner. On the table is a now somewhat old-fashioned portable radio, with its lid open, and a pile of silver cutlery, together with equipment for cleaning them. We watch them for a few seconds, enjoying each other's antics.

Outside the scullery, Hawk is approaching along the passage. The radio can be plainly heard. He marches up to the scullery door and opens it quickly. The music instantly stops, and Effie and Boots are quietly cleaning the silver. Hawk glares at them and shuts the door again. We cut back to inside the scullery. Effie and Boots are dancing again, the radio blaring away, as if there had never been an interruption at all. Outside the door, Hawk has taken two or three paces along the passage, but now returns, on tiptoe. His hand goes to the door knob.

Inside, Effie and Boots are dancing. But suddenly, as if by some form of telepathy, they both stop instantly. They both grab a duster in one hand and a piece of silver in the other, and Boots knocks the lid of the radio shut with his elbow at the same time, causing the music to stop instantly, so that by the time Hawk has got his head round the door again, all is as it should be. He glares again, shuts the door, and immediately opens it again. This causes things to get rather out of step, in a strange way, because, as he opens the door, Boots lifts the lid of the radio, and he and Effie start to dance. Hawk stares at them, and shuts the door. They immediately close the radio, and start cleaning silver. Hawk opens the door again, and they open the radio and start to dance. He shuts it, and they clean the silver. He opens it – and, as the music starts yet again, we see a puzzled Hawk in close-up.

Lesley is coming into the house. It is now quite dark – the grandfather clock chimes eleven.

Downstairs, in the drawing room, all is deserted. Hawk is emptying ashtrays and finishing up any liquor in the odd glasses dotted around the room. Lesley looks in, sees no one except an obsequious Hawk, and starts towards the staircase.

Somewhere upstairs, all the guests are murmuring goodnight, and going to their rooms. We see Carol give Twist a good-night peck, Giles going into his room, and Twist into his.

Inside Mrs Brassett's room, the good lady is clad in a large towel, ready for a shower. She enters the bathroom, knitting, as usual. This time it is a very large sock, a rugby sock, or something similar. She steps behind the shower curtain, and throws her towel out. We hear the water turn on, and Mrs Brassett splashing about.

Lord Twist is in his room, in his striped underpants. He removes his singlet, and does a few knees-bend exercises – up and down twice, inhaling and exhaling as he does so. On the second knees-bend there is a sharp snapping noise, and he comes to a standing position very carefully. He starts to remove his shoes.

In the shower, Mrs Brassett has turned off the water – reaches an arm out for the towel, and a second or two later emerges with it round her, still knitting. The rugby sock has now shrunk to about half its size *(or maybe a little smaller)*.

Giles is climbing into bed. He settles down, and reaches up to the light switch, which is one of those pull-string affairs into the ceiling. He pulls it, and the light goes off.

Lord Twist is in bed. He, too, reaches up to pull the light switch, and the light goes off.

The light comes on in Giles's room. He looks round, startled, sees nothing, and pulls the string again. His light goes off.

Twist's light comes on. He, too, looks round and then pulls the string, putting out the light.

Giles's light comes on again. He puts it out.

Twist's light comes on. He puts it out.

We see the front of the house. Quite a few lights on – but in one wing we see the alternating lights of Giles and Lord Twist, off and on, off and on.

Then we see Giles, who is standing on the bed, winding the string of the light round the pillar of the four poster. He pulls it, and hangs on to it.

We see the light go on in Twist's room again. He, furious, gives a great tug at his light switch.

We see the front of the house again. All the lights in the house go out at once. There is a second's silence, then we hear mutterings and murmurings coming from the house.

Inside the house, the chattering is growing. The guests are all creeping about, trying to find out what has happened. The mutterings are interlaced with little shrieks and cries as people meet each other in the dark. Old Jack is bumping into everything, and Carol is outraged at least twice. So far we have seen nothing of them – just the occasional silhouetted shape, vague and unrecognisable.

In the servants' quarters, Hawk, lit by a candle, is just finishing mending the fuse. He goes to insert the new fuse into the circuit-box.

We are in the hall. The chattering has reached a crescendo. Suddenly all the lights go on. Everyone is standing in various positions in the hall, on the stairs, on the landing. They all freeze, and look at one another. They chattering stops instantly. As they stare around at each other, we see: Mrs Brassett, dressed entirely in wool – woollen pyjamas *(double-knit)* and a sort of pixie hood. Old Jack, in a night shirt with a pocket for his deaf-aid. Lord Twist, in union jack pyjamas. Carol, her hair in curlers, with a chin strap on, which doesn't match her flimsy night-dress at all. Lesley, in a surprisingly daring baby doll pyjama suit, and finally, Effie and Boots, looking more embarrassed than anyone. Boots is wearing a winceyette-type striped pyjama top, and extremely tight, thin, cotton pyjama trousers with large spotted pattern, and Effie is wearing striped winceyette trousers which look enormous on her, and a thin, cotton pyjama top with a large spotted pattern, which matches Boots's trousers exactly. They look at each other's clothes and realise what they have done in their haste. Everyone shuffles off in different directions, in an embarrassed silence – and Saturday is over.

Sunday morning. Birdsong; sunshine; church clock striking ten.

Cook is approaching, down the corridor, dressed in her Sunday-best-going-to-church-clothes. She sweeps up to the door of the scullery, and goes in, revealing the two tweeny maids behind her, in their Sunday best. Inside the scullery, Boots is in his Sunday best, playing darts. The dart-board is on the scullery door. Cook looks in, indicates with a jerk of her head that it's time they were on their way, and leaves again, closing the door. Boots throws a dart into the board, followed by another. Effie, doing something to her make-up, takes the darts from Boots, and has her turn – giggling a little at her low score. Boots pulls out the darts, and prepares to throw again.

Hawk is now approaching along the corridor. He wears a butler-type blue suit, and bowler hat.

We see a dart land in the board.

Hawk is at the scullery door.

The second dart lands in the board.

Hawk opens the scullery door.

The third dart lands in Hawk's bowler.

He glares stonily in close-up.

Giles is seen, going into the lavatory. He is not in his Sunday best, but in very comfortable tweeds. He carries a model yacht. The lavatory door closes.

Hawk is on his way to Carol's room, with the Sunday papers. He knocks and rushes in, hoping to catch Carol unawares. Surprisingly, she is up and dressed, in tight slacks and an over-crowded sweater. Hawk notices a rolled-up towel and a pair of sunglasses on the bed. Carol gyrates into her bathroom for a moment and Hawk, quick as a flash, unrolls the towel. Sure enough, inside the towel is a bikini. He stuffs the bikini into his pocket, and rolls up the towel again, just in time. Carol emerges from the bathroom, picks up the rolled towel and, putting on the sunglasses, wobbles her way out of the room, bowed out by Hawk. We see Hawk's face, absolutely trembling with anticipation, as he watches her go.

The door of the lavatory. The chain goes, deafening, cacophonous. A large amount of ceiling and plaster falls on cook, who is just about to go out of the front door. Her hat now resembles a Christmas cake.

Outside, Carol is walking through the woods, on her way to the lake. Behind her, in the distance, we see Hawk, who is following her – concealing himself behind trees and bushes.

Then we see Carol again, but this time the film is overcranked, so that she floats in slow motion through the trees.

We cut to Hawk, dodging from tree to tree. This time undercranked, so that he moves jerkily and extremely quickly from one hiding place to another.

Carol again, floating: Hawk again, whizzing.

Carol floats down to the edge of the lake, and settles. Hawk skids to a halt and, concealing himself in the bushes, waits, with baited breath. Now, at normal speed once more, Carol begins to undress, starting with the sweater. Hawk's eyes are sticking out like chapel hat-pegs. Carol is seen, from the back, as the sweater comes off. No bra.

A cow, grazing in a field, looks up, and does a double-take on Carol (*reverse film optical*).

Carol opens the towel, and discovers there is no bikini inside. Hawk's face is a study. Carol's face is a dilemma – she looks round, sees no one, and decides to go in for a swim anyway, costume or no. In very long shot, from Hawk's point of view, we see her remove her slacks, and prepare to dive into the lake. Hawk, trembling, produces a pair of binoculars. As he raises them to his eyes, some heavy instrument is brought down with a crash onto his bowler. He collapses, stunned. The heavy instrument turns out to be a large telescope, which Giles, his assailant, immediately focuses onto Carol's nude form splashing about in the lake. He watches appreciatively for a few moments.

In another part of the ground, Old Jack is sketching a landscape – a stream, hedges, a large tree in the background.

Mrs Brassett enters the lavatory in the house.

Jack is mixing his paints in the grounds.

Mrs Brassett pulls the chain. Deafening.

The tree in Jack's landscape falls, disappearing out of sight behind the hedges. He looks up to paint it – it is gone.

At the side of the lake, Hawk is regaining consciousness. He sits up, and blinks. Carol is still in the water. Hawk looks for his binoculars, but they are gone. He gets a devilish idea – he will hide Carol's clothes. He creeps down towards the lakeside on his hands and knees. In doing so, he puts both hands into a boggy piece of ground, and his hands come out covered in thick mud. He crawls on, and reaches the pile of clothes. He wipes his hands on the towel – we plainly see the two muddy hand prints. Seeing the mess he has made, he quickly puts the towel down on the ground again, clean side uppermost. He then grabs the clothes, keeping out of sight of Carol behind the low bushes, and crawls away, hiding them in the foliage. He looks back, and realises he has left the towel. He begins to crawl back towards it, but too late – Carol is coming out of the water. He stares, fascinated as long as he dare, and then scuttles away into the undergrowth. Carol arrives at the towel, and finds her clothes gone. Her face is puzzled, then alarmed, realising someone has been spying on her.

Back in the garden, near the house, Old Jack is looking at a small statue. He walks round it, studying it. He suddenly tries to push it over, to no avail. He tries lifting it, but can't. He kicks it, leans on it – it doesn't move an inch. Satisfied, he steps back to his easel, where we see he has already sketched it. He begins to apply paint to the sketch, keeping an eagle eye on the statue, for fear that it should disappear, like the rest of his subjects so far. Suddenly he looks up. Hurrying towards him, along a path towards the house, comes Carol, clad only in her towel. It barely covers her essentials, and she is clutching it tightly round her, top and bottom. The aged gardener, still with his manure wheelbarrow, is creeping along at a snail's pace towards her. He disappears from view behind a clump of bushes. Carol, too, has to pass behind the bushes on her way to the house. Old Jack watches, and after two or three seconds the aged gardener reappears trudging on his weary way. Carol also appears again on the opposite side of the bushes, still hurrying towards the house. Old Jack stares at Carol's back view. Two muddy hand-prints are planted firmly on the towel, covering Carol's buttocks. We know that Hawk put them there, when he wiped his hands down by the lake, but Old Jack doesn't, and he stares at the receding gardener with amazement. Effie, standing in for Hawk, appears on the steps with a gong, and bangs it for lunch. Lesley and Giles, talking and laughing, are crossing the lawns.

An hour or so later, a small van drives up to the entrance of the house. The driver delivers a large wicker basket to Hawk, and drives off.

Giles and Lesley are in the drawing room having coffee, when Hawk enters, and whispers discreetly in Giles's ear. He is delighted and, taking Lesley's hand, leads her out to where the basket is standing in the hall. They open it, and we see printed on the side "Fox Ltd, Costumiers". Inside are various large brown paper parcels. The other guests drift in, and each receives a parcel from Giles, who is reading the names on the labels. As they receive their parcels, they go upstairs to their respective rooms. The last to receive his parcel is Hawk and he, too, disappears to get dressed.

Lord Twist is in his bedroom, with a pair of tights on, but still wearing his sports jacket. He is ferreting about in his package, and brings out a long feather. He looks at it.

Mrs Brassett has got into a large black bombazine dress – she is obviously going to be Queen Victoria.

Old Jack is struggling into a roll-neck jersey, with large horizontal stripes.

Lesley is in a buckskin skirt with tassels, and is about to put on the jacket.

Carol is struggling into a glittering, silver-lamé top, close fitting, with long sleeves.

And Giles has got on a pair of white trousers.

Outside the house, Hawk is driving the Rolls-Royce up to the entrance. He parks it, and gets out – he is clad in furs and skins – we don't quite know what he is supposed to be. He walks round the side of the house, and out of sight.

In the hall, people are appearing in their fancy dress. Twist is standing, looking rather sheepish, as Robin Hood. Mrs Brassett, as Queen Victoria, is knitting. Lesley comes downstairs, very pretty as an Indian maiden, closely followed by Old Jack, as a burglar, complete with flat cap and eye-mask. He carries a small black leather bag marked "SWAG". The others laugh and chatter. Old Jack looks rather stony-faced. Giles comes down the stairs as Buffalo Bill, and gets a few murmurs of approval. Then Carol makes her entrance. Joan of Arc – in silver-lamé armour, fitting her as if it was her own skin, the light reflecting off her salient points. She receives a round of applause. They all troop out to get into the car.

A large poster: "Grand Summer Fête" etc. The words "Fancy Dress Parade" are prominent. As we pull back, we see the fête is already in progress – lots of stalls, and country people enjoying themselves. Various shots of different stalls – darts, rolling pennies, ball in the bucket, etc. A stall where you knock down tins with mop-heads. A large sign saying "One win – anything off the bottom shelf." On the bottom shelf sits a little old woman, smoking a home-made fag-end. She looks bored. A tin hits her on the head. She still looks bored.

A boy, about ten years old, is throwing rings over goldfish bowls. His first throw is successful – the ring goes over the bowl. The stall-minder – a lady who looks as if she might be the vicar's wife (remember, this is a fête, not a professionally run funfair) hands him a small goldfish in a large polythene bag full of water. The boy throws again – again he wins a fish. His third throw misses, but his fourth wins another fish. The whole thing is obviously much too easy. We leave him as he is buying more rings, and trying to cope with three bags full of water.

The Rolls-Royce is arriving at the entrance to the fête. Giles gets out, as a small crowd begins to gather, staring at the car. We realise that not many of the crowd have bothered to come in fancy dress. Twist gets out, and opens the rear door of the car. Out steps Queen Victoria. The crowd parts, and Mrs Brassett sweeps through them, receiving a few unconscious curtseys and bows from the villagers. She is followed out by Old Jack who, by contrast, looks a ridiculous figure in his burglar's outfit. Lesley, meanwhile, has got out of the door on the other side, and is talking to Giles, and laughing at Jack's stony-faced reception of the crowd's amusement. The last to come out is

Carol. She is very conscious of the crowd, and strikes a pose with one foot on the running board of the car. Applause and approval, especially from the male villagers. They follow Queen Victoria through the crowd, Giles and Lesley going last. Giles is fiddling with an "instamatic" type Polaroid camera.

The goldfish stall is doing a roaring trade. People are winning goldfish left, right and centre, and walking away with water-filled bags.

A canvas latrine, marked "MEN". The canvas finishes about nine inches from the ground. Old Jack stops and stares at the gap below the canvas. There are three feet protruding from under it, and two sticks.

Jack is puzzling this out, when the three feet and two sticks move away, and out of the latrine comes an old yokel with a walking stick, followed by a man with a wooden leg. They go off in different directions.

Giles is bowling at skittles. The sign says "Win a Pig." Lesley is with him, cheering him on. He is doing well and the skittles are flying in all directions. As he lets fly with his third ball, the man with the wooden leg crosses the line of fire. The ball hits his wooden leg, and he is bowled over.

Hawk is arriving at the fête on his motor bike. He is dressed in furs, as before mentioned. He dismounts, and from a box strapped to his pillion he takes out a viking's hat, with the horns. Removing his crash helmet, he swaps it for the horned hat. There is very little difference. He marches off into the crowd.

Old Jack is at the shooting gallery, run by a curate. The curate is rather nervous of guns. We see Old Jack taking aim at a row of clay pipes. He fires, and hits a fancy plate on the shelf of prizes. It shatters. He fires five more times in rapid succession, and each time shatters a prize. He is cheered by a couple of callow youths nearby, and points to the clay pipes, beaming. The curate hands him a clay pipe and Jack goes away, delighted, leaving the curate mystified.

A "treasure hunt" – a plot of sand on the ground about six feet square, with little flags stuck in it. A few feet away, a "Muffin the Mule" type wooden horse, painted silver, for children's rides, the kind you put sixpence in, and it jogs up and down.

This is being looked after by a rather neurotic middle-aged lady. Next to the horse, a coconut-shy booth. Between the horse and the coconuts stand two old farmers, talking away. The one nearest the horse takes a match out of his waistcoat pocket, and strikes it on the horse's hindquarters, to light his pipe. The lady looks livid, and tells him not to do that. He grins and nods apologetically. She turns to attend to a child, and he does it again.

A group of yokels standing round a pen, in which is a prize cow. They are staring at it, as country yokels do. Hawk approaches, and leans on the fence, looking at it. The cow looks up, sees Hawk's horns and backs away. The yokels all stare at Hawk. He smiles uneasily and hurries off.

The farmer has just struck his match on Muffin the Mule again, and the lady, furious, gets some of the Boy Scouts who are guarding the "treasure hunt" to move the horse to another part of the ground. The farmers are still talking, oblivious to the fact that it has gone. Two men, carrying some fencing, or part of a collapsible booth, make their way between the farmers and the coconut shy, causing the farmers to step back, so that they are adjacent to the treasure hunt. They are still talking. Carol is walking along, looking at things, with Giles and Lesley in the background. The boy scouts ask her to try her luck with the treasure hunt. She takes a flag and bends over, trying to decide where to place the flag. Giles, a few yards behind her, raises his Polaroid camera, and we see, from his point of view, Carol's silver-lamé bottom sparkling in the sunshine. The farmer, without looking, strikes a match on it, still talking. Giles and Lesley suppress their mirth with difficulty.

Old Jack is rummaging round a rummage stall. He puts down his leather swag bag, in order to look at something. Someone picks it up, buys it, and goes away. The village policeman is wandering round the fête. Large, sweating, not too bright. He stops, and watches Old Jack the burglar, rummaging. Finding nothing to suit him, Old Jack drifts away, picking up a lady's handbag from the stall as he does so, in mistake for his swag bag. The policeman eyes him suspiciously and follows at a respectable distance, tailing him.

Nearly everyone in the crowd is now carrying a goldfish.

Giles and Lesley are playing "Knock his hat off". Three youths, with assorted hats – a top hat, a ladies picture hat covered in flowers and birds, etc. – are walking up and down behind a canvas screen, which is just head-height, so that only the hats are showing. The competitor, in this case Giles, has to throw tennis balls, to try and knock off a hat as they move to and fro. We see Giles miss a couple, and purchase more tennis balls from the stall holder. Old Jack is wondering along, tailed by the policeman. He goes behind the "Knock his hat off" stall, staring at the youths who are wandering up and down for no apparent reason.

We see Giles again, preparing to throw. Old Jack, being short, is not visible to Giles behind the screen. Suddenly a policeman's helmet moves slowly along the top of the screen.

From the back, Old Jack finds there is no way out at the far end of the canvas screen. He turns back, and the policeman passes him, so as not to arouse suspicion.

From the front, Giles is taking aim. The helmet arrives at the end of the screen, turns, and begins to move slowly back again. Giles lets fly, and catches it – a beauty. It disappears. Old Jack wanders away past Giles, as Giles collects his prize. The policeman is dusting his helmet behind the canvas screen. He then moves, helmet in hand, to keep Jack in his line of sight. Next to the canvas screen is a large square of plywood, with an oval hole cut in it, at about head height. From the policeman's point of view, through this hole, we see the tiny figure of Old Jack in the distance. The policeman moves up and puts his face through the hole, watching. From the front, we see for the first time that the plywood has on it a crude painting of a headless fat lady in a terrible bathing costume, a real seaside dirty postcard look, the sort used by beach photographers. The policeman is supplying the head, and is greeted by a ragged cheer from the onlookers. Giles is there, with his Polaroid camera, and snaps it, as, of course, does the photographer who is running the stall.

Everyone, but everyone, now has a goldfish in a bag of water. We see a small girl carrying one in close-up. Suddenly, it springs a leak, the water streaming out in an arc, unnoticed by the child.

From the dais, the vicar is announcing the fancy dress parade. The microphone is over-modulated, and keeps cutting out, with the result that we hear one word in four, and that very crackly. People start to drift round to the fenced-off portion of the ground near the dais, as the competitors, including all Giles's guests, get ready for the parade. Most of the goldfish bags are leaking now, but people don't seem to notice. Music starts to play from an amplifier, and the competitors begin to walk round. They all have numbers pinned on their backs by a young lady near the dais as they enter the arena. Shots of people still approaching the fences and watching – all with leaking goldfish bags. A long shot of the parade going on. The policeman is still following Old Jack as he goes into the arena. The young lady pins a number onto the policeman's back – no. 49.

A shot of three yokels, standing against the fence, watching the parade. First, from the back, we see they all have bags of goldfish. Then, in profile, we see the three of them, grinning at the fancy dresses. Three jets of water are streaming out through the open fence, at just the right height. After a few seconds, two of the streams slowly drop down and peter out, but the one in the middle carries on, strongly. His obviously is bigger and contains more water. We cut to his face – oblivious – a great, red, shiny country face. Back to the three-shot, with the steady stream showing no sign of letting up.

A long shot of the parade. Then, a quick shot of the sky, darkening rapidly. There is a sudden clap of thunder, and down comes the rain, in buckets. Umbrellas go up all over the ground, and people all break for cover. Shots of everything getting soaked. Close shots of the ground, with puddles rapidly forming – Lesley, with her one Indian feather drooping – Hawk terribly bedraggled, water dripping from his fur – everyone scattering, and all the guests making for the Rolls-Royce. They arrive at the car and Giles, bending his head to get into the driving seat, shoots about a gallon of water out of the brim of his ten-gallon hat, onto the ground. Hawk, in his horns, is bundling people into the rear door as fast as he can. Carol, as she is bending to get in, drops her sword, and Hawk picks it up, butting her in the behind with his horns as he does so. The doors slam, and they drive away.

The large poster, advertising the fête – saturated, all the paint running: and finally, a large puddle, and in it, several goldfish swimming about happily, their lives saved in the nick of time by Mother Nature.

The House. Everyone has changed into their ordinary clothes, and is preparing to leave. Mrs Brassett is knitting, and Old Jack clutches his easel and one canvas, on which he has the painting of the statue. Carol is now wearing an evening dress – a diaphanous affair with a long train at the back. Giles is shaking hands with them all – they are chattering away as usual. As they come out onto the steps, we see that the storm has passed, and it's a fine summer evening again. Hawk helps them into the car *(this time he has a chauffeur's cap on – he is driving them to the station).*

Old Jack, staggering into the car with his easel, catches it on the side of the door rather violently, causing him to drop his one remaining canvas. He recoils from the impact and puts his foot through the picture. He bends down to pick it up, planting one end of his easel down on the train of Carol's dress as he does so. Hawk helps Carol into the front passenger seat at this moment, and the whole of her skirt is ripped off as she climbs in. Hawk slams the door, and then notices the skirt on the ground, just as Old Jack slams his door. Hawk's face in close-up – delighted at the prospect of driving next to a skirtless

Carol. He rushes round to the driving seat, leaps in, and the car disappears down the drive.

Giles is waving from the steps, chuckling. Lesley appears round the door frame, from inside the house. Giles looks surprised and indicates the receding car. Lesley grins and points downwards, indicating that she intends to stay a little longer. Giles is delighted, and takes her hand and pats it. Suddenly, from inside the house, we hear a strangled cry of delight, and the oriental gentleman rushes out, between Giles and Lesley, flinging his arms wide in relief at having found his way out of the house. Muttering joyously, he rushes down the drive in undercrank, leaping and dancing in his ecstasy.

Giles and Lesley look at each other and, hand in hand, go into the house, shutting the door behind them.

As the door closes, the stone ball falls off the balustrade, and rolls down the drive.

We pull out, slowly.

The Two Ronnies:
The Two-Handers

onnie Barker first met Ronnie Corbett socially at the actor's club
– The Buckstone – in 1963. Three years later they found themselves part of David Frost's team (alongside John Cleese) for *The
Frost Report*. Over the years they developed a strong friendship and
performing rapport, so much so that in 1971 Bill Cotton, then head
of BBC Light Entertainment, suggested poaching them from ITV and
giving them their own show on the BBC. (In fact, Cotton never realised
that just days before his offer the Ronnies had been dropped by ITV,
over contractual problems the network had developed with Frost.)

All the show needed was a title. "They asked what we should call it,"
says Ronnie, "and someone in the office said, 'Well, they're always called
the two Ronnies, so why not call it *The Two Ronnies*?' So we did."

Over the 12-season, 94-episode run of *The Two Ronnies* (plus
Christmas specials) Gerald Wiley contributed a vast amount of material. Although the show provided both Barker and Corbett with plenty
of solo moments, some of "Wiley's" best pieces were the two-handers
between Ronnies B and C, from their classic pub exchanges, to the
tramps and yokels, via a short-sighted opticians through the aged
armchair-bound ramblings of Godfrey and Humphrey, to a shop-
keeper dealing with a man who, to all intents and purposes, appears
to be asking for "Four candles"...

FORK HANDLES

or "Annie Finkhouse?"

*An old ironmonger's shop. A shop that sells everything – garden equip-
ment, ladies' tights, builders' supplies, mousetraps – everything.*

A long counter up and down stage. A door to the back of the shop up left. The back wall also has a counter. Lots of deep drawers and cupboards up high, so that RC has to get a ladder to get some of the goods RB orders.

RC is serving a woman with a toilet roll. He is not too bright.

RC: There you are – mind how you go.

(Woman exits. RB enters – a workman. Not too bright either.)

RC: Yes, sir?

RB: Four candles?

RC: Four candles? Yes, sir. *(He gets four candles from a drawer.)* There you are.

RB: No – fork handles.

RC: Four candles. That's four candles.

RB: No, fork handles – handles for forks.

RC: Oh, fork handles. *(He gets a garden fork handle from the back of the shop.)* Anything else?

RB: *(looks at his list)* Got any plugs?

RC: What sort of plugs?

RB: Bathroom – rubber one.

(RC gets box of bath plugs, holds up two different sizes.)

RC: What size?

RB: Thirteen amp.

RC: Oh, electric plugs. *(Gets electric plug from drawer.)* What else?

RB: Saw tips.

RC: Saw tips? What you want, ointment?

RB: No, tips to cover the saw.

RC: Oh. No, we ain't got any.

RB: Oh. Got any hoes?

RC: Hoes? Yeah. *(He gets a garden hoe from the garden department.)*

RB: No – hose.

RC: Oh, hose. I thought you meant hoes. *(He gets a roll of garden hose.)*

RB: No – hose.

RC: *(Gives him a dirty look.)* What hose? *(He gets a packet of ladies' tights from a display stand.)* Pantie-hose, you mean?

RB: No, "O"s – letter "O"s – letters for the gate. "Mon Repose".

RC: Why didn't you say so? *(He gets ladder, climbs up to cupboard high up on wall, gets down box of letters.)* Now, "O"s – here we are – two?

RB: Yeah.

RC: Right. *(He takes box back up ladder and returns.)* Next?

RB: Got any "P"s?

RC: Oh, my Gawd. Why didn't you bleedin' say while I'd got the box of letters down here? I'm working me guts out here climbing about all over the shop, putting things back and then getting 'em out again. Now then, *(he is back with the box)* how many? Two?

RB: No – peas – three tins of peas.

RC: You're having me on, ain't yer? Ain't yer! *(He gets three tins of peas.)*

RB: No, I ain't. I meant tinned peas.

RC: Right. Now what?

RB: Pumps.

RC: Pumps? Hand pumps or foot pumps?

RB: Foot.

RC: Footpumps. Right. *(He goes off, returns with a small footpump.)* Right.

RB: No, pumps for your feet. Brown pumps, size nine.

RC: You are having me on. I've had enough of this. *(He gets them from drawer.)* Is that the lot?

RB: Washers?

RC: *(exasperated)* Windscreen washers? Car washers? Dishwashers? Hair washers? Back scrubbers? Lavatory cleaners? Floor washers?

RB: Half-inch washers.

RC: Tap washers! Here, give me that list, I'm fed up with this. *(He reads list and reacts)* Right! That does it. That's the final insult. *(Calls through door)* Elsie! Come and serve this customer – I've had enough!

(RC stalks off. Elsie enters – a big, slovenly woman with a very large bosom. She takes the list. Reads it.)

ELSIE: Right, sir – what sort of knockers are you looking for?

HUMPHREY AND GODFREY (1)

RB and RC in armchairs in their London club.

RC: I say, Godfrey.

RB: What is it, Humphrey?

RC: How's your headache?

RB: She's out playing bridge.

RC: Come now, Godfrey, you shouldn't talk about the old gel like that, you know. Love makes the world go round.

RB: So does a punch on the nose, old lad. No, I've had bad luck with both my wives. The first divorced me and the second one won't.

RC: It was a case of love at first sight with me.

RB: Then why didn't you marry her?

RC: I saw her again on several occasions.

RB: So you married someone else?

RC: Yes, she's very slow.

RB: Slow? What at?

RC: Everything. It takes her a day to make instant coffee. Trouble is, I'm hen-pecked.

RB: Oh! Mustn't be, old lad. Stand up to her. Show her who's boss.

RC: I'm going to. I've made up my mind I'm going to pluck up courage and tell her something I've been wanting to tell her for ages.

RB: What's that?

RC: I must have a new apron!

THE CASE OF MRS MACE

A police station – a room or office within the station itself. RB as plain-clothes North Country detective, sits at a desk. RC enters.

RC: Good day, Inspector Jay.

RB: Morning, Dorning. Any news of the Girder murder?

RC: Yessir. He's been shot at Oxshott. Bagshot got him with a sling-shot full of buckshot.

RB: He's a good shot, Bagshot. Well, you must be pleased that situation's eased.

RC: The relief is beyond belief chief. My mind is once more a blank. And I've only you to thank.

RB: Alright. Never mind the fawning, Dorning. I'm glad to hear your head's clear: it means there's more space for the Mrs Mace case to take its place.

RC: The Mrs Mace case? Have they traced the face? (*Points to photofit blow-up on wall.*)

RB: No – and the night-dress is still missing.

RC: Is she sure it was the right night-dress? She's not mistaken about what was taken?

RB: How come, little chum?

RC: Well, to the voluptuous Mrs Mace, all her night-dresses are equally seductively attractive and attractively seductive. Whatever she wore, she'd still be a bountiful, beautiful nightie-full.

RB: She's certainly a grand lady to have as a landlady. I've been told that her teapot's never cold.

RC: I'd be delighted to be selected to inspect her, inspector. Any prospects of any suspects?

RB: Yes – two. Two of them are actors who lodge with Grace – Mrs Mace, at her place in the Chase. Leo Mighty, the leading man, known for his portrayals of charmers, farmers and men in pyjamas. And the other one is Roger Mainger, the stage manager, who once played a mad stranger in a film starring Stewart Granger called Deadly Danger.

RC: May I add another to your list? If I'm not being too bumptious or presumptuous?

RB: Who?

RC: Sergeant Bodger!

RB: What? That replacement constable from Dunstable? You must be crazy.

RC: It's just a theory, dearie. May I sit down?

RB: Please – make yourself comfy, Humphrey.

(RC sits.)

RC: It's just that Bodger has got a face like a fit: which fits the face on the photofit in the first place, and he's often to be found at her place, in the Chase, filling his face with fish.

RB: Fish?

RC: Fried by Grace – Mrs Mace. Mostly dace or plaice.

RB: But what about Leo Mighty? He's there nightly – isn't it slightly more likely? She obviously looks very flighty in her nightie – he's the sort of toff that might try to pull it off.

RC: Possibly – but here's something you don't know.

RB: I don't?

RC: No. I've spoken with Roger.

RB: Roger?

RC: The lodger.

RB: Oh – Roger Mainger, who played the stranger with Granger.

RC: He says he saw Leo take the night-gown. He was staring through the keyhole in Mrs Mace's bedroom door.

RB: He dared to stare through there? Would he swear he saw Leo Mighty take the nightie?

RC: He'll do plenty of swearing. No wonder he was staring – it was the one she was wearing!

RB: What? Surely not!

RC: He stood on the bed, and pulled it over her head. She went red, and he fled. He locked himself in the shed, and wished he were dead. She was going to phone her cousin Ted, but felt dizzy in the head, so she lay on the bed instead, and went red.

RB: So you said. Roger is a liar!

RC: Have you any proof, you old poof?

RB: I've seen where Mrs Mace sleeps. It's an attic! So the story about pulling the garment over her head is false. He would have to pull the night-gown right down! There's no headroom in her bedroom!

RC: So Roger's lying! Then he must be the culprit! Game, set and match, chief! And so ends the disgraceful Grace Mace case.

RB: *(picks up phone)* I'll just tell the Chief Constable – what a relief, constable. *(Into phone)* Hello, sir – we've solved the Mace Case. I'm happy to tell you that Leo is innocent and so is Sergeant Bodger. Yes, sir: in other words – 'twas not Leo Mighty who lifted the nightie, t'was Roger the Lodger, the soft-footed dodger, and not Sergeant Bodger, thank God!

LIFE IN THE TRENCHES (Part 2)

A trench. 1914–18 war. Heavy and noisy gunfire. RB and RC discovered. RB a captain, RC a corporal.

RB: We're cornered, corporal. We'll be lucky to get out of here alive.

RC: Yes, sir – probably later than that, I shouldn't wonder.

RB: What?

RC: Later than five, sir – probably nearer half-past.

RB: Get out alive, I said – not get out by five.

RC: Oh, sorry sir. It's these damn guns, sir. I can't hear properly, sir. Are we cut off from the others, sir?

RB: I think so. We can either lie low until morning, or you can find a high vantage point to see if we can spot the enemy. *(Hands him binoculars.)* What do you say?

RC: Thank you, sir. *(For the binoculars.)*

RB: No, I mean: what do you think?

RC: Oh. Up to you, sir.

RB: Alright, corporal – I think you'd better get up a tree, and risk it.

RC: Oh good, I could just do with one.

RB: What?

RC: Cup of tea and a biscuit, sir.

RB: I said: get up a tree and risk it!

RC: Oh. Oh dear.

RB: Well, go on – make a start.

RC: Bake a tart, sir?

RB: Make a start, man, make a start. Do I have to repeat every stupid little word?

RC: No need to be personal, sir.

RB: What do you mean?

RC: Calling me that, sir.

RB: I said "stupid little word".

RC: Oh, sorry, sir. I thought you said something else.

RB: Well – off you go then, corporal.

RC: Excuse me sir, but I can't climb trees, sir.

RB: What?

RC: Never could, sir. Ever since I was a small boy at Wimbledon.

RB: You never told me that.

RC: What, sir?

RB: You were a ball-boy at Wimbledon. I've always loved tennis.

RC: Who, Dennis the cook, sir?

RB: Tennis, man, tennis! Look, never mind all that. One of our tanks is just up there on the ridge. We must try to recapture it.

RC: Yes, sir.

RB: But be careful. Jerry snipers are everywhere. Anywhere near a tank is a hot-spot.

RC: No, I don't think we are, sir.

RB: Are what?

RC: Anywhere near a Lancashire hot-pot, sir.

RB: Hot-spot, damn you, hot-spot!

RC: Sorry, sir. Please sir – I can't go, sir.

RB: Why not, corporal?

RC: My gun's all wonky, sir.

RB: Well, it's nerves, it's only natural.

RC: No, my gun, sir.

RB: Oh. What's the matter with it?

RC: It was in my trouser pocket and it went off half-cock, sir.

RB: Oh, well you'd better report to casualty when we get back. Looks as if I'll have to go.

RC: Yes, sir – thank you, sir.

(RB climbs up the trench. He is shot, and falls back.)

RC: Any gravy on your pie and peas?

RC: Are you alright, sir?

RB: Of course, I'm not alright! I'm shot.

RC: Yes, so am I, sir, it is hot.

RB: Shot! Not hot!

RC: Oh, sorry, sir. Shall I get stretcher bearers, sir?

RB: No, it's too late for that. Just go and let me die in peace.

RC: Yes, sir – any gravy sir?

RB: What?

RB: I didn't say go and get me pie and peas! I said go and let me die in peace. Goodbye, corporal. You're a good chap. We haven't always seen eye to eye. Or ear to ear for that matter.

RC: No, sir. It's the guns, sir.

RB: Yes – but if you get through safe and sound, at least when I get up to heaven they'll say "he died – saving an ordinary man".

(Big gun explosion.)

RC: Save what, sir? (He is about to go over the top.)

RB: An ordinary man!

RC: I certainly will, sir.

RB: What?

RC: Save you a strawberry flan.

(He goes, and RB dies of annoyance.)

HUMPHREY AND GODFREY (2)

RB and RC in armchairs in their London club.

RB: *(looking at newspaper)* I say, Humphrey.

RC: What is it, Godfrey?

RB: It says here, "A firm bust in four weeks".

RC: That's nothing – my brother's firm went bust in a fortnight.

RB: No, no old boy, it's an advert – for women.

RC: Don't answer it, old chap, you've already got one. Talking of women, seen the new maid in the bar?

RB: Yes. I've seen better legs on a piano. And with a piano, you get one extra. Bit of a gold-digger too.

RC: Really?

RB: Yes. I can read women like a book.

RC: What system do you use?

RB: Braille.

RC: Trouble with life is, when you're young you can't afford women. By the time you have money to burn, the fire's gone out.

RB: Like my brother. He still chases his secretaries round the desk but he can't remember why.

HEAR HEAR

RB sits at desk. A large sign on the wall – "Hearing Aid Centre".
Enter RC. He approaches the desk.

RC: Is this the hearing-aid centre?

RB: Pardon?

RC: Is this the hearing-aid centre?

RB: Yes, that's right, yes.

RC: Ah. I've come to be fitted for a hearing-aid.

RB: Pardon?

RC: I said I've come for a hearing-aid.

RB: Oh, yes. Do sit down. I'll just take a few details. Name?

RC: Pardon?

RB: Name?

RC: Crampton.

RB: Pardon?

RC: Crampton.

RB: Oh, Crampton.

RC: Pardon?

RB: I said Crampton.

RC: Crampton, yes.

RB: Right, Mr Crampton. Now I take it you are having difficulty with your hearing.

RC: Pardon?

RB: I said I take it you're having difficulty with your hearing?

RC: That's correct.

RB: Pardon?

RC: I said that's correct.

RB: Which ear?

RC: Pardon?

RB: Which ear?

RC: The right.

RB: Pardon?

RC: The right ear.

RB: Ah. Could you cover it up with your hand, please. *(RC does so.)*

RB: Now can you hear me?

RC: Pardon?

RB: Can you hear what I'm saying?

RC: It's very faint.

RB: Pardon?

RC: It's very faint.

RB: I can't hear you.

RC: Pardon?

RB: Try the other ear.

(RC covers it up.)

RB: Now, what's that like?

RC: I still can't hear you.

RB: Can you hear me?

RC: Pardon?

RB: Hm. Definitely need a hearing-aid.

RC: I thought so.

RB: Pardon?

RC: You can't hear me, either, can you?

RB: Pardon?

RC: Why don't you wear one?

RB: You're still very faint.

RC: A HEARING-AID! Why don't you wear one?

RB: I am wearing one.

RC: Pardon?

RB: Pardon?

RC: I said "Pardon".

RB: Oh. I said "Pardon".

RC: Oh, to hell with it – I'll get some new teeth.

(He exits.)

THE GROCERY SHOP

A village shop, sells mostly foodstuffs, but has a toy section, stationery, gardening equipment, etc. RB, as proprietor, potters about. RC enters, with shopping list.

RB: Morning, sir.

RC: Morning. Erm – we've just moved into the village, and as a matter of fact, you've been recommended to us.

RB: Oh, lovely. That's probably 'cos we're the only shop in the area. Still, what can we do for you, sir?

RC: Well now, my wife has given me this list and her handwriting is not all that easy to decipher, I ...

RB: Let's have a look – I get used to reading people's terrible writing. *(Takes list, reads.)* No, I can't understand a single word of that, sir. *(Gives it back.)*

RC: Well, I can read some of it. Now – what's this first one? – "A large tin of bears".

RB: Bears? Bear's what?

RC: Just bears.

RB: Must be pears.

RC: No – it's beans.

RB: Oh, beans!

RC: Yes. "Preferably Cress and Blackwell".

RB: Oh, right. Here we are. Next?

RC: Some Cornish Panties.

RB: Panties? Let's see. *(Takes list.)* Oh, that'll be pasties, sir, pasties. How many would you like?

RC: Er, two. The wife eats them all the time.

RB: What size?

RC: Outsize.

RB: Right – they're nice ones today, sir, with the nice frilly edges. There we are. One pair of frilly pasties. Will they be large enough for the wife, sir?

RC: Yes, they look about her size.

RB: 'Cos if they're not big enough for her, tell her to pop by and drop 'em in the shop and I'll change them for her. Now, what's next?

RC: Looks like slippy soap. No – sticky loofah. No – Loopy Loop.

RB: Loop the loop? That's soup.

(Goes to get soup.)

RC: No. Stinky loam?

RB: Oh. Fertiliser.

(Goes to get fertiliser.)

RC: No, spicy love?

RB: Oh, that's paperbacks.

(Goes to get paperbacks.)

RC: Sliced beef?

RB: Ah –

(Goes to refrigerated counter.)

RC: Got it – sliced loaf.

RB: Are you sure, sir?

RC: Yes, look, it says "wholemeal" in brackets.

RB: Thank God for that. What's next?

RC: "Jolly Christmas".

RB: Eh? *(Takes list.)* "Jelly crystals". Right. Now. "A small union man". Would that be you, sir?

RC: A small union man?

BOTH: "A small onion flan".

RC: Good, now we're getting the hang of it. Er – dolls' puddles.

RB: Doll puddles? Oh, I know what that is. *(Goes over to toys.)* Here we are. The new dolly, sir – wets its nappy and then comes out in spots all over its little BTM. Then you rub this special cream on it and its hair grows.

RC: No, that won't be it. Perhaps it's "dog puddles".

RB: Oh, I hope not.

RC: Ah! I suddenly saw it. "Dill pickles".

RB: Oh yes, right.

RC: It's funny how you can suddenly get used to someone's handwriting, isn't it? Now, *(reads)* "Two large stiff and kindly pigs".

RB: No, no, sir. *(Looking at list)* That's "Two large steam and kidney pills". She means these, sir. *(Shows packet.)* Knock a horse out, these would.

RC: No – it's "two large steak and kidney pies".

RB: Oh yes, of course. Are we nearly there?

RC: Won't be long now. "Two topless molls".

RB: Two towel rails.

RC: Two toilet rolls.

RB: *(taking list)* A bot of raspberry jim. A large bot or a small bot, sir?

RC: That's for the wife too.

RB: Oh, a large bot. Right – a tin of diced parrots, *(gets each object as he says them)*, a pond of self-rising flood, a large bedroom, half a new member and a bunch of ruderies. *(I.e. tin of carrots, bag of flour, large beetroot, half a cucumber and a bunch of radishes.)* Right, sir, do you want these delivered?

RC: Please. Cash on delivery?

RB: Certainly, sir.

RC: Right. There's my address.

RB: *(reading address from paper)* Mr and Mrs Spith, Number Twanky Foop, Thigh Streek, opposite the Pouf's Office.

RC: That's it – good morning!

(Exits.)

End.

MARK MY WORDS

A pub. RB at bar, drinking a pint – flat cap. RC enters – flat cap. They speak throughout without any sign of emotion at all.

RC: Evening, Harry.

RB: Hullo, Bert. What you having?

RC: Oh ta, I'll have a pint of, er–

RB: Light?

RC: No, er–

RB: Brown?

RC: No–

RB: Mild?

RC: No–

RB: Bitter?

RC: Yes, bitter. Pint of bitter.

RB: *(calls)* Pint of bitter, Charlie.

(Barman attends to it.)

How are you then?

RC: Mustn't grumble. I just been up the–

RB: Club?

RC: No, up the–

RB: Dogs?

RC: No–

RB: Fish shop?

RC: No–

RB: Doctors?

RC: Doctors, yes. Up the doctors. I just been up the doctors. I've been having a bit of trouble with my, er–

RB: Chest?

RC: No, with my–

RB: Back?

RC: No–

RB: Side?

RC: No–

RB: Backside?

RC: No, my wife.

RB: Oh.

RC: My wife. She seems to have got it into her head that I'm a, I'm a–

RB: What, annoyed with her?

RC: No, a–

RB: A martian?

RC: No–

RB: A pouf?

RC: No, a bit under the weather. But he's examined me all over. Nothing wrong at all. He told me to drop my–

RB: Really?

RC: And he looked at my–

RB: Go on.

RC: And he said there was nothing to worry about at all. No, on the contrary, he said I was, er– I was er–

RB: First class?

RC: No–

RB: Fascinating?

RC: No–

RB: Friendly?

RC: No, fit.

RB: Oh, fit.

RC: Perfectly fit for a–

RB: Change.

RC: No, for a man of–

RB: Ninety?

RC: For a man of my age. It's nice to know, isn't it? 'Cos I only went up there on the–

RB: Bus?

RC: No, on the off chance.

RB: Oh, off chance, yes.

RC: Have you been up there lately? It's all different now up there. He's got a marvellous great big new, er– big new er–

RB: Rolls Royce?

RC: No, a big new er–

RB: Waiting room?

RC: No, big new er–

RB: Receptionist?

RC: Receptionist, yes. Big new receptionist. Oh my word, she's got it all er–

RB: Up here?

RC: No–

RB: Down here?

RC: No–

RB: Where then?

RC: She's got it all er–

RB: All over?

RC: No, she's got it all organised up there. Up at the doctors. 'Cos it used to be such a mess, but now it's completely reorganised. I just stood there in a, in a–

RB: Queue?

RC: No, in a–

RB: Vest?

RC: No, in a–

RB: Draught?

RC: No, in amazement.

RB: Oh, amazement, yes.

RC: Oh yes, it's like a conveyor belt up there. Mind you, it's all sex equality up there. You don't have separate cubicles. All the men had to take off their shirts and stand against one wall, and all the women took off their dresses and satin, er – satin–

RB: Blouses?

RC: No, satin, er–

RB: Panties?

RC: No, rows. Sat in rows along the other wall.

RB: Oh, I see, yes.

RC: I tell you who was up there. That young Julie.

RB: Julie?

RC: Yeah, you know. Her mother's got them big, er–

RB: Teeth?

RC: No, them big–

RB: Bay windows?

RC: No, them big Alsatians. You know, them ones she keeps taking up the common and they keep biting people in the er–

RB: Leg?

RC: No, in the er–

RB: Bushes?

RC: No, in the evenings. Well, her kid, Julie. She was up there.

RB: Oh, what was she up there for?

RC: Well, she was telling me, she went out one night with some young lad, and they fell in the duck pond, and now she's er–

RB: Pregnant?

RC: No, er–

RB: Stagnant?

RC: No, now she's er–

RB: Fragrant?

RC: No, she's off work with a cut foot. Doctor said she was lucky, with that duck pond, it could've been a lot worse. It could have been a septic er–

RB: Septic tank?

RC: Toenail. Septic toenail. Here, I had a lucky escape last week.

RB: Oh, yes?

RC: Well, I was in the canteen, sitting opposite a woman with one of those, er–

RB: One of those looks in her eye?

RC: No, one of those er–

RB: Hourglass figures?

RC: No, one of those apple turnovers.

RB: Oh, yes. Go on.

RC: She's got this turnover and she kept er–

RB: Turning it over?

RC: No, she kept toying with it.

RB: Oh, toying with it.

RC: Yes. Well anyway, we was sitting right opposite, at this little table, and suddenly I felt her er–

RB: Hand on your knee?

RC: No, I felt her–

RB: Hand on your other knee?

RC: No.

RB: You felt her what? What did you feel?

RC: I felt her looking at me. And I could tell she fancied me, see. So we got talking, about gardening, and it came up in the conversation that I was very good on er–

RB: On the lawn?

RC: No, I'm very good on er–

RB: Friday nights?

RC: No, very good on pest control. So she said, what are you doing Saturday afternoon, she said. And I told her this week I'm going shopping for the wife, 'cos she'll be resting in bed with er–

RB: With any luck.

RC: No, with her trouble. So, anyhow, this woman said, why not come round Saturday afternoon for a couple of hours, she says. I can sunbathe on the patio, and you can have a look at my big ...

RB: Big what?

RC: Bigonias.

RB: Oh, bigonias, yes.

RC: They're covered in blackfly, she said. Well, I was taken by surprise, rather, so at first I said I couldn't, as I hadn't got a long enough, er–

RB: What?

RC: You know, a long enough, er–

RB: Garden spray?

RC: No, a long enough shopping list to be out that long.

RB: Oh. So didn't you go then?

RC: Yes, I went, eventually, 'cos she pleaded with me. She said if I didn't, she would have to spend all afternoon lying there on her, er–

RB: On her back?

RC: No, on her–

RB: On her front?

RC: No, her–

RB: Begonias?

RC: No, on her own.

RB: Oh, her own.

RC: So, anyway, there she was in her sun suit, and after I'd sprayed her blackfly, we walked down the garden, and I said, "I would like to kiss you," I said, and she immediately got on her, er–

RB: Hands and knees?

RC: No, her high horse.

RB: Oh, her high horse, oh yes.

RC: Certainly not, she said, I think you're a little, er–

RB: A little raver?

RC: No, a little–

RB: A little drunk?

RC: No, a little premature.

RB: Oh, a little premature drunk.

RC: "I've only known you half an hour," she says – "You'll have to wait another ten minutes," and she disappeared indoors. So I spent the next ten minutes rearranging her rock garden, and then went indoors, and there she was in the all, er– in the all, er–

RB: In the all-together?

RC: No, in the 'all of the 'ouse. Anyhow, we had a lovely time, and afterwards she gave me a round of, er–

RB: Round of applause?

RC: No, a round of, er–

RB: Round of golf?

RC: No, a round of toast and a cup of tea. But I was a bit worried when I got home. The wife was waiting for me. I thought she'd found out. Do you know what she gave me?

RB: Which reminds me – I'm late for me supper. Cheerio, Bert, see you in the canteen for an apple turnover!

(He exits, and the barman approaches.)

BARMAN: I couldn't help overhearing, Bert. You've got me all interested now – what happened?

RC: Well, I was a bit worried when I got home, 'cos the wife was waiting for me. I thought she'd found out. Do you know what she gave me?

BARMAN: What?

RC: As soon as I walked in, she gave me a bunch of ...

BARMAN: A bunch of fives right up the throat?

RC: No, a bunch of begonias! Ta-ta, Charlie!

HUMPHREY AND GODFREY (3)

RB and RC in armchairs, in their London club.

RB: I say, Humphrey.

RC: What is it, Godfrey?

RB: You know, no matter how hot the day is, at night it gets dark.

RC: Yes. It's the same in America.

RB: Just come back, haven't you?

RC: Mm.

RB: Did you go for pleasure, or did the wife go with you?

RC: Went alone. Very grand hotel.

RB: Really?

RC: Yes. So grand that even the guests have to use the service entrance.

RB: That is grand.

RC: Funny people, the Americans, though. On the plane going over, a woman collapsed. Doctor, sitting on one side of her, refused to help. Said he was on holiday.

RB: Amazing.

RC: Chap sitting other side of her said "That's disgraceful." Doctor said "Would you carry on your profession if you were on holiday?" "I certainly would," said the other chap. "Alright, what is your profession?" he said. "I'm a fishmonger," said the other chap, and he picked the woman up, loosened her clothing and sold her two pounds of haddock.

LIMERICK WRITERS

A hotel lounge. A large banner saying "23rd Annual Convention of Limerick Writers". RC is in very cheap suit, RB very grand.

RC: How de do?

RB: How de do?

RC: My name's Dear. Arnold Dear. I come here every year.

RB: My name's Algernon Crust. You write limericks, I trust?

RC: No – I'm only here for the beer. *(RB looks disdainful.)*
Just a joke, just a rhyme and a joke
I can't help it
I'm that sort of bloke–
Just a joke and a rhyme
And a jolly good time.
(confidentially) What I really came for was a–

RB: *(offers cigarettes)* Smoke?

RC: No, I won't. Please don't think that I'm rude
Smoking's fine if you're in the right mood;
I smoke with my food
My wife smokes in the nude
(As long as it doesn't intrude!)

RB: Tell me, what sort of rhymes do you do?

RC: Oh, just things about ladies from Crewe
Who step from a train
Catch their foot in a drain
And the porters all – what about you?

RB: Oh, I've published a book – and it sells;
It's described by the Bishop of Wells
As the best of its kind
And my work is confined
To the loo walls of 4 star hotels.

RC: Oh, of course, published by the AA!

RB: Recommended by Egon Ronay,
Yes, it's perfectly true–
And BBC 2
Made it into a *Play for Today.*

RC: You're the wit who writes things about marriages
On the walls of first-class railway carriages!
Please tell me once more
The classic you saw
On the seat of the boys' room at Claridges!

RB: *(Ah!)* "My mother, a born intellectual
Made me a complete homosexual"
Underneath wrote some fool
"If I gave her the wool
Would she make me one?" – not ineffectual!

RC: That's the stuff that I wish I could write
But I sit and I ponder all night
I end up with some tale
Of a cow and a pail
And the last line's a load of–

RB: Quite, quite.
My room's pretty grotty – how yours?

RC: Well, there's woodworm in both of the doors
There's a hole in the floor
But what worries me more
Is the dry-rot I found in my drawers.

RB: Have you noticed that little blonde tart?

RC: Oh – how pretty she is – bless her heart.

RB: She's a right little goer!

RC: Oh, how well do you know her?

RB: Well, she's not a real blonde, for a start.

RC: With her looks, I don't think I'd quibble.

RB: I must say, I fancy a nibble–

RC: She's inspired you, no doubt,
  With the urge to give out–

RB: Yes – let's go to the gents for a scribble.

"HIGH NIGH"

"Harrid's" linen and haberdashery department. RB is being served by a young male assistant.

ASSISTANT: Anything else, sir?

RB: Yes, I'd like some tiles.

ASSISTANT: Tiles, sir?

RB: Yes – bathroom tiles.

ASSISTANT: Are these for fixing yourself, sir?

RB: Fixing myself? No, they're for drying myself. Tiles, man. After the bath, give yourself a good brisk tiling dine.

ASSISTANT: Oh – towels – yes, sir – I'll show you a selection. Excuse me a moment.

(He goes.)

(RC appears, also an upper-class type.)

RC: *(recognising RB)* Hello, Charles!

RB: Hello, Aubrey! Bit of shopping, what?

RC: Rather! Damn good place this. Everything for the Heiss.

RB: Absotively. I often come here for the Old Spice.

RC: Old Spice? Wrong department, old boy. Toiletries, second floor.

RB: No, no – the wife – the speiss, the little woman. I'm buying for.

RC: Ah. I'm here for soup.

RB: Oh, what kind?

RC: Brine.

RB: Ah. Bit too salty for me, brine.

RC: No, brine. Brine Windsor. Wife brought up on the stuff. Lived very near here, you see. She's a sly person.

RB: What, Angela? Oh, I wouldn't say that. Little devious at times, but–

RC: No – sly – she was born in Sly. Maidenhead, Sly and Windsor, you know.

RB: Ah.

RC: Food department here excellent. Fish, pâtés, game.

RB: Cheeses.

RC: What's the matter, old boy?

RB: No, I was just saying cheeses. Wonderful cheeses, all rind.

RC: We don't eat the rind.

RB: No, all rind. Generally.

RC: Oh yes, rather. I say – did you hear what happened to Roger?

RB: Roger Kimboley-Dimbleby? From Wimbledon?

RC: Kimber-Dimber-Wimbers, yes.

RB: Haven't heard abite him for years. Last time I saw him he was a little tight.

RC: Drunk?

RB: No, a little tite for a bookmaker. A bookmaker's tite. Going around with a gel called Poopsie Benedict.

RC: He left her, old boy. Consistently lied.

RB: Did she? Deceitful, what?

RC: No, lide, old dear. Consistently noisy.

RB: Ah.

RC: No, he's with Dulcima Paget at present. They're both in trouble. He was fined in the park, you know.

RB: Fined? Fined for doing what?

RC: No, fined – discovered. By the park keeper. And she was beside him on the grind.

RB: Good gracious! Scandalous. I don't know what he sees in her.

RC: Well, he said that although she hasn't got an attractive face, she has a wonderful mind.

RB: Well, yes, she's got two wonderful minds, we know that. Stick out a mile.

RC: No, brain, old fellow. Got it up here.

RB: Oh, got you. Listen old chap, it's awfully nice to see you – fancy a drinky-poos?

RC: What about your tiles?

RB: Can't be bothered to wait. Fancy a bite to eat?

RC: Well, I am a bite to eat myself.

RB: Quite a big bite too! Come on.

(They start to move off.)

RC: Yes, we'd better hurry. When I came in there was a man with a placard saying "The end of the world is nigh".

RB: *(as they exit)* What, absolutely right nigh? This very minute? Good lord *(etc. etc.)*

(They are gone.)

HUMPHREY AND GODFREY (4)

RB and RC in armchairs, in their London club.

RC: I say, Godfrey.

RB: What is it, Humphrey?

RC: You've got your shoes on the wrong feet.

RB: Impossible. These are the only feet I've got. Anyway, my head's in no fit state to think about my feet.

RC: Hung over?

RB: Absolutely draped, old chap.

RC: Well, cheer up old lad – no one ever died of a hangover.

RB: Don't say that, Humphrey. It's only the hope of dying that's keeping me alive.

RC: Who were you with, Godfrey?

RB: Geoffrey, Humphrey. We both left the party together. He was so drunk I couldn't see him. I took him to the West End for coffee.

RC: Should never give coffee to a drunk. All you get is a wide-awake drunk. Is he better now?

RB: Getting better. He's in hospital.

RC: Hospital? Why?

RB: We were sitting on Westminster Bridge, playing who could lean over the farthest, and he won.

HUMPHREY AND GODFREY (5)

RB and RC in armchairs, in their London club.

RC: I say, Godfrey.

RB: What is it, Humphrey?

RC: My doctor has advised me to give up golf.

RB: Why? Did he examine your heart?

RC: No, he had a look at my score card.

RB: Ah. Does he play at all?

RC: My doctor? Yes. Terrible cheat. He always puts down one stroke less than he actually took. We caught him out the other day, though.

RB: How was that?

RC: He got a hole in one and he put down nought.

LOOK HERE

A small optician's in the high street. RC enters – he wears thick pebble glasses.

RC: Hello – anyone there? *(He moves to large mirror on wall behind counter.)* Ah, good morning. *(He leans, by mistake, on bell-push on counter.)* Oh, sorry.

RB: *(Emerging from behind curtained alcove – he, too, is wearing thick pebble glasses.)* Ah, good morning, Miss Prendergast. You're early.

RC: Ah, good morning. *(turning vaguely in RB's direction)*

RB: *(approaches, stands near him, but facing slightly in the wrong direction.)* Oh, sorry. Good morning.

RC: Er – two pounds of potatoes, please.

RB: No, sir – this is an optician's.

RC: What?

RB: Optician's, sir – it says so over the door.

(Points in the wrong direction.)

RC: Oh, how silly of me. I was coming in to see you this morning anyway. Look, it's on my list – optician's and greengrocer's. *(Holds up list to side of RB's head.)* See?

RB: *(not seeing)* Oh, I see. Oh good.

RC: Yes, it was the wife's idea actually.

RB: I understand, sir – won't you sit down?

(He indicates a small table with a spikey ornament on top. RC is about to sit, but straightens up again.)

RC: You're new here, aren't you?

RB: About six months I've been here.

RC: Yes, I thought I hadn't seen you in here.

RB: No, the other lady left to get married.

RC: You're not a lady, are you?

RB: No, no – I took her job. Do sit down.

RC: *(This time he sits in the swivel chair.)* Thank you.

RB: Cup of tea? I've just made it.

RC: That would be very nice.

(RB picks up milk jug from tea tray, pours milk into nearby plant pot.)

RB: Well now, sir, what seems to be the trouble?

RC: Well, I've got a feeling my eyes aren't quite as good as they used to be.

RB: Oh dear, what makes you think that?

RC: Well, it started when I bumped into someone I hadn't seen for ages.

RB: Oh, who was that?

RC: Someone I work with at the office every day. And I suddenly realised I was always bumping into them: and it was ages since I'd seen them properly.

RB: I see. Milk?

(He picks up small copper watering can and pours water into cup: then hands it to RC.)

RC: Can be damned inconvenient at times. Do you ever wear glasses?

RB: Er – occasionally, yes. Just for reading and seeing things.

RC: Anyway, as I was passing, I thought I'd look in.

(Drinks tea, reacts in surprise.)

RB: You obviously need something a bit stronger.

RC: Possibly, just a bit.

RB: Well now, let's try a bit of a test with the wall charts. *(He presses a button on the counter, and a revolving police bulb lights up on the other side of the stage, near the chart. RB steers himself towards it.)* Right, now then, take your glasses off. *(RC does so.)* Are they off?

RC: Yes.

RB: Right, now read the letters, starting from the top.

RC: *(peers into space)* Er – no – could you just wave your arms about, I'm not quite sure of the direction.

RB: *(waves his arms)* Over here – here we are.

RC: *(peering)* No. No, that one's stumped me, I'm afraid.

RB: Don't worry. Try this one. *(He reveals the next one – this just has a large "E" and underneath it "I" and "C".)* There, how's that?

RC: Er – "A"?

RB: *(peering closely at it)* No.

RC: "B"? "C"?

RB: Keep going.

RC: "D"?

RB: No.

RC: "E"?

RB: That's it. Next line.

RC: *(peering)* No.

RB: I'll give you a clue. What do you see with?

RC: Your eye.

RB: "I", good. Now, what do you do with your eye?

RC: See.

RB: "C", good, good. Try the next line.

RC: Is there a next line?

RB: *(peering closer)* Probably not.

RC: I really couldn't see any of that last chart, you know.

RB: Don't worry, we'll get it sorted out. Just a matter of trial and error. Now then, try this. *(He pulls a cord – the curtains covering the right-hand wall part, revealing a single six foot "A".)*

RC: Ah, er – "A".

RB: Good, excellent. No help from me either.

RC: "I".

RB: No, that's the hat stand–

RC: "H".

RB: *(as we see a shot of the "H"-shaped bookcase)* No, you're reading the furniture now. Just hang on–

RC: Sorry.

RB: *(Takes a long, thin lathe of wood from where it stands by the wall, near him, and points it in the direction of RC.)* Now – see if you can grab this long stick.

(RC manages to grab it eventually. RB feels his way along it, hand over hand, homing in on RC until he reaches him.)

RB: Thanks awfully. Excellent. Now, I'll just get the test frames and lenses. Shan't be a jiffy– *(manages to locate the trolley, pushes it down towards RC, hits chair with a crash.)* Oops, careful. Now, let's put these test frames on for you – just sit still, that's it– *(he has arrived the wrong side of RC and puts the frames on the back of his head. He feels RC's hair.)* Ah – well you know your trouble, don't you?

RC: What?

RB: You've let your hair grow over your eyes.

RC: No, no – I'm round here. Follow the sound of my voice.

RB: Oh yes, sorry. *(He finally gets the frames on RC's nose.)* Now then *(picks up lens, slots it in)* Is that better or worse?

RC: Er – worse.

RB: *(Picks up spoon, slots it in.)* How about that?

RC: Fractionally better, I think.

RB: Bit better. I'll leave that one in then. And this?

(Adding another one.)

RC: No, worse.

RB: Right. Well, that looks about it then. Have a look at some frames now, shall we? Follow me, would you?

(They walk in opposite directions, RB to counter, RC towards wall.)

RB: No, over here!

RC: Oh, sorry. *(They make contact at the counter.)*

RB: Now, *(takes off RC's glasses, puts them down on counter)* try these frames. *(Puts on ordinary large pair of frames.)* There, have a look in the mirror. *(Indicates a photograph of a grey-haired lady in spectacles.)*

RC: *(peering at it)* Mm, yes – I think they make me look a bit older. What do you think?

RB: *(looking at photo)* Yes, I see what you mean. *(Takes off his own glasses.)* Just a minute. This isn't a mirror, it's a photograph of an old lady.

RC: Haven't you got any others?

RB: *(puts down his own glasses, picks up RC's, in close-up)* Well, there's these–

RC: *(gropes around, picks up RB's glasses.)* What about these? *(Puts them on.)* Good heavens. These are marvellous! I can see perfectly!

RB: No, they're mine–

RC: No, they're not. *(pointing)* You've got yours in your hand, look.

RB: Have I? *(Puts them on.)* Good heavens! I say, it's amazing. Everything's becoming clear to me.

RC: How can I ever thank you? You'll send me the bill, naturally?

RB: Of course not – wouldn't dream of it. Fair's fair. I've benefited as well.

RC: True. Cheerio, then!

RB: Bye! *(RC exits. RB looks round him.)* So – this is where I work, is it?

KNOTTY PROBLEM

A haberdasher's shop – old-fashioned. RB as assistant.

RB: Can I help you, sir?

RC: Yes, please. I want a pair of laces.

RB: Certainly, sir. Boot or shoe laces?

RC: Shoe laces, please.

RB: Black or brown, sir?

RC: Black, please.

RB: Short or long, sir?

RC: Short.

RB: I thought so. Do you prefer nylon or cotton?

RC: Oh dear. I think I'll have cotton ones, please.

RB: Do you prefer the rounded type or the flat ones?

RC: I'll have the flat ones, please.

(RB turns to drawer behind him and looks through contents.)

RB: I'm afraid that we haven't got any short black cotton flat shoe laces, sir.

RC: Round ones, then?

RB: No, sir – no short black cotton ones at all.

RC: Nylon ones then?

RB: No sir, sorry. No short black ones of any description.

RC: Well, all right. I'll have brown ones.

RB: No brown ones either, sir. No short laces at all.

RC: All right – long ones then.

RB: No, sir – no long ones either.

RC: Well, what have you got?

RB: Nothing. We don't sell shoe laces, sir. This is a fish shop.

RC: A fish shop. It says "Haberdasher" over the door!

RB: That's my name, sir. George Haberdasher.

RC: But if it's a fish shop, why doesn't it look like one?

RB: Lowers the tone of the neighbourhood. Sorry about the laces, sir.

RC: Never mind – just give me a piece of cod and sixpennyworth of chips.

RB: Right, sir.

(RB reaches below counter and produces a piece of newspaper and shovels hot, steaming, sizzling, succulent chips – not old, tired, dry ones – onto it – adding a tender piece of cod. Camera goes in on this delicious sight.)

THE YOKELS

Two village idiots meet on a stile.

RC: Morning.

RB: Afternoon.

RC: Nice evening, isn't it?

RB: It's not as nice an evening as it was yesterday morning.

RC: No. Yesterday morning was a lovely evening.

RB: I blame the weather, you know.

RC: You're the village idiot, aren't you?

RB: Yes.

RC: I'm the next village idiot.

RB: How do you know?

RC: I'm the idiot from the next village.

RB: Oh. Were you elected?

RC: No, picked. They put the names of the three daftest people in the village in a hat and mine was picked out.

RB: Who were the other two?

RC: The Vicar and the local MP.

RB: Oh, you were lucky then.

RC: I had an unfair advantage. My name was in the hat twice.

RB: How was that?

RC: It were my hat. You always put your name in your hat, don't you?

RB: I don't.

RC: What do you put in your hat, then?

RB: Me head.

RC: Oh. How did you get the job?

RB: It was who had the funniest nose. And they all picked mine.

RC: I wouldn't pick your nose.

RB: And I wouldn't pick yours.

RC: How's the wife?

RB: I haven't got a wife.

RC: No, but how is she, anyway?

RB: She's very well. We're getting married next month.

RC: What, both of you?

RB: 'Course.

RC: Who to?

RB: Each other.

RC: Oh, that's a coincidence.

RB: She's being married in white.

RC: What colour will you be in?

RB: Me best suit. The one I had for me birthday.

RC: You going to be married in your birthday suit?

RB: Yes, why not?

RC: It'll need pressing. Will she carry something up the aisle?

RB: Yes, her father, most likely.

RC: Oh. Well, I wish you Joy.

RB: Who?

RC: Joy. The Parson's daughter. I'm in love with her. I'm learning to write so I can write to her. Look what I wroted.

(Shows RB a note.)

RB: You writted all that?

RC: Yes, all rot by me, that is.

RB: What's it say?

RC: Dunno, I ain't learned to read yet.

RB: That Parson's a funny-looking bloke. I wonder who picked his nose?

RC: Eh?

RB: I wonder who picked the parson's nose?

RC: Yes, roll on Christmas.

RB: They buried old Jack yesterday, in Shropshire.

RC: Oh? What part?

RB: All of him.

RC: What did he have?

RB: The shepherd's pie, I think.

RC: What were his last words?

RB: Let me out, I'm not dead. Does your mum know you're courting?

RC: No, my mum don't approve. Her and my dad hate each other, but they can't get a divorce.

RB: Why not?

RC: They're not married.

RB: Oh, so you were born out of wedlock?

RC: No, I was born out by Matlock. You got any kids?

RB: I've got three children and half of them are boys.

RC: Oh, what's the other half?

RB: They're boys as well.

RC: Are they triplets?

RB: Two of them are.

RC: What's the other one?

RB: A window dresser.

RC: Oh. A Kentish man?

RB: He is a bit, yes. Well, I'm going home for me supper.

RC: What do you have for supper?

RB: Pie. If I'm hungry, I cut it into four pieces and eat all four pieces. If I don't think I can eat four pieces, I only cut it into two pieces.

RC: I'm harvesting my corn tomorrow.

RB: Oh, yes? Do you grow corn?

RC: No, it grows itself. I fertilise it. And the wife.

RB: Well, we all know that.

RC: I hope it's better than last year. It was so small the rooks had to kneel down to eat it.

RB: You want to try sparrows.

RC: Yes. Well, I'm off.

RB: Oh, it's you, is it? I thought something was.

RC: Are you going to help me with the harvesting tomorrow?

(Orchestra begins intro to song.)

RB: Oh, yes – I love the harvest time.

(Song: to the tune of "Come, Landlord Fill the Following Bowl" trad.)

BOTH: The harvest time is here again
   The church is decked with barley
   The vicar's wife is all dolled up
   And looks a proper Charley.
   She's pinned some barley on our coats
   And tied a wheatsheaf round our throats
   Very soon we'll get our oats
   Hurrah, hurrah, the harvest.

RB: Miss Jackson's home-made cowslip wine
   It states upon the labels
   Is vintage nineteen forty nine
   It takes the paint off tables

RC: Old Mrs Johnson's got a rare
   Display of apples over there –
   But you should see her daughter's pear!

BOTH: Hurrah, hurrah, the harvest!

RC: Our organist is Mister Keys
   A man of many troubles–
   There's water in his pipes 'n' he's
   Forever blowing bubbles.

RB: His bellows they are real antiques
   His pump is full of squirts and squeaks
   He sits among the peas and leaks

BOTH: Hurrah, hurrah, the harvest!

(Segue into tune of "Lincolnshire Poacher" – trad.)

BOTH: At harvest time we make the hay and a-reaping we shall go.

RB: We're off in a lorry with Winnie and Florrie and Jennifer-Jane and Jo.

RC: The lorry it stops in a shady copse and we're out in the corn all day.

BOTH: But there's never a doubt, when the moon comes out, we'll
all be making hay. Oh! there's never a doubt, etc.
At harvest time we make the hay and dance upon the green–

RC: It's clap your hands to a cheerful band and crown the village
Queen
Now, young Doreen's our village queen
But she can't be with us today
So a feller called Stanley, who's not very manly, is going to be
Queen of the May!

BOTH: So – a feller called Stanley, etc.

BOTH: At harvest time we make the hay and hold the village fête–

RB: There's home-made tarts and hoops and darts, and guess young
Phyllis's weight
Young Phyllis's weight was eight stone eight and Febbrey, March
'n May
Now it's ten stone three and it's plain to see that's she's been
making hay!

BOTH: Yes, it's ten stone three and it's plain to see that she's been
making hay!

(They exit.)

HOTEL LOUNGERS

A general (RC) and an admiral (RB) sitting in an hotel lounge – potted palms and a tea-time trio playing out of vision. They sit, in uniform, in easy chairs. They are very old. A pretty waitress in a short skirt delivers tea to the admiral. The general ogles her legs. She goes.

RB: Thank you, Dulcie.

RC: Nice legs.

RB: Yes. Very good tone as well.

RC: What?

RB: The piano.

RC: No, the waitress. Nice legs.

RB: A trim craft. Fond of women, are you?

RC: I used to be.

RB: Gone off 'em, have you?

RC: Not at all. Just as keen as ever.

RB: It's just opportunity really, isn't it?

RC: Yes. Lately I never seem to get the chance to show my prowess.

RB: How long is it?

RC: What?

RB: How long is it? – since you had, since you made, since you were, er, since you did, er the er made love. To a woman, I mean.

RC: I don't see that's any of your business.

RB: No, no. I'm sorry.

RC: Since you did, I bet a pound.

RB: What?

RC: When did you last make love?

RB: If you must know, it was round about 1945.

RC: 1945? Ha! Well, that's a damn long time ago!

RB: Not really. *(Looks at watch)* It's only 22.30 now.

(RB winks at the waitress, who winks back. RC looks amazed.)

TRAMPS

A series of nine quickies – RB and RC sitting by the side of a country road, their paraphernalia around them.

1: "RICH"

RB: I wish I had enough money to buy an elephant.

RC: What do you want an elephant for?

RB: I don't – I just want the money. What is the largest known diamond?

RC: The Ace, isn't it?

RB: No – diamond. Jewellery, you know.

RC: Oh. The Kohinoor.

RB: The Cohen what?

RC: Kohinoor.

RB: Oh. 'Course, you might know it would be Jewish.

RC: It's Indian.

RB: Nice to own that, wouldn't it?

RC: You'd have to be Rockefeller to own that.

RB: You know, if I was as rich as Rockefeller, I'd be richer than Rockefeller.

RC: How?

RB: I'd do a bit of window-cleaning on the side.

2: "FOOD"

RB: Have you seen the evening paper?

RC: No, what's in it?

RB: My lunch.

RC: Can I have some of it?

RB: No. Get your own.

RC: Where did you get it?

RB: That woman up the hill.

RC: Oh, her. Terrible cook, she is. I broke a tooth on her gravy once. She gave me some cold spinach. Eat that, she said. It'll put colour in your cheeks.

RB: Yeah, it will. But who wants green cheeks?

RC: I'm never going to her again. I nearly went blind drinking her cocoa.

RB: You can't go blind drinking cocoa.

RC: I nearly did.

RB: How?

RC: I left the spoon in the cup.

3: "MONEY"

RB: It says here "there is no recession". All I can say is, if this isn't a recession, it must be the worst boom in history.

RC: No. Everybody's got more money than they used to have.

RB: I haven't. I'm skint.

RC: Didn't you just have an uncle die?

RB: No, I've got an Auntie Di. Married to Fred.

RC: Oh, it was your Auntie, was it?

RB: No, Auntie didn't die, she's alive. It was Fred. He's dead.

RC: Fred.

RB: Dead.

RC: How much money did he leave?

RB: All of it; you have to. But none of it to me. I am truly borassic.

RC: Like me. I haven't got two half-pennies to scratch the soles of me feet with. But I don't need money.

RB: I do. I've asked for money, I've begged for money, I've cried for money–

RC: Why don't you work for it?

RB: Well, I'm going through the alphabet and I haven't got to "W" yet.

4: "PRISON"

RB: The ladder of life is full of splinters, but you never realise it until you start sliding down.

RC: Do you know that the only time you're allowed to spit in a policeman's face is when his beard's on fire?

RB: What is that to do with sliding down life's ladder?

RC: My brother has slid down it. And he's got the splinters to prove it. In his head.

RB: His head?

RC: Splinters of a policeman's truncheon.

RB: Ah. 'Cos he spat in his face, when his beard wasn't on fire.

RC: Zackly. He's in prison now.

RB: Bit of a slur on the family name, isn't it?

RC: Not really. The family name is Pentonville, anyway.

RB: What's he in for?

RC: He was imprisoned for his beliefs.

RB: Really?

RC: Yes. He believed the night watchman was asleep.

5: "MEAN"

RB: Here, lend us a match, will you?

RC: I ain't got no matches.

RB: Eh? You sure?

RC: 'Course I'm sure.

RB: Funny. I could have sworn you had some. Check your pockets, see if you have.

RC: I haven't, I tell you! I have not got any matches!

RB: Oh, dear. Oh well, I'll just have to use me own then.

(He takes out matches.)

RC: Cor, dear! That is mean, isn't it? That's what I call a really stingy dirty trick.

RB: Not as stingy and dirty as my sister's husband. Now he is really stingy and dirty. He went and stayed with my mum for a fortnight. He arrived with a spare shirt and a pound note, and never changed either. Miserable so-and-so he was, an' all. Even when he won the sweepstakes down the pub. "You don't look very cheerful, considering you won the sweep," I said. "No, I'm not," he said. "What annoys me is, I bought two tickets."

6: "TELESCOPE"

They are eating chips or scraps from a screwed-up newspaper.

RB: It says here they've invented a telescope what can see 93 million miles.

RC: Impossible.

RB: Nothing is impossible.

RC: Must be something.

RB: No.

RC: I'll tell you something that's impossible.

RB: What?

RC: It's impossible for a worm to fall over.

RB: Ah, that's different – I mean in space, and that.

RC: I don't trust these space scientists. If they're so clever, why do they count backwards?

RB: Ah well, yeah.

RC: 'Zackly. One of them telescopes wouldn't be no good to me. I got spots before me eyes.

RB: You got new glasses – didn't they help?

RC: Sort of. They didn't get rid of the spots, but I can see 'em much clearer now.

7: "SHOES"

RC: Cor, dear. My arthritis is playing me up this morning.

RB: I didn't know you suffered with arthritis.

RC: 'Course I do. What else can you do with it? Talking of which, what's the matter with your feet? I noticed you was walking funny.

RB: It's these shoes. They're flaming killing me.

RC: Well, why do you wear 'em, then?

RB: Listen – I've got no money, I can't afford tobacco or beer. I haven't got a television, I'm all alone in the world – no decent girl will look at me, and even if she did, I couldn't afford to take her out. And after a long day's tramping in the heat or the pouring rain, I think of all my troubles and I feel suicidal. Then I take off these damn shoes – and oh boy! That's the only pleasure I ever get.

8: "MARRIAGE"

RC: Do you think marriage is a lottery?

RB: No. In a lottery you do have a slight chance.

RC: But you like women, don't you?

RB: Oh yes. Just give me my pipe, the great outdoors and a beautiful girl, and you can keep the pipe and the great outdoors. Still, that's nothing to do with marriage, is it? It's just the opposite sex.

RC: The what?

RB: You know what the opposite sex is, don't you?

RC: Yes. It's the tart who lives across the road.

RB: Talking of which, my sister-in-law has just had quads.

RC: That's pretty rare, isn't it?

RB: Rare? Certainly is. Doctors say it only happens once in one million six hundred thousand times.

RC: Blimey. It's a wonder she ever found time to do any housework.

9: "AGE"

RB: I'll have to lose some weight, you know. Can't go knocking on people's doors saying I haven't eaten for three days looking like this.

RC: It's middle-aged spread, that.

RB: I know.

RC: Lot to be said for middle-aged spread.

RB: Yes. It's good for married couples – brings them closer together.

RC: A lot of advantages come with age.

RB: Yes. My old grandad, for instance. Now he can whistle while he brushes his teeth.

RC: 'Zackly. 'Course there's disadvantages, too. I went to the doctor about me memory. It's really going. I told him I can't remember anything.

RB: What did he say?

RC: He was very reassuring – he told me to just forget about it.

YOU CAN SAY THAT AGAIN

A pub. RB at bar. RC enters.

RB: Hello, Bert – what are you going to have?

RC: Oh, hello, Charlie. I'll have a pint of, er–

RB: Light?

RC: No, a pint of–

RB: Brown?

RC: No, a pint of–

RB: Mild?

RC: No–

RB: Bitter?

RC: Pint of bitter.

RB: Pint of bitter. Pint of bitter, Alan. Haven't seen you round the factory lately – been off sick?

RC: No, I packed it in. They told me I had to change me, er, change me, er–

RB: Hours?

RC: No, change me–

RB: Habits?

RC: No, change me–

RB: Socks more often?

RC: No, duties.

RB: Oh, duties.

RC: Change my duties, that's it. Well, I wasn't having that, 'cos I had a good job. Cushy little number. *(Barman delivers pint.)* Ta. Cheers.

RB: Cheers, Bert. What exactly was your job then, there?

RC: Same job as I'd done for twenty years. I always worked with, er–

RB: Pride?

RC: No, I worked with, er–

RB: Within reason?

RC: No, with, er–

RB: With your overcoat on?

RC: No, with Harry Hawkins.

RB: Oh, Harry Hawkins, yes.

RC: We always worked together. He used to give me his, er–

RB: Whole-hearted support?

RC: No, his, er–

RB: Athletic support?

RC: No, his ginger nuts.

RB: Oh, nice.

RC: And I used to dip them in, er–

RB: His tea for him?

RC: No, in the chocolate.

RB: Oh, the chocolate, I see. That's the job, is it?

RC: Me and him made all the chocolate ginger nuts. Then suddenly they decide a woman can do my job, and they put me on to, er–

RB: Short time?

RC: No, on to–

RB: Short cake?

RC: No, sherbert fountains. Messy job, that, dreadful. Everything gets covered in it. You go home, strip off, and find you've got a coating of sherbert all over, er–

RB: All over the weekend.

RC: Precisely. And the wife doesn't like it.

RB: Oh, that makes it worse. So you can't even–

RC: Meanwhile, the woman refused to work with Harry Hawkins. She didn't like the way he handled his, er–

RB: His ginger nuts?

RC: His machinery, and she thought he was, er–

RB: Nuts?

RC: No, she thought he was, er–

RB: Ginger?

RC: No, incompetent.

RB: Oh, incompetent, yes. So you went back with Harry, did you?

RC: No, I decided I'd had enough. I went home to the wife and I found she was up, er–

RB: Up to her knees in sherbert?

RC: No, up, er–

RB: Up to her old tricks with the milkman?

RC: No, up her mother's. So I thought, why not go up the Job Centre, I thought. 'Cos I mean, if you're really looking for a decent job, that's the place to, er–

RB: Steer clear of.

RC: No, be fair. They vary, don't they? My brother went to one for a job as a removal man, and within a week they'd already given him a–

RB: Fortnight's holiday?

RC: No, they gave him a–

RB: Set of tea chests?

RC: No, a hernia.

RB: Oh, hernia, yes.

RC: Still, this place was quite nice. I went up to this girl sitting behind this sort of grill, and she was filing–

RB: Filing her nails?

RC: No, filing the, er–

RB: Filing the bars trying to get out?

RC: No, filing these jobs in this portfolio thing.

RB: Oh, jobs, yes.

RC: Yes. Big girl she was, with these two, er–

RB: Oh yes, I get the picture, yes.

RC: Either side like.

RB: Well, they would be, yes.

RC: And I asked about jobs, and these two, er–

RB: Yes, I know, yes.

RC: They sprang up.

RB: Eh? How was that, then?

RC: Sort of in excitement, like, and–

RB: Good Lord.

RC: And they came towards me.

RB: Did they?

RC: Yes. Oh, what are they called? Clerks.

RB: Oh, clerks, oh my mistake.

RC: Turned out she was a sort of trainee. She'd just got off the er–

RB: The train?

RC: The course.

RB: Oh, course. Of course.

RC: So they sprang up and said, "There's a job that might very well suit you," they said. "We're looking for a man with short, er–"

RB: Legs?

RC: No, short, er–

RB: Short shirts?

RC: No, er–

RB: Shortcomings?

RC: Here, do you mind? Shorthand and typing – they needed a man with shorthand because they were, er–

RB: Short-handed?

RC: No, understaffed at the Town Hall. So, of course I didn't get the job.

RB: Oh dear – so you're still out of work, are you?

RC: No, they only had one other post available, so I took it.

RB: Go on–

RC: Yes, I've now got a job with the sweet, er–

RB: With the sweet factory again?

RC: No, a city job – a job with the sweet, er–

RB: With the sweet smell of success?

RC: Not exactly. I'm in charge of the "gents" at Waterloo Station! Cheers!

BARMY ARMY

A dug-out or tent in the front line. 1915.

RB is seated at rough table, studying a map. RC enters.

RB: Oh, it's you, Hugh. Did you get through to HQ?

RC: At two minutes to.

RB: Two minutes to? Good for you.

RC: They must have realised I was due to get through. They cleared the line.

RB: Divine. What news of support?

RC: Nought.

RB: Nought?

RC: Lord, Gort up at the fort thought we ought to have sought support before we went out and fought.

RB: All a bit fraught. We're going to get caught! Pass the port. Here we sit grounded, surrounded and utterly confounded. Cut off by the Krauts.

RC: Oh dear – I feel queer. I think I'll have a brandy, Sandy.

RB: Do, Hugh.

RC: *(pouring brandy)* I've been thinking.

RB: Drinking?

RC: Thinking.

RB: Oh, thinking and drinking.

RC: We're not rapped completely, Captain Wheatley. There are one or two very tight gaps in the Jerry-type chaps. Here's one of the maps of the gaps. Take a "garnder", Commander.

RB: Good grief, O'Keefe! You expect me to squeeze through these? A man of my size, with my thighs? Hardly a holiday, Halliday.

RC: O'Keefe, sir.

RB: Quite. What a night! I feel thoroughly misbegotten, hot and rotten. And what a stench in the trench! If we're not caught by Jerry, we'll die of beri-beri! Damn the Kraut, I've got to get out!

RC: I agree, it's pretty infernal, Colonel.

(Restraining him.)

RB: *(pushing him aside)* That's the understatement of the year, you little queer! I've had it up to here!

RC: Now don't get manic and panic–

RB: It's no good, chummy. *(Breaks down)* Oh, lumme – I want my mummy!

RC: Here – suck this dummy. *(Puts dummy in his mouth.)* Now, on the bed and rest your head. Just try to unroll yourself and control yourself while I give you the low-down on this show-down. We may have run out of ammo, but we've still got an MO and he's conquering disease by degrees. There aren't very many places with beri-beri cases – Private Schwartz has got warts, Private Doyle's got boils and Private Wurzel's pet weasel's got the measles. And Corporal Clappy is not a happy chappy. Still, you can't be a saint with his complaint.

RB: No, nobody smiles with piles. Still, it's worse for the nurse. God, what a barmy army.

RC: Sir – fancy a flit? Shall we slip out of this hell-hole?

RB: I'd certainly rather be in Solihull than sitting shivering in this stinking load of shrapnel. What's your plan, little man?

RC: Frank's tank. It's up on the bank.

(Points outside.)

RB: Frank?

RC: Frank Messiter. The cricketer from Chichester.

RB: Oh, him. I thought he name was Jim. Is he no longer with us, Smithers?

RC: Not any more – he's gone before. Jerry threw a grenade. There sat Frank, in his tank, dreaming of cricket, and a straight middle wicket. The grenade came over the wall – Frank thought it was a ball; caught it and bought it.

RB: So there stands his tank – and we've got Frank to thank. Can you drive it, Private?

RC: I think so – without being egotistical, my vehicle test verged on the artistical.

RB: Would you mind repeating that?

RC: I'd rather not try.

RB: I can quite see why. When shall we leave?

RC: As soon as you feel partial, Field Marshal.

RB: So – it's off we go – bravo. We're all set – let's have a wet.

(Reaches for bottle.)

RC: Talking of wet – will you excuse me, Generalissimo? I must go outside for a–

RB: Yes, I know. So must I – but watch out for a hun with a gun. You go first; if I hear a short burst, I'll fear the worst.

RC: And if you hear a long sigh, you'll know I'm high and dry.

(He exits. The field telephone rings. RB answers it.)

RB: Forty-fifth fusilier here, HQ. Eight two, how are you? Ah! They are? How far? Hurrah! I'll see you in the bar and buy you a cigar! Ta-ta!

(RC re-enters.)

RB: We're relieved!

RC: You as well?

RB: That was Sergeant Bone on the phone. Captain Hooper's turned up trumps with twenty-two troopers – fired a howitzer and hit the Kaiser squarely in the trouser. They've all retreated, much depleted.

RC: Then now's our chance. Before we get hurt and dropped in the dirt, let's put on a spurt and desert, Bert.

RB: Desert? It's an idea, my dear. Can we start a new life together, Merryweather?

RC: Of course we can, you silly man.

RB: You've made an old man very happy, you dear chappy.

RC: Call me Mary, you old fairy.

(They exit.)

SAY IT AGAIN, SAM

A tiny snug bar in a pub. RB sits drinking at the bar. RC enters.

RB: Hello, Bert, what you gonna have?

RC: Oh, thanks, Harry, I'll have a pint of, er–

RB: Pint of light?

RC: No, a pint of, er–

RB: Pint of brown?

RC: No, er–

RB: Pint of mild?

RC: No, er–

RB: Pint of bitter?

RC: Pint of bitter. Yes, ta.

RB: *(calls to barman)* Pint of bitter, Charley.

RC: Lovely. I thought I'd pop in on my way to, er–

RB: What, the off-licence?

RC: No, on the way to, er–

RB: Alcoholics Anonymous?

RC: No, on the way to the darts match. Up the club. *(The beer arrives.)* Oh. Ta, Charley.

RB: *(raising glass)* Well – merry Christmas, Bert.

RC: Merry Christmas, Harry. It's all Christmas now, isn't it? Christmas decorations, Christmas parties, Christmas carols, Christmas cards–

RB: Yes, well, it's the time of year, isn't it? It's seasonal. You always get a lot of Christmas things going on at Christmas, don't you?

RC: Suppose it's inevitable. Talking of Christmas celebrations, we had ours the other night. Up the club.

RB: Oh, yeah?

RC: Funny old do it was an' all. Same every year, it always takes the form of an egg and, er–

RB: Egg and spoon race?

RC: No, an egg an' er–

RB: Egon Ronay gourmet banquet?

RC: No, an egg and chip supper.

RB: Oh, I see, yeah.

RC: Took the wife along, of course. Well, she's useful for laying the, er–

RB: Laying the eggs?

RC: No, laying the, er–

RB: Laying the foreman?

RC: Laying the table. She lays the tables. It was all very nice. The men all get cigars and the woman all get, p– er–

RB: Pie-eyed?

RC: No, the women get p–er–

RB: Pickled?

RC: No, er – picture hats.

RB: Oh. Picture hats, yes.

RC: Mind you, they also get pis–

RB: Well, they would.

RC: Pistachio nuts.

RB: Oh, pistachio nuts, oh I see. Very nice.

RC: And, of course, the beer was flowing like there was no, er–

RB: Whisky left?

RC: Like there was no tomorrow. This waitress was going around with these big jugs.

RB: Oh – topless, was she?

RC: Yes, flat as a pancake. Well, I was sat next to that Wendy from accounts. You know, her with the enormous, er–

RB: What, Filofax?

RC: No, the enormous, er–

RB: Inflation rate?

RC: No, enormous rubber plant on her desk.

RB: Oh, that's what it's made of, yeah.

RC: We got chatting about this and that. She fancies me; I know that 'cos she once gave me a bit of, er–

RB: A bit of this and that?

RC: No, a bit of, er–

RB: A bit of this, that and the other?

RC: No, a bit of, er–

RB: A bit of the other without the this and that?

RC: No, a bit of her seedy cake in the canteen. Suddenly, she leans over and kisses me on the cheek.

RB: Go on!

RC: I thought "Hello!" 'Cos she's already kissed me on the, er –, on the, er–

RB: Ear?

RC: No, on the–

RB: Face?

RC: No, the–

RB: On the other place?

RC: No, on the Thursday.

RB: Oh, I see. On the Thursday, right.

RC: Well, lucky enough, the wife didn't see, 'cos she was out laying the, er–

RB: The tables?

RC: No, the foreman, as it happens.

RB: Oh, I was right the first time.

RC: Well, I pretended not to notice, kept eating me supper, and then suddenly her fingers sort of crept forward and pinched one of my, er–

RB: Go on, really?

RC: Yes, she pinched one of my, er–

RB: Just the one, like?

RC: Yes, oh yes, only the one. Well, I'd only got two.

RB: Naturally.

RC: Chips.

RB: Oh, chips, yeah.

RC: And she popped it in her, er–

RB: Her mouth?

RC: No, popped it in her, er–

RB: Where? There's nowhere else to pop it.

RC: Her handbag. She popped it in her handbag, for later.

RB: Oh, I'd forgotten her handbag.

RC: Then the boss stood up and proposed the toast.

RB: Oh, you got toast an' all, did you?

RC: The loyal toast, to our great Queen and all the, er–

RB: All the little Queens?

RC: No, all her dominions.

RB: Oh, yeah.

RC: And may she remain in good health and be protected against the dreaded, er – the dreaded, er–

RB: Dreaded Lurgy?

RC: No, the dreaded, er–

RB: Dreaded corgi?

RC: No, the dreaded–

RB: Dreaded Fergie?

RC: No, the dreaded foe.

RB: Oh, foe, yes.

RC: Then we all got up for a dance, and this Wendy grabbed me in the, er–

RB: Heat of the moment?

RC: No, in the, er–

RB: Seat of the trousers?

RC: No, in the Gentlemen's Excuse Me.

RB: Ooh, painful.

RC: And she pulled me to one side, and said, "We were made for each other, because I'm also a little sh– a little sh–"

RB: Short at the end of the week?

RC: No, shy. "I'm a little shy myself," she said. "But if you're interested, when you leave here, go to the bicycle sheds, and I'll be round, er–"

RB: Round at the back?

RC: No, round, er–

RB: Round at the front and back?

RC: No, round the corner in the bushes. So of course, I went.

RB: Go on? What happened?

RC: Well, there she was, reclining, and she said, "Now's your chance," she said. "You can have anything you want."

RB: And did you?

RC: Not half. I grabbed her by the hand, er – the hand, er–

RB: The handiest bit you could get hold of?

RC: No! Do me a favour. I grabbed her by the handbag and pinched me chip back! Cheers!

The Two Ronnies: Monologues & Spokespersons

O ne of the unique aspects of *The Two Ronnies* as a double act was that they were never really a double act. "Certainly I remember feeling quite strongly about that," remembers Ronnie Corbett. "We said we wouldn't do chat shows together or interviews together."

To emphasise this, every episode of the show featured at least one solo moment for each Ronnie – Ronnie C's took the form of his weekly seat-bound, rambling shaggy dog story, while Ronnie B chose to deliver a wide array of spokespeople for a bizarre collection of institutions, charities, government ministries and so on. These were often *tour de force* moments of performance, which highlighted Ronnie's fascination with, and playful love of, language as a writer. As Sir Peter Hall (a collaborator with Ronnie in his theatre days back in the 1950s) has noted of these pieces: "His scripts are very precise. Very immaculate, very particular. And they relate to his extraordinary ability as an actor to time accurately in the way he says a line. I think the actor and writer kind of coalesce in their precision, because although he's an anarchic comedian in some respects, as a performer he's about precision."

〇〇

PISMONOUNCERS UNANIMOUS

RB: Good evening. I am the president for the loyal society for the relief of sufferers from pismonunciation; for people who cannot say their worms correctly. Or who use the wrong worms entirely, so that other people cannot underhand a bird they are spraying. It's just that you open your mouse, and the worms come turbling out in wuk a say that you dick knock what you're thugging a bing, and it's very distressing. I'm always looing it, and it makes one feel umbumfter-kookle; especially when going about one's diddly tasks – slopping in the sloopermarket, for inkstands. Only last wonk I approached the chuckout point, and showed the ghoul behind the crash desk the contents of my trilley, and she said, "Alright, grandad, shout 'em out." Well, of course, that's fine for the ordinary man in the stoat, who has no dribble with his warts, but to someone like myself, it's worse than a kick in the jackstrop. Sometimes you get stuck on one letter, such as wubbleyou, and I said, "I've got a tin of whoop, a woocumber, two packets of wees and a wallyflower." She tried to make fun of me and said, "That will be woo pounds and wifty wee pence." So I said "Wobblers" and walked out.

So you see how dickyfelt it is. But help is at hand. A new society has been formed by our mumblers to help each other in times of ex cream ices. It is bald "Pismonuncers Unanimous" and anyone can ball them up on the smellyfone at any tight of the day or gnome, 24 flowers a spray, seven stays a creak, and they will come round and get you drunk. For foreigners, there will be interpreters who will all squeak many sandwiches, such as Swedish, Turkish, Burkish, Jewish, Gibberish and Rubbish. Membranes will be able to attend tight stool for heaving grasses, to learn how to grope with the many kerplinkities of daily loaf. Which brings me to the drain reason for squawking to you tonight. The Society's first function, as a body, was a Grand Garden Freight, and we hope for many more bodily functions in the future. The Garden Plate was held in the grounds of Blenheim Paliasse, Woodstick, and guest of horror was the great American pip-singer, Manny Barrowload. The fête was opened by the Bleeder of the Proposition, Mr Neil Pillock, who gave us a few well-frozen worms in praise of the Society's jerk, and said that in the creaks and stunts that lie ahead, we must all do our nut-roast to ensure that it sucks weeds. Then everyone visited the various stalls and abruisements, the ruda-bouts, thingboats and dodgers, and of course the old favourites such as cocoshy nuts, stry your length, guessing the weight of the cook, and tinning the pail on the wonkey. The occasional was great fun and, in short, I think it can safely be said that all the men present and thor-oughly good women were had all the time.

So please join our Society. Write to me – Doctor Small Pith (*caption:* "DR PAUL SMITH") The Spanner, Poke Moses (*caption:*

"THE MANOR, STOKE POGES") and I will send you some brieflets to browse through and a brass badge to wear in your loop-hole. And a very pud night to you all.

AN APPEAL FOR WOMEN

RB: Good evening. My name is Arnold Splint, and I am here tonight. (*Caption – "An appeal for Women".*) This is an appeal for women only. No, please don't switch off – because it's you men I want to talk to, especially tonight. I am appealing to you, for women. I need them desperately. I can't get enough – and the reason I'm appealing to you men is that I don't appeal to women. But I still need them. So this is how you can help. If you have an old woman you no longer need – send her to me. Simply tie her arms and legs together, wrap her in brown paper, and post her to me, care of the BBC, with your own name printed clearly on the bottom. Because that's the bit I shall undo first. Of course, I cannot guarantee to make use of all women sent to me. It depends on the condition, so make sure you enclose a self-addressed pair of knickers. Send as many women as you like, no matter how small. I assure you, all those accepted will be made good use of by me and my team of helpers – who, incidentally, carry on this work, many without any form of support.

I do hope you can find time to send me something: we did originally start collecting with a van, from door to door, but this scheme was abandoned owing to the wear and tear on the knockers.

I think we should remember that Christmas is on its way. And when it comes, and you are sitting at home by your own fireside, warming yourself beside a roaring great woman, think of all those poor unfortunate people who are having to go without this Christmas. Why not send them an old flame or two, to warm the cockles of their hearthrug? I'm quite sure that many of you have women lying about in drawers, that you haven't touched for years. Please, post them off today. Help us set up our Women On Wheels service for old men who can't move about. I know it's not easy. It requires self-denial, patience and an enormous amount of string; but I'm sure you'll feel better for it. I know I shall. Good night.

SWEDISH MADE SIMPLE

We start on the above title as a caption, over RB as the professor. He is dressed as a head waiter – tails, black bow tie, etc. Suitably stupid music under opening shot – which fades as RB starts to talk.

RB: Güten abend, grutte Erfund, Good evenink. My name is Professor Gewister *(raspberry)* fitten, and tonight we have a Swedish lesson for you, but with a difference. It is in Norwegian. Now I expect some of you are wondering why I am dressed as a waiter. It is because tonight our lesson is entitled "In the Restaurant" or as we say in Sweden "Im de restaurant". And before we go over to the scene, let me explain that, as we act out our little drama for you, there will be on the screen sub-titles. Which, as you know, are used in Swedish films and, which are necessary to explain to English people what is going on in the bedroom scenes. But to make it easier, we spell it out for you. We used only one letter for each word. Instead of putting thus *(Super caption "Hello")* Hello, we put this *(Super caption "Lo")* "Hello". You see – "Hell–lo."

(Cut to three pictures – photo blow-ups behind him. Zoom in on the first one: a picture of a ragged child being given money.)

And similarly, here we have "Pity" *(super "PT")*

(Pan to next photo – general view of St Paul's, etc.)

And here "City" *(super "CT".)*

(Pan to next photo – bikini girl with big boobs.)

And er … *(super "TT")* … and so on. So come with me and we will begin the lesson.

(He walks into little café set. Two tables, one door to kitchen. Minimum of detail. RC, as customer, is already seated alone.

N.B. just before each line is spoken, the sub-titles appear at the bottom of the screen in bold capital letters, without full-stops, but a reasonable distance apart.)

RC: LO.

RB : LO.

(Looks at camera briefly with a "remember this bit?" sort of look.)

RC: RUBC?

(Takes menu from RB.)

RB: SVRBC.

(A waitress walks past carrying ham on a dish.)

RB: LO.

WAITRESS: LO.

RC: LO.

WAITRESS: LO.

RC: FUNEX?

RB: SVFX.

RC: FUNEM?

RB: 9.

RC: *(suspiciously)* IFCDM.

RB: VFN10EM!

WAITRESS: (*popping her head round kitchen door*) A! VFM.

RC: R!

RB: O?

WAITRESS: C – DM.

(*Shows him ham on dish.*)

RC: OK – MNX.

RB: MNX.

RC: FUNET?

RB: 1 T?

RC: 1 T.

RB: OK – MXNT (*shouts to kitchen*) MXNT41!

WAITRESS: (*appearing*) VFN10EX.

RC: UZUFX.

RB: (*shouting*) YFNUNEX?

WAITRESS: IFE10M!

RB: (*to camera*) SILLYCOW.

AN EAR IN YOUR WORD

RB: A very good one to you all and evening. My name is Willie Cope. I am the president of the "Getting Your Wrongs in the Word Order" Society, and I've been asked by the BCB to come a night too long to aim the society's explains, and picture you firmly in the put.

(*Caption over – President, Getting Your Words in the Wrong Order Society.*)

Firstly, I would like to say here and now – but I can't. I always say to seem now and here which nose me absolutely get-where. And most of our troubles have this member. It is very difficult to undersay what people are standing, especially if, as I did then, people only get half their back words-wards. As you can imagine, funny and gentlemen, you get some ladies combinations.

Now this certainly vocabs down your cutlery. You obviously have to avoid words like auspices and titillation for a start. Last week, for instance, I went to the barbers, and asked for my usual on the top, and not too much off the backside. But the society is doing most of its ut to ensure that both men and women who are live have comfortable members. Why not come down to Head-Head in Surrey and visit our hindquarters? Members can stay for the weekend, or weak members can stay for the end. End members can, of course, stay for the week.

Both men and sports can enjoy the pastimes and women. Indoor games include ping, billiard-winks and tiddley-pong. Outdoors one can swim through the country lanes, or go for a long hike in the swimming pool. Facilities also include a nine-course golf-hole, and a three lunch hot course at the restaurant, where the menu will offer you a wide choice of waiters to taste your suit. Anything from beef toad to hole in the wellington.

The club house is a favourite drinking place for meters, as is the local pub, the Three Feathers; often one hears the cry "Meet you in the three tails for a cock-feather". The club house also offers accommodation for visitors, so if your lady-friend arrives, she can be put in the club, up the house, overnight.

However, I would hate you to get the skittle that it's all beer and ideas. I myself give lectures every aftermorning and noon, five weeks a time. I have an assistant, Miss Help, who Witherspoons me out most weekends. She always crowds very large drawers. We need new members – who doesn't? So if you would like to join the shy, don't be course. Write to me, naming your state, and enclosing a recent problem (head and shoulders only, please) together with a stamped addressed photograph. Here is the address – *(Super caption as he speaks)* Dr Willie Cope, 21 North Place, St Johns Wood, London WC, I'll just repeat that: *(Second caption)* Dr WC Cope, 21 John Willie Place, Northwood, London N8. And just to make sure, I'll repeat it again: *(Third caption)* Dr J Wood Willie, 21 WC Place, North London 8. May I wish each and every year of you a Merry Christmas and a happy new one. Goodnight.

THE MINISTER OF POETRY

RB: Good evening. May I say at once, without further ado,
How nice it is to speak to each and every one of you.
No matter where you all may be, on land or sea or foam,
Whether climbing up Mount Everest or kicking about at home,
I broadcast to you all tonight, on BBC TV
To tell you of the creation of a brand new Ministry.

(Caption – "Ministry of Poetry". RB puts on big floppy black hat.)

"Here, just a mo," I hear you cry – now what's all this about?
"A Minister of Poetry?" "Good God, who let him out?"
It's Margaret Thatcher's brainchild, this – our venerable prime
    Missis.
I'll tell you, if you'll all pin back your aural orifices.
Last Friday week I left the House of Commons just on eight
The wife was out at Bingo, so I knew that she'd be late.
I popped into the local – I was feeling rather frail –
And there stood Maggie Thatcher with her foot upon the rail.
"What you having, Jack?" she cried, her beady eyes aflame –
"I'll have a pint of Mild," I said. She said, "I'll have the same."
Well, seventeen pints later – God, how that girl can booze!
We sat on the Embankment and she came out with the news.
"For many years," she mumbled, as she munched the crisps I
    bought her,
Tidily folding up the bag and chucking it in the water,
"For many years I've longed to see this ancient land of ours
Return to former glories – and the pubs to longer hours.
Those grand old days of Shakespeare when the folk all spoke in
    rhyme,
And the language wasn't full of swear words, all the bleedin' time.
How nice it must have been to hear a lilting line that lingers,
When the worker to the foreman gave two verses, not two fingers.
If we could re-create the old-world charm of this great nation,
The voters would forget the shrinking pound, ignore inflation.

And you're the man, dear Jack," she said, "who can that promise
    keep.
Romance is not yet dead!" With that, she burped, and fell asleep.
I covered her with newspaper and left her on the grass
Looking every inch a lady and completely upper-class,
In a powder-blue ensemble with her hair all freshly done,
And across her chest, another chest, from page three of *The Sun*.
And that is how the Ministry was created overnight.
And now it's up to you, my friends, to see you do it right.
Pray, have no fear, the task is not as hard as it may sound
For inside every Englishman, good English rhymes abound,
And each of you has, at some time, I'm sure (as haven't we all?)
Inscribed a simple stanza on some by-gone wash-house wall.
So off you go and don't forget, just like the old graffiti,
Keep it short, and keep it snappy, keep it fruity, keep it meaty.
Just think of all the joy you'll cause when on a bus you leap,
At dawn, one chilly morning, when the world's still half asleep.
"A single fare – to Euston Square," you warble to the driver.
"The cost to me is 20p," and offer him a fiver.
As he looks for four pounds eighty change, what gay thoughts fill
    his head–
With any luck he'll hand you out a fourpenny one instead.
The world can be a better place, if each man does his best
To choose his rhymes to match the times, so get it off your chest!
Beneath the old stiff upper lip the ancient fire still flickers–
Come, fan the flames, and let us get the lead out of our knickers.
Press onward, England, do your best – revive our former glories –
Let's raise our beers and give three cheers. Goodnight and up the
    Tories.

A SERMON

*A vicar enters a pulpit. Organ music over. Caption: "Vicar of St Cain
and Abel church, Hampstead Heath". Organ music stops and he
addresses us.*

VICAR: Now many of you gathered here tonight in the church of St Cain and Abel in Hampstead Heath will know that these words are Cockney rhyming slang. Cain and Abel means table and Hampstead Heath means teeth. We are glad to welcome tonight a large group of Cockney worshippers to Evensong; and it is to them that I wish to address my sermon. I want to tell you a story.

A long time ago, in the days of the Israelites, there lived a poor man. He had no Trouble and Strife – she had run off with a Tea Leaf some years before – and now he lived with his Bricks and Mortar, Mary. And being very short of Bees and Honey, and unable to pay the Burton-on-Trent, he was tempted to go forth into the Bristol City, and see what he could Half-Inch. And he would say to Mary, his Bricks and Mortar – "I will take a Ball of Chalk into the town, and buy some tobacco for my Cherry Ripe." And he would put on his Almond Rocks, and his Dicky Dirt and his Round the Houses, and set off down the Frog and Toad, until he reached the outskirts of the Bristol.

One day his Bricks and Mortar gave him some money, saying, "Here is a Saucepan Lid – go and buy food. A loaf of Uncle Fred and a pound of Stand at Ease. But do not tarry in the town and bring me back what is left of the money to buy myself a new pair of Early Doors, for my present ones are full of holes, and I am in a continual George Raft." But instead of returning with the Bricks and Honey for his Bricks and Mortar's Early Doors, he made his way to the Rub-a-Dub, for a Tumble-down-the-sink. And he became very Elephant's Trunk, and Mozart; and when the landlord of the Rub-a-Dub called Bird Lime, the man set off back towards his Cat and Mouse, reeling about all over the Frog and Toad, and drunkenly humming a Stewed Prune.

And it came to Khyber Pass that as he staggered along he saw on the pavement a small brown Richard the Third. And he stared at it, lying there at his Plates of Meat. And he said, "Oh, small brown Richard the Third – how lucky I did not step on you." And he picked it up and put it on top of a wall, where no one could step on it. And a rich Four-by-Twoish merchant, who witnessed the deed, put his hand into his Sky Rocket, and took out a Lady Godiva, and handed it to the man, saying, "I saw you pick up that Richard the Third and remove it from the pavement and that was a kindly act. Take this Lady Godiva for your Froth and Bubble." And the man took it and went on his way. And the Richard the Third flew back to its nest.

When the man arrived home, his daughter was sitting by the Jeremiah, on her favourite Lionel Blair. And the man said unto her – "Here is a Lady Godiva, which I earned by a kindly act." And the woman was overjoyed and said, "Thank you, father. Now I can have my pair of Early Doors." "And I can have my drink," said the man. "Verily, that kindly act has ensured that we both have enough to cover our Bottle and Glass."

I thank you all.

PISMONUNCUATION (2)

RB at plain desk.

RB: Good evening. I'm squeaking to you, once again, as chairman of the loyal society for the prevention of pismonunciation. A society formed to help people who can't say their worms correctly. I myself often use the wrong worms, and that is why I was erected charming of the society. Firstly, let me try and put you in the puncture, regarding our mumblers. Peach and every plum of them have dickyfelty in conversing with the people they meet in everyday loaf – their murk-vates at the figtree or the orifice; even in their own holes, min and woof, sather and fun, bruzzer and thistle, unable to comainicute. This can be an enormous bandy-chap to our tremblers at all times, but especially at Bismuth time; because Bismuth is a season of grease on earth and pigswill to all men, when the family get together to eat, drunk, and be messy – to gather round the fireside, cracking nits, smelling Tories, and singing old pongs and barrels. Many of our rumblers lose out on these skinful pastimes – a very close fringe of mine, for instance, once went carol slinging with the local church queer, but instead of slinging "Good King Wenceslas stuck out. And his feet were steaming", he sang: "Go rest your belly, gentlemen, Let nothing rude display", which, of course, caused havoc among the queer, and deeply up-ended the knickers wife. This is just one instance of what my tremblers have to stiffer with a lipped upper stuff.

What we need now is money, to build clubs and calamity-centres, where people don't have to bother with the right worms. Places where they can greet each other with a cheery "Good afternuts, how nice to squeeze you" – a place where they can play a game of ping-tennis, table-pong, scribble, or newts and crutches.

Many famous people are patrons of the society. Piddyticians like

Widdly Whitelaw, Sir Geoffrey Who and Mr Denis Holy. Also famous TV Nosebleeders like Reggie Boozenquart, Angela Ripe'un and Anna Floored. And, of course, Mrs Hairy Whitemouse; not to be confused with Mrs Woodlouse, the hog-dangler. Among the aristocracy, there is Lord Longfelt – the Duchess of Bedbug, and Lord Monty-boo of Goolie. But patronage is not enough.

Remember the worms of William Shakepiece, our great national poe-face: "A Horse, a House, my kingdom for a Hearse". And of course, eventually, he got all three.

What we need is printed matter – any sort of printed matter – no mitter what sort. Send your magazines, nose-papers, dicks and booktionaries. Do it now. Bungle it up in pustules and post it to one of our mini branches dotted all over the Bottish Isles:

Minchester, Herminbum, Loverpill, and as far North as the Firth of Filth. And we are also busy setting up outposts in foreign pants, too, all over the glob. In fact, we have just opened a branch in Siam, and, in confusion, I would like you to join me in slinging the Siamese Notional anthem, to the tune of God Save the Queer.

(Audience and RB sing, as words are supered over lowerthird, or whatever.)

RB AND AUDIENCE: Owa Tana Siam
   Owa Tana Siam
   I Yamut Wit
   Owa Taphoo Lamai
   Owa Taphoo Lamai
   Owa Tana Siam
   Owa Tanit.

RB: Goodnight.

MORE WORMS

(From an idea by David Nobbs.)

RB: Good evening. Last year I spoke to you, appealing for help for those who, like myself, have trouble with worms. They can't pronounce their worms properly. Now, I am the secretary for the Loyal Society for the relief of sufferers from Pismonunciation. The reason I am once more squeaking to you tonight is that many people last time couldn't understand what I was spraying – so I am back again on your little queens to strain it and make it all queer.

It's a terrible thung to be ting-tied; it's even worse when your weirds get all muxed up, and come out in wuck a say, that you dick knock what you're thugging abing. Like I did just then, only crutch much nurse. It can be cured by careful draining at special draining-stools, which the Society has fcd up all over the Twittish Isles, and for the really dicky felt cases we have a three-week bash course on the Isle of Fright, where the doctors can get to grips with the patients, and the nurses can get to grips with the doctors, and everyone has a dolly good climb. Except the patients of course, who find it Dudley Dell. Doddly Dill. Diddly Doll – or, in other words, bitefully flooring. People have tried to cure themselves. They stand in front of their bodroom mirror and say, "Every day in every way, I get bitter and butter." But it doesn't cure them, you can bot your wife. And most of them usually do. The disease is spreading. It affects people from all walks of loaf; members of the Swivel Service, lawyers, silly-sodders, commercial drivellers, cop sheepers and wactory furkers, especially on the night shirt – and famous piddly-titians like Widdly Hamilton. Not forgetting Peanock Owl, and stars of screege and stain like Black Mygraves, Frantic Howerd and Peculiar Clarke and Rude old Newry-eff, the ballet dangler.

How can you help? Well, for a tart, it's no good simply trying to correct people when they suffer from this complaining distress. My wife does it to me all the time. Lucky old you, I hear you squirt. No, I mean she corrects me when I get any ring thong, and it makes me lavvy and Ingrid. Last time I backed her up the kickside.

We need money. Your minny. You may row ashore that it will be put to the best possible use, by myself and my large and loyal stiff. Send your chocs or pistol orders today. Smash open your baggy pinks. Dip your hand into your wife's bags and send us a few cod hoppers. Or why not simply slip a pond newt into an envelope? Send your donations to me, Poctor Podger Smish, at my new address, 51 Duberry Road, Kidling, Dorset. I'll just repeat that – Dictor Smidger Posh, whifty fun, Doberry Rude, Diddling, Corset. Thank you for glistening, good night, and a crappy isthmus.

THE SEX EQUALITY MONOLOGUE

RB discovered as spokesman – dressed half as a man and half as a woman. Half a long blonde wig, half a black moustache, half a frilly dress, half a suit jacket, half a bosom.

RB: Good evening. I'm from the Ministry of sex equality, and I'm here tonight to explain the situation man to man – or as we have to say now – person to person.

(Super caption: "A Spoke Person".)

RB: My name is Mr Stroke Mrs Barker. But I don't advise any of you to try it. Stroking Mrs Barker, that is. Now due to this new law, no one is allowed to be called male or female, man or woman. This has already caused a great deal of argument in Parliament, so they are all going for a Parliamentary conference at Personchester. They will all stay at a Nudist colony and air their differences. Members only, of course.

But where do you come in? Is it easy to become unsexed? Well, it can be done. And I represent the proof. At least, half of me does, the other half's quite normal. The first thing we have to realise, is that for too long, women have been beneath men – not only in the home, but at the office. And there are many ways in which we can change that. Vertical desk tops for a start. The main area of change, of course, will be in the language. The "man in the street" will become the "person in the street". Whoever you are, whether man or woman, you will be the person in the street. Incidentally, when I was in the street the other day, I nearly fell down a person-hole, so be careful.

Certain professions will have their names changed. From the Chairperson of a large company, right down to the humble Dustperson. (Not to be confused, of course, with the famous film star, Dustin Hoffperson.) Speaking of films, there will be special feature films made, showing the equality of the sexes. Already in production, a new musical called *Seven Persons for Seven Other Persons* starring Paul Newperson and Robert Help-person, with music by Persontovani and His Orchestra.

Now, dress. Of course, you won't be expected to dress like this. This sort of costume is much too expensive. Half a nicker certainly doesn't cover it. No, each person can of course choose what to wear, provided it includes the customary shirt, bra, underpants and a handbag. Shoes can be black or brown, according to individual taste. I myself find that black shoes taste better than brown shoes.

Jobs, too, will be entirely sexless; with one or two obvious exceptions. What are they, you may ask? You may ask, but I'm not telling you on this programme. But here is a clue. They have jam on them, and appear at tea time. A job must be open to either a whatsit or a whoosit – that is, of either sex. For instance, certain advertisements will not be allowed. This one here says *(holds up newspaper cutting)* "Bar staff required for West Country Pub, male or female. Must have big boobs". Now that won't be passed by the Ministry at all. What they should have said was "Bar staff required, male or female. Must be attractive in the Bristol area". That would have got past.

A recent idea by the Ministry, to avoid confusion, is to call a man a doings, and a woman a thingy. This offends no one, and makes conversation clearer. Thus we instantly recognise the book called *Little Thingies* or the play by George Bernard Shaw called *Doings and Superdoings*. There are times, however, when it sounds better to stick to the word "person". "The person in the street" is still better than "The doings in the street". That is something to look out for and steer clear of.

Finally, don't let this new law alter your life. After all, what's in a name? As the great John Greenpimple once remarked – a rose by any other name, doth smell as sweet. Or a Henry. Goodnight.

PLAIN SPEAKING

A spokesman desk, as on TV. RB enters in old-fashioned dinner jacket, drunk. A floor manager sits him in the chair.

FM: *(whispering)* We're just about on the air, Sir Harry. Your speech is on the autocue.

RB: What? *(Clutches notes in his hand.)* I've got me notes.

FM: No, look, the words on the prompter there, all written up. *(Cut to stand autocue, see it rolling.)* Just read them out. I'll take those.

(Tries to get notes.)

RB: Get off!!

(Snatches them away. They fall on floor. FM leaves the set, RB bends to pick them up. Music starts in wide shot – then cut to close-up of RB's backside. Super caption "A Spokesman". Cut back to wider shot. RB turns, recovers, starts to speak.)

RB: Good, er, it is – evening. I am a, er, spokesman for the Ministry of, er, what is it? – communications. And we all thought it would be a good idea, if I came along this evening, and told you all, what was, I mean tried to explain the whole, er put you, in it. The hole. The picture. As to what the f– what the folk, up at the Ministry think they're pl– think they're doing – know they're doing. And I should know what they're doing, because I am one of them. One of them. And I should know what I'm doing, but I don't. Want you to think that we at the er, where is it? – the Ministry are sitting down on our fat, er, fat chance we get to sit down at all because we are constantly on each other's toes, and secretaries, are, I mean she's always buzzing round, making tea and ends meet, and giving her utmost to whoever needs it, and when I say utmost, I mean most of her ut. Not that I want you to think. That we have anything. To hide. The Ministry of, er Communickers, Commu Knickers, cami-knickers, cami-knickerasians is not a – cannot be compared with a, I mean is nothing like, a, er, water closet. Er, water, Gate, Watergate. Nobody's going round bugging each other, thank goodness, because I mean these people who do go around bugging other people are, er, I mean they are absolute b–, er I mean there's only one word to describe them, and that is, er, they are simply, er, rotten bugbears.

As the Minister himself said, "We don't want any bugs in this ministry. I'm the only big bug around here," and he's absolutely, er, parded, er perfectly right. I say, it's absolutely stifling in here – does anybody mind if I open a bottle? Thanks.

(He takes a half-bottle whisky flask from his pocket, pours whisky into carafe glass. Picks up carafe, pours water into glass as well. As he puts down the carafe, the floor manager's hand comes and takes the glass away. Not even noticing this, RB drinks from the whisky flask.)

RB: That's better. Now, thirdly, I come to my second point. Inflation. Doctor Kissinger of whom it has been said – many times – and indeed, who am I? ... I repeat, who am I?

(He looks inside his jacket to read name.)

Oh yes. Who am I, a mere Moss Bros, to argue with him? He said, at the last Common Market assembly and here I quote *(looks at notes)*
"Trousers to cleaners, liquid paraffin, boots". And what a sorry picture that presents of the country today. We stand figuratively

speaking at the crossroads. The men and women of this country having been taken to the cleaners, trouserless, not knowing which way to look – to turn; and some of us are already, er, on the turn, slipping and sliding, our boots filled with liquid paraffin, on the downwards path that leads to the upward spiral of inflation, knowing that we must move, in ever decreasing circles, finally disappearing up our only chance, is to stand firm, and sleep it off – sweat it out. Back to back, noses to the wall, best foot forward, knees together and legs astride, we must all push in the same direction, see, and I would be the first to join in the fun, bearing in mind, er, that I include women in this, because women are, in a sense, lumped together. At least the ones I know are.

Finally, in confusion I would like to say unrequir, unrequilier, but I can't. But what I can say is this. Peace, perfect peace – that's what we all want. And we cannot get it alone. We must combine with the rest of Europe; in a spirit of comradeship and conviviality. And that is why I am meeting the French Minister for Communications directly after his broadcast. In his own words, "We go out and get peace together." Goodnight.

The Two Ronnies: Assorted Sketches

STAR TREK

Original opening captions if possible, with RC's voice-over, as Captain Kirk. If not available, we copy as near as possible.

After captions, cut to: Scene 1: The control room. As near as possible to the original. Essential are sliding-doors at entrance, which appear to be automatic, a computer-type piece of equipment, with hole for things to come out of and an overlay "viewer" on which we see stars and a planet (zoom in on caption boards for this). Also a seat for Captain Kirk, Lieutenant O'Hara and Mr Scott. The above three principals, plus a couple of extra men, are in position at the start of this scene.

SCOTT: Approaching unidentified planet now, sir. Warp three.

RC: *(As Kirk – seated at controls)* Distance?

SCOTT: 3,800 miles, captain.

RC: Velocity?

O'HARA: *(a white girl)* 7,500 miles per hour, captain.

RC: Chronometric scale?

O'HARA: Similar to our own, sir. 21st century AD.

RC: Precise time at present moment?

SCOTT: Three minutes past eleven.

RC: You don't say – where the hell's the coffee? And come to think of it, where's Mr Spock? I want him to run checks on this planet before we land.

SCOTT: He just slipped out for a moment, captain.

RC: What for?

SCOTT: He's only human, sir.

RC: That's just it, he's not. He's a Vulcan. He told me they never had to go at all. Keep a steady course, Scotty, I'm going to find Spock. *(He rises)* Hey! *(Looks down at himself)* I'm much smaller than I used to be! What's happened? Scotty! Look at me!

SCOTT: Sir?

RC: I've got smaller. Come over here.

SCOTT: *(approaching)* Good gracious, so you have, sir. How could that have happened?

(The automatic doors open – RB enters, with pointed ears, as Mr Spock.)

RB: Pray excuse me, captain, I was delayed. *(He stares)* Captain Kirk, I don't know if you are yet aware of it, but certain physical changes have taken place in your body, resulting in a somewhat abbreviated version of your erstwhile good self.

RC: Never mind my body, Mr Spock – what about yours?

RB: I regret that I, too, have become affected, but in a different direction – that is, outwards, as opposed to downwards. I am approximately twice as heavy as I was. I suggest we take steps to investigate the phenomena immediately – especially in your case, captain.

RC: Why me more than you?

RB: With respect, captain, if a thing swells it can only get bigger, but if it shrinks, it could disappear altogether.

RC: What?

RB: You are very small, captain.

RC: And you're like the side of a house!

RB: Verbal fisticuffs will get us nowhere, captain. Let us consider – has anyone else on board been affected?

RC: Lieutenant O'Hara certainly looks the same size and shape to me – still as attractive as ever.

(A shot of her, at her controls.)

RB: *(eyeing her)* Hmm. One detail may have escaped your notice. Yesterday she was a negro.

RC: You're right, Mr Spock! *(calling)* Lieutenant O'Hara! How do you feel?

O'HARA: Oh, I'se just fine and dandy, Captain Kirk. Don't you worry yo' head 'bout lil ole me!

RB: It's still working on her.

SCOTT: *(who has been looking into viewer on "computer" device)* Captain Kirk, sir!

RC: What is it, Scotty?

SCOTT: There seems to be something wrong with the computer banks, sir. I'm getting no information on the planet at all.

(RC and RB move to computer.)

RC: Spock?

RB: *(peering into "viewfinder")* There appears to be a malfunction in the electronic brain-cells themselves, captain. Some force is being exerted which has the effect of twisting the cell-patterns, producing a kind of insanity within the machine.

RC: Insanity? That's crazy!

RB: That is another way of putting it, certainly.

RC: Here – let me feed it a question. *(Switches on and speaks into small microphone.)* Co-ordinates, please, of the planet in our immediate flight-path.

(He presses button once.)

(The computer chugs and tings and bangs away for a few seconds – then a final twang – and a card comes out of the output hole. RC picks it up.)

RC: *(reading it)* "Your weight is 8 stone two, and you will meet a short dark stranger." That's ridiculous. *(Into mic. again)* Precise details, please. Type of planet. Land mass. Atmosphere. Life forms.

(He presses button four times. The "viewer" flashes four times, then same noises as above. After final "twang" – RC takes out strip of paper from the hole and holds it up.)

RC: Four passport photos.

RB: Allow me, captain. *(He speaks into mic.)* Full report please, on computer brain itself. Self-analysis and diagnosis on "over-ride sanity" circuit. *(To Kirk)* That should do it, if anything will, captain.

(Same noises as before. Then we cut to the actual opening in the computer, through which the messages come. A paper cup, being filled up with black coffee. Spock's hand comes in and takes it out.)

RB: I think we may safely deduce that the computer is completely out of its tiny mind.

RC: That does it. Scotty – prepare to beam us down to the planet's surface. This force must be coming from down there, Spock.

RB: I'm quite certain you're right, captain. We must investigate at once.

RC: Let's go. As soon as we enter the transporter-room, beam us down, Scotty – and then circle the planet and stand by.

(They exit.)

SCOTT: Aye, aye, sir. *(He crosses to computer and tastes the cup of coffee)* Well, I'll say one thing – you make a lovely cup of coffee.

(The computer burps.)

Scene 2: *The transporter room.*

RB and RC are already standing in position.

RC: Okay, Scotty – beam us down. Go!

SCOTTY'S VOICE: *(over intercom)* Aye, aye, captain. Beaming now.

(RB and RC start to fade, but don't disappear completely.)

RB: Increase power, Mr Scott. We haven't gone yet. *(RB disappears completely, RC still half there.)* Spock has gone, Scotty. I seem to be stuck.

(RC disappears – RB fades back a bit.)

RB: Something's wrong with the machine – I'm back.

(RC flicks back suddenly.)

RC: Me too. Over-ride, Scotty! I'm beginning to feel like a yo-yo.

(They both fade away and disappear. A pause.)

RC'S VOICE: We're still here. For Pete's sake, Scotty!

RB'S VOICE: Try the booster, Mr Scott.

(They begin to fade back – but only the bottom half of RB shows.)

RB'S VOICE: This is ridiculous. *(The legs walk round RC.)* I'll try and fix it – I'll join you later.

(The legs walk away, out of shot. RC fades in and fades out as we cut to: camera zooms slowly in on planet, surrounded by stars.)

RC *(voice-over)*: Captain's log, star-date 2150. Mr Spock and I finally managed to land on the planet XJ 340, after trouble with the ship's computer. We set out to search for the source of the strange evil force which had changed our shape.

Scene 3: A room in the palace of Kanhuth, on the planet.

RC and RB enter, ray-guns in hand.

RC: Seems deserted.

RB: It would appear so, captain. However, Mr Scott beamed us down as near to the force-field as possible. We must be within a few feet of it. We should proceed with caution.

RC: Search the room.

(They begin to do so. In the centre of the room, a sort of plinth, on top of which is a black metal box, with a knob on the top. RC is searching in a corner. RB approaches the black box, touches the knob. Then he lifts the black box up by the knob. Underneath, like a large cheese on a dish, is a head – green, with wires coming from its temples. It looks to be completely detached, resting on a chromium square block. It is obviously alive. It looks at him evilly. RB puts back the cover before he realises what it is. He has moved away, and suddenly stops.)

RB: Captain!

(He beckons RC over and then lifts the cover off again.)

RC: Good grief.

HEAD: Greetings, earthman.

RC: Greetings. Are you in charge here?

HEAD: There are many kinds of life-form who serve me.

RC: So you're the head?

HEAD: I am the Master.

RB: Tell me, Headmaster, is it you who have been disrupting our starship and changing our physical shapes?

HEAD: The ray emanates from the machine behind me. I control it by thought waves.

RC: But why? Why?

HEAD: Revenge! Revenge!

RC: I see! I see! Go on – go on.

RB: Captain, if we're going to say everything twice we're never going to get out of here. I suggest once is enough.

RC: I'm sorry, I'm sorry. I mean, I'm just sorry. Once.

RB: Revenge, I believe you said.

HEAD: Yes – I loaned my body to the scientists for experiments – *(furious)* and they never returned it. They left me here with this machine – using my brain as a sort of clockwork machine! Me! Who used to love life! Wine, women and song! I lived for them!

RB: Well, at least you can still sing.

RC: Does no one bring you food?

HEAD: What good is food? I have no stomach.

RC: Tough.

RB: And women?

HEAD: The same thing applies.

(RB looks at RC.)

RC: *(explaining)* He has no inclination.

HEAD: I'm becoming a vegetable.

RB: *(takes RC aside)* What is your opinion, captain?

RC: *(to RB, quietly)* I think he's off his head.

RB: True. An evil force that must be dealt with.

HEAD: I'd be better off dead.

RB: I think that could be arranged.

(*He suddenly slams the cover over the head and then runs to the machine which is emitting the ray. He turns it onto the black box, then moves forward to the black box and is about to pick it up.*)

RC: Spock! Keep back – you could get contaminated!

RB: Leave me, captain – beam aboard and wait for me on the starship.

RC: I'll have the medical unit stand by.

(*He exits. Spock removes the black cover. Underneath is a cabbage. RB stares at it. Then a strange thudding noise is heard. RB looks apprehensive and backs away from the door. We fade.*)

Scene 4: Captain Kirk's cabin on the starship.

A small affair, one door; the main essential is an overlay blue window in the back wall – three foot tall by four foot wide. (Note: the impression to create here is that RC is now six feet tall so everything to scale.)

RC is standing next to a couch-type bed. O'Hara, who is now a negress, and must be about eight inches shorter than RC, is offering him a drink from a tray.

RC: *(taking it)* Thanks, Lieutenant O'Hara. Glad to see you've got your colour back. I'm back to my normal six feet again. Spock must have overcome the creature and nullified the ray. The question is, is he OK? *(Enter Scotty)* Scotty – is Spock back yet?

SCOTTY: *(on monitor)* No, captain. And I don't like it, being down here on the planet's surface. Permission to blast off again, sir?

RC: Certainly not, Mr Scott. Not without Spock.

(*He looks out of the "window" where we see the planet's surface – typical backcloth à la science fiction magazine.*)

RC: Somewhere out there, there are many life-forms – who knows – one of them may have got Spock!

(The thudding noise is heard again. They freeze. Then in through the window peers the vast head of RB (on overlay). The head fills the window.)

RB: Good day, captain. I've come to say goodbye.

RC: Goodbye? Spock, what's happened?

RB: I became contaminated – and just grew and grew. I intend to stay here until I become normal size again. Farewell!

RC: But that's terrible. Terrible!

RB: Don't worry, captain. You were right about the other life forms – one of them did get me. Say goodbye, Angelique.

(An enormous under-dressed girl peers in, displaying a bosom about four feet across. She smiles and waves, then stands up and turns round, displaying a bottom about four feet across. It walks away from us and we see Spock eventually, walking with her. An amazed look from RC, and we bring up the music, as per original.)

DR SPOONER IN THE BOOKSHOP

A Victorian bookshop. Enter Dr Spooner. A lady assistant appears.

ASSISTANT: Good day, sir.

SPOONER: Good day. My name is Spooner. Spoctor Dooner. I was just frassing the punt of your shop, and I thought I'd book in for a look. Look in for a book. Do excuse me, I sometimes get one word nuddled up with a mother. I'm stequently made a laughing frock.

ASSISTANT: Ah yes – Dr Spooner, of course. You're most welcome, sir. Which book did you require?

S: How about the complete shirks of Wakespeare? Or a book of poetry by Kelly, or Sheets?

A: I'm afraid we're rather low on poetry at the moment.

S: Oh, pot a witty, pit a wotty. It was to be a gresent for my pud lady.

A: Your pud lady, sir?

S: My wife, the dear thing.

A: Ah! If it is for a lady – perhaps something fairly easy to read – nothing too taxing for the female brain.

S: On the contrary, nothing too simple. My wife is a right little bl ... a bright little reader.

A: A romantic novel then? *The Vicar of Wakefield*?

S: Possibly – providing it doesn't arouse her animal instincts. She likes red beading – beading in red, that is. Last month I bought *Wuthering Heights* for her, and the following evening I found her needing it in the rude.

A: I see.

S: So I don't wish to encourage her to leap out of her vicars for *The Knicker of Wakefield*.

A: Quite.

S: How about Chickens?

A: Pardon?

S: Chickens. Darles Chickens. One of our most nipping grovellists. Perhaps *David Kipperfield* or *Knockerless Nickleby*? Or the one about the lady with the large chest, who advertises it for sale in the local newspaper ...

A: By Dickens, sir?

S: Yes, yes. Ah! Got it. *The Tale of Two Cities*.

A: I'm afraid not, sir – we could order the book for you.

S: I need it at once – you see, she has gone to Wigan, to the seaside. She's coming back tomorrow. I wanted to give her the wook, when she got see from the backside at Biggun. That is, I wanted to give her the whack, when se got big from the wee-side at ... I wanted the book for the whack on the backside ... I wanted to give her the Biggun. I do hope I've made myself clear.

A: Perfectly clear, sir.

S: Perhaps I'll buy a book for myself instead. What have you to interest me? A charm from your obvious parts. Er – apart from your obvious charms.

A: *(coyly)* It is difficult without knowing your taste. Perhaps something of an instructional nature? A text book?

S: Ah! Now, one of my gobbies is hardening.

A: Oh dear. You need a copy of *The Complete Home Doctor*.

(Offers it.)

S: What? No, no, gardening! How I love my garden. When the shun is signing and the twirds are bittering, how wonderful it is to rip out and pick a few noses. Perhaps a book on flowers?

A: *(taking up a book) Familiar Wild Flowers, From Stinkwort to Periwinkle?*

S: Ah no – not wild flowers. There is no room in my garden for the Periwort or the Stinkwinkle. No, no – cultivated flowers – tupins and lulips, coxgloves and farnations – sweet bees, pooh-bells and dainty little net-got-me-fors. Do you have a gouse with a harden?

A: No – I live in furnished rooms.

S: How sad! May a say you are most welcome to visit mine – and if you like it, I'll ladly give you the goose of it. Why not come round tomorrow for key and trumpets?

A: I would love to.

S: Good, then will sonsedder it kittled. I must be off.

A: I fear we still haven't found you anything to read.

S: Don't worry – if it hadn't been roaring with pain outside, and if I hadn't left my haincoat at Rome, I wouldn't have bum in for a cook in the first place. Good day!

(He exits.)

GEORGE'S BEDROOM

RC in bed with attractive wife. She is asleep. He stirs, restlessly, then sits up. As he thinks, we hear his voice-over.

RC: *(Voice-over):* Now I really can't sleep. Or perhaps I'm dreaming. Hm. People usually pinch themselves to see if they're awake. I'll try that. *(Does so.)* No, can't feel a thing. Therefore I must be dreaming. *(Looks at wife.)* Is she asleep? Or am I just dreaming she's asleep? I'll pinch her as well. *(Puts his hands under the bedclothes – no reaction.)* She didn't move. But if I'd really pinched her, she would have woken up. Therefore I only dreamt that I pinched her. Therefore I'm definitely not awake. Right. Walking then.

(RC walks out of bedroom door.)

Cut to: street door. (He comes out through it. He looks back, puzzled.)

RC: Funny. Our bedroom's usually upstairs.

Exterior. Street – Day.

(He walks along the road in his pyjamas. A man on a bicycle passes him, also in striped pyjamas. RC approaches a pub. Its lights are on, a hum of noise from within.)

RC: Perhaps I'll pop in for a drink. *(Approaches, then hesitates.)* Hang on, I don't drink. Ah yes, but that's when I'm awake. I can do what I like when I'm dreaming.

(Enters the pub.)

Interior: pub.

The pub is quite full and lively, everyone is in nightclothes – all the men in pyjamas, the girls in nightdresses. Cut to: one old lady in curlers. The barman, also in pyjamas, greets RC.

BARMAN: Yessir, what can I get you?

RC: Er – half of shandy, please.

BARMAN: Horlicks or Ovaltine?

RC: Pardon?

BARMAN: Do you want it mixed with Horlicks or Ovaltine?

RC: Oh, er – Ovaltine, please. And a packet of crisps.

(Barman gives RC crisps. RC opens packet. It contains only one enormous crisp. He shakes the packet, looks in, then eats the poppadum-like crisp. Drink arrives. RC takes it, looks around. Sees a man dressed in bib and brace overalls, with old suit coat and a cap.)

RC: *(to barman)* Why is he dressed differently to everyone else?

BARMAN: He's on nights.

RC: Oh.

(Door opens. A policeman (RB), in striped pyjamas with pointed helmet, enters. Goes to RC.)

RB: Is that your car outside?

RC: What car?

RB: *(Goes back to door, opens it. Back projection of Brands Hatch. Cars, racing by in profile. One car has stopped on the verge.)* That red one. Rotten bit of parking, that.

RC: My car is at home in the garage.

RB: Oh? How did you get here then?

RC: I'm not here. I'm at home in bed, asleep.

RB: Have you got anyone who can vouch for you?

BARMAN: I'll vouch for him. We all will, won't we, lads?

(Everyone shouts agreement.)

RB: Well, don't let me catch you at home asleep again.

(RB opens the door again – the cars race by, but the parked one has disappeared.)

RB: He's hopped it, the swine. Oi!

(RB shuts the door. Terrible screaming of brakes and crunching of gears. The pub customers laugh.)

A street: Day.

(RC walks along. The houses are terraced back-to-back types, opening on to the street – no gardens. A woman, in nightdress, sweeping the front step. She stares at RC.)

RC: 'Evening. *(Walks on, then turns his head again)* What are you staring at, you silly old cow?

Cut to: real cow, standing in a different doorway. It stares back.

(A girl in a shortie nightie approaches RC. As she passes him, she smiles at him. He looks back and then goes round a corner. We pick him up the other side of the corner. He looks startled. Cut to: his point of view. The same girl approaches again. Again, she smiles, and goes round the corner.)

(Now we see him from behind – the same girl comes from behind camera, overtakes RC and smiles back at him. She carries on and enters a house further ahead. Immediately she comes round a second corner up ahead and approaches RC, smiles and passes him.)

(RC puzzled. He approaches the house the girl went into – it is near the second corner. He looks in the window.)

GIRL: *(off)* Coo-ee!

(RC reacts, looks round.)

GIRL: *(off)* I'm round the corner!

(RC goes towards corner. Close-up of RC as he comes round the corner into completely different, much grander street. The girl stands by the gate of a detached house. She beckons.)

GIRL: Hurry up.

(RC hurries over to her.)

RC: You're the receptionist girl, aren't you? His wife, he said.

GIRL: That's right. Come on!

RC: Where?

GIRL: You're in love with me.

RC: Certainly.

GIRL: Come on then, quick.

RC: What about him? The psychiatrist?

GIRL: He's out on a case.

RC: What of?

GIRL: Scotch. Come on.

(She takes out a key, which is on a string round her neck, and unlocks the door. They go in.)

Outside the girl's bedroom.

(They walk along a corridor. Policeman (RB), in pyjamas and helmet, stands by the door and salutes as they start to go into bedroom.)

RB: Evening all.

(RC stares, but the girl takes no notice.)

RC: What's he doing there? That's not your husband in disguise, is it?

GIRL: No, nothing like him.

RC: Same build.

(Unconvinced)

GIRL: He's not in our dream. Don't worry about him.

(They go into bedroom and close the door. Cut to: clock. It says two o'clock. The hands move round to 3.30. Then they whizz back to eleven, then round and round. Finally, the clock explodes.)

Part of the bedroom.

Close-up of RC and girl in bed.

RC: Good gracious, is that the time?

GIRL: Don't go.

RC: I must. It's a long walk.

GIRL: Haven't you got wheels?

RC: No, feet. At least I usually have.

(He lifts bedclothes to look down.)

GIRL: I mean, have you any means of transport?

RC: No.

GIRL: Take mine – it's in the garage. Keys on the dressing-table.

RC: How will I get it back to you?

GIRL: Come back in it tomorrow.

(She smiles.)

Outside the garage.

Close-up on RC as he fiddles with keys. Cut wide – he is sitting on a single brass bed with a steering wheel attached. He is trying to work the clutch. The girl appears from the house.

RC: It won't go.

GIRL: Here. *(She sits on the bed with him.)* You've not switched on. I'll drive you.

(They leave with her at the wheel. Various shots, as they travel the streets. They turn a corner and the policeman (RB) steps out and stops them.)

RB: Excuse me. Have you got a licence for that?

GIRL: For what?

RB: Two in a bed.

RC: You need need a licence?

RB: Certainly. Marriage licence.

RC: *(to girl)* Come on, let's get out and walk.

RB: You can't leave that here.

RC: What?

RB: Not unless you've got double yellow lines down your pyjamas.

RC: What?

RB: This is a no-snoring zone. Hot water-bottle holders only.

RC: What?

RB: Is that all you can say?

RC: What?

(Hooters are heard. Cut to: a line of five single beds all with two people in them. Close-up of a bed knob "honked" like a car-horn.)

RB: Go on, drive on, you're holding up the traffic.

(RC and girl sweep off out of frame as policeman (RB) goes to sort out the angry drivers.)

RC's house.

(RC and girl sitting in the bed by the kerb.)

RC: Well, thanks for bringing me home. It's been lovely, hasn't it?

GIRL: Smashing.

RC: I never dreamt that a dream could be so real. If I didn't know I was dreaming, I would swear that I'm wide awake. I suppose I didn't just dream that I dreamt it, did I? May I pinch you?

GIRL: Depends where.

RC: There.

(Pinches her arm.)

GIRL: Ow!

(She pinches him back.)

RC: Ow! Yes, that really hurt. I really am dreaming this. I'm so grateful to your husband for suggesting I go for a walk.

GIRL: So am I. *(Kisses his cheek)* See you tonight?

RC: Only if I can't sleep!

(He gets out of bed, tiptoes to door, turns, waves, goes in.)

RC's bedroom.

(RC enters and stares. The psychiatrist is in bed with RC's wife.)

RC: Here! What's all this?

RB: Sorry, old chap. I couldn't sleep either!

WELCOME M'LORD

Old lord and wife at dinner in ancestral home.

LORD: Where's the food? We've been sitting here ages. That new butler is very erratic. Wait for ages, then he brings all the food at once. What's more, he's damned impudent.

LADY: Oh, do you think so? He's always very polite to me.

LORD: Well, he's not to me. Impudent bounder.

(Enter butler, puts down plate in front of lady.)

BUTLER: Your game, Milady.

(Gives her a leer and starts to go.)

LORD: I say, Blenkinsop, hurry up with my roast pork. Make sure it's a nice fatty bit!

(Butler appears to ignore him, and exits.)

LORD: There you are – ignores me.

LADY: Don't make such a fuss. He's very efficient.

LORD: Damned rude, I call it.

(Butler enters, with another plate. Places it in front of lord.)

BUTLER: Your fat, Milord.

(He exits.)

LORD: How dare he! I'm going to have to sack him.

LADY: Steady on – we have enough servant trouble as it is. The handyman's about to leave us, and the plumbing is in a terrible state.

LORD: Oh, that reminds me, the lavatories ...

(Butler enters with dessert – he places it in front of lady.)

BUTLER: Your sweet, Milady.

(He leers again.)

LADY: Oh, thank you, Blenkinsop.

(He goes to sideboard, brings dish to lord.)

BUTLER: Your nuts, Milord.

(Turns away.)

LORD: Cheeky swine! *(Calls to him)* How am I supposed to break these open – with my teeth?

(Butler returns to table.)

BUTLER: Your crackers, Milord.

(Hands him nutcrackers, and exits.)

LORD: That does it! Staff shortage or no staff shortage – he goes!

LADY: Well, you know best, dear. What were you saying about the lavatories?

(Butler enters, pushing a large trolley.)

LORD: They're broken. Out of order. Up the spout and down the drain.

LADY: What? And we've sacked the handyman! How are we going to manage?

(Butler, at table by the trolley, takes cover off a bucket, hands it to lady.)

BUTLER: Your pale, Milady.

(Takes cover off another object.)

Your potty, Milord.

MILEAWAY

A pretty country road. A high shot, as a little open sports car comes over the hill. In it sits RC. A mild-mannered civil servant, and his wife, a tall, forbidding blonde. The car draws to a halt by a signpost. Muriel (the wife) consults a road map on her knees.

RC: *(looking at sign)* Podmores End. Never heard of it. Are you familiar with Podmores End, dear?

MURIEL: *(icily)* Not at all.

RC: Lucky Podmore.

MURIEL: Don't make pathetic jokes, Brian. You haven't the faintest idea where we are, have you?

RC: I know exactly where we are, Muriel. We are lost. That's where we are. *(Looking at sign)* What's that other name? I can't see from here.

MURIEL: Well, get out then.

(RC gets out of car to inspect sign. A close-up of sign. It says "Mileaway – 1/2 mile".)

RC: It's a place called Mile-away, half a mile away. But it's only a footpath.

MURIEL: Well, at least there will be someone who can tell us where we are.

RC: Righto. Are you staying here?

MURIEL: No, it's too hot. I'm being bitten all over by gnats as it is.

RC: I think they're attracted by your aftershave.

MURIEL: Brian!

RC: Perfume. Sorry – Freudian slip. And talking of Freudian slips, mind where you put your feet round here.

(She descends from the car.)

MURIEL: Do you think there will be anywhere we can spend the night?

RC: Bound to be some sort of pub or inn. Might be nice.

MURIEL: Mm. A single bed, mind.

RC: What, for the two of us?

MURIEL: Don't be facetious, Brian. You know how set I am on a single bed. I won't be moved on that.

RC: I wouldn't dream of trying to move you on any kind of bed, dear. Come along.

(They set off down the path. Cut to them emerging from a cart-track, or similar, into a village street. A close-up as they stop and stare. Music over. We cut to their point of view. The village street we see is a street of Elizabethan times. Peasants with carts, ragged children, horses and sheep in the street. The locals give them strange stares as they go about their business. One middle-aged peasant approaches them.)

PEASANT: Good day, Master, Mistress. I do see by your apparel, in shape and form most foreign to mine eye, that you be strangers to this valley and these lands. I give you welcome, Master.

RC: Thanks awfully. Er – sorry to disturb you on your carnival day. We were wondering if there was an inn where we could spend the night. Single beds, of course.

PEASANT: There be the inn, good master – yonder, there.

Cut to: inn – close-up sign "The Boar's Head".

PEASANT: But I must warn you straight, the landlord here
True to his title, "land-lord" doth possess
And is in sooth the Lord, of all these lands.
He is our Thane, our Duke, our governing Peer
And he doth rule, and over all hold sway.

RC: Ah yes, I know the type. *(To Muriel)* Bit of a big-head.

PEASANT: Shall I convey thee to my good Lord's door?

RC: Yes, certainly. I'll soon sort him out. He's not even in the *Good Food Guide*.

(Suddenly, shouts off. Cut to: the door of the inn. Bolts are drawn, the door is flung open – chickens hurtle out. A nearby child looks terrified. A servant girl is propelled out, held by the scruff of the neck by RB as the landlord – a Henry VIII type figure, of Falstaffian proportions.)

RB: Thou poxy wench! If I do but catch thee once more with thy greasy hand in my money-bags, I'll wrap thy legs round thy neck and hang thee up by thy garters for the crows to peck at! Now, be gone!

(He kicks her into the street. As he does so, he spies RC and Muriel. He struts over to them.)

RB: What have we here? Upon my troth, look now,
'Tis bold Sir Thomas Thumb, I do declare!
Thrice welcome, good Sir Tom, and to thy spouse.
(aside) If that is what she be – such frozen looks dispute she is Mistress of his bed.

MURIEL: Single beds, Brian.

RC: Yes, good evening. Do you think you could accommodate us? In single beds? Both of us, that is. Separately.

MURIEL: In the same room.

RC: But facing different ways. What I mean is, can you put us up?

RB: What, put you up? I, marry, that I shall!
My microcosmic Lord, thou shalt be up
As tall as any subject in the realm.
Thou shalt take dinner seated on a cask
Of good red claret, earmarked for the feast.
Astride this mount, its tap between thy legs,
Thou shalt replenish all the serving maids.

(Muriel looks disdainful.)

RB: Put up indeed, the highest in the land
Thou shalt sit here, with me, on my right hand.
Thy frosty spouse, however, by my crown

Should not be up, nay, she should be laid down.

MURIEL: That reminds me, Brian. Hot water bottles.

RC: Ah yes – are the beds warm?

RB: There is a wench, who for an honest groat
Will warm thy bed with warming pans of coals
Or whatsoever method you devise
'Twixt she and you – the girl knows all the ways. *(Looking at Muriel)*
As to this glacier – this Siberian stone.
Give me its latch-key, I will warm it straight. *(He slaps her roundly on the roundel of her rear.)* Come, enter, and prepare ye for the feast.

(Music as he sweeps inside, scattering children and chickens. Muriel is standing aghast.)

RC: Come on then, dear. *(They start to follow him)* I hope he takes Barclaycard.

They enter the inn. Mix to: inside the inn.

A tracking close-up of goblets being filled from a jug by a serving wench. Lots of raucous noise. The faces of the diners, laughing, eating. The serving wenches, queuing up to fill their jugs from the cask, on which sits RC, legs astride it. RB on his left – pan to the frosty-faced Muriel.

Shots of the crowd stuffing their faces – a jester wanders round, hitting people on the head with a sheep's bladder balloon. RB, eating and tearing at a chicken. He burps, then throws one leg of chicken over his shoulder.

It hits a footman standing behind him. RB throws the other leg. It lands in the cleavage of a enormously busted middle-aged woman, who stares down at it. The footman laughs, RB throws his tankard over his shoulder. It hits the footman, who stops laughing. Large-busted woman laughing. A drunk passes, holding chicken bone. Sees woman's cleavage, removes her bone, replaces it with his one, goes off eating hers.

The musicians – maybe four or five – start up a dance with drum and tabor. People get up to dance. RC is grabbed by the big-bosomed woman and led onto the floor. The dancers, as part of the dance, suddenly draw each other closer and part again. RC's face splats into the large lady's bosom, recoils, and is dragged in again. Muriel sits on her own, frostily. The crowds laugh and applaud, the dogs eat scraps from the rush-covered floor. Muriel is suddenly surprised by something under the table. It is RC, who emerges.

RC: It's alright, it's only me, dear.

(He is dishevelled.)

MURIEL: You promised you would never touch me there, Brian.

RC: I'm sorry, Muriel – I didn't mean to grab your bad knee. I'm hiding from that woman. I had to suddenly drop down. Luckily, she's got such a big bosom, she can't see the floor.

MURIEL: I think I would like to go to our room now, Brian. I want to listen to *Book at Bedtime* on Radio 3.

RC: Yes. Bit hectic, isn't it? They're always the same, these Henry VIII Suppers. I don't even know which room we're in.

MURIEL: Well, ask him.

(Indicating RB, who is involved with a serving wench.)

RC: *(crossing round to RB)* Excuse me, mine host, but we'd like to retire.

RB: So shall you, good Sir Tom – sweet dreams. *(They start to go.)*
But stay!
Afore ye go, there's reckoning to be made
Thou must, for this night's work due recompense
In full account of cost be now discharged.
This is the custom in these whereabouts–
No man shall sleep until he pay his dues.

RC: *(to Muriel)* Oh, obviously a Union man. Barclaycard? Or perhaps used fivers?

(He produces both.)

RB: *(staring at the money)* What? Papers, bills and promissory notes? Nay, this is not a London counting house! Were not the vittals real?

The meat not warm? Was not the wine wet, did the cheese not bite? How then can we accept some airy pledge? The promise of some future settlement? *(Grabs him, threateningly)* One shilling in the silver of the realm. The honest coin that bears our good Queen's head.

MURIEL: A shilling?

RC: Oh, well, why didn't you say so? *(To Muriel)* Must be National Trust, or the Arts Council. Lord Montague's probably behind it. *(Hands over coin)* There you are, my man. There's 5p. Come along, Muriel.

(They start to leave.)

RB: Stop! This coin is counterfeit! Restrain them!

(RC and Muriel are grabbed.)

RB: Bear witness all – that some strange alien face doth masquerade hereon for Good Queen Bess. "Elizabeth the Second" the legend bears. We know, God knows, that there be only one!

RC: But look ...

RB: But me no buts, thou scurvy knave.
This counterfeiting is a heinous crime.
The punishment is clear, and widely known.
The forfeiture of all your goods and wealth,
And for your further humblement and shame
To spend the night imprisoned in the stocks.
Away with him.

(He is taken out.)

RB: Yet hold his wife close by.
She, being but a chattel of his house
Is likewise forfeit to our royal claim.
Go, woman, and prepare her for the night
With perfumes, unctions – dress her all in white.
The ice is white that floats in Arctic sea –
But ice must melt – and melt then so shall she!

(A cheer as she is taken out.)

Cut to: RC in stocks – or rather, a pillory – hands and head.

(He stands there, deserted. Camera pulls back, he is on a box. The stocks are under a large tree.)

RC: This would never have happened if we'd stuck to Trust House Forte. *(He looks round at the twilight)* It's going to be damn cold standing here all night. At least they could have given me something on my head.

(Above him, in the tree, a boy drops a hen's egg. It lands and bursts on RC's head.)

RC: Sorry I spoke.

Cut to: a bed-chamber, a large four-poster.

(RB carries in Muriel, in revealing night attire. He throws her onto the bed. As she bounces, she shows a lot of leg and promise. A close-up of her, bosom heaving, as we hear sounds of RB tearing off his clothes.)

Mix to: next morning. Sunny.

(Muriel is hurrying along, looking only slightly the worse for wear. She emerges from the footpath, to find RC sitting in the passenger seat, his arms and hands in the air, as if still in the stocks.)

RC: Ah – there you are, dear – are you alright?

MURIEL: I'm not sure – I think I'm possibly quite well. Why are you doing that, Brian? You look silly.

RC: The stocks, dear. I've just sort of set like it. You'll have to drive. Have you had much sleep?

MURIEL: Not a lot.

(She half-smiles to herself.)

RC: I've just noticed. That sign isn't there any more. The one that said "Mileaway". *(We see that it isn't.)* Muriel, do you think we dreamt it? God, what a nightmare.

MURIEL: Oh, I don't know ... *(she smiles warmly at him)* All set, Brian, dear?

RC: Fine. You're very relaxed this morning.

MURIEL: I'm just looking forward to the drive, that's all.

RC: Well, don't drive too fast. In this position, I might fly away.

MURIEL: *(laughing)* Let's have a little music, shall we? *(She turns on the radio.)*

Cut to: a radio.

(It is standing by the four-poster, in which RB sits, dressed in night cap and Elizabethan frilly night shirt. He is smoking a cigarette and counting fivers. He comes across RC's Barclaycard – opens a small box on the bedside table, and throws it in with the rest. The Irish DJ's voice comes from the radio.)

DJ: Well, now, with such beautiful weather you should all be out in the country, not sitting indoors listening to this rubbish – why, there's places out there that you've never even heard of. Believe me, it's worth it. Go and find yourself an adventure. It may change your life.

Cut to: RC and Muriel.

(She smiles at him as they drive along. He turns to her and manages to flap one hand at her as they zoom off over the horizon.)

UPSTAIRS DOWNSTAIRS

Credits:

We copy the steel engraving-type captions of the series, finishing with an engraving of the outside of the Bellamy house. We go in on this, mix through to studios.

Scene 1: The drawing room – a May morning, 1907.

Mr Bellamy (RC), suave, elegant, an MP, sits reading a letter. His wife, beautiful and witty, is toying with some embroidery.

MARJORIE: Well?

RC: What?

MARJORIE: What does it say?

(She is eager.)

RC: I haven't quite finished reading it. Be patient, my dear.

MARJORIE: Patient? A letter is delivered by hand from no less an address than Buckingham Palace itself, and my husband asks me to be patient. Richard, really!

RC: I'm sorry, my dear, to be a trifle slow. Reading wasn't my best subject at Eton. That's why I had to give up any ideas of following a profession and become an MP.

MARJORIE: Well, how far have you got?

RC: Well, I'll tell you this much, it's addressed to both of us.

MARJORIE: Here, let me read it. *(He gives it to her.)* To Sir Richard and Lady Bellamy ...

RC: There you are, I'm right so far.

MARJORIE: I have the honour to inform you that His Majesty – oh! – would deem it a privilege to dine with you on May the 21st at eight o'clock, at your residence in Belgrave Square. His Majesty will, of course, be incognito. I have the honour to remain, etc. Arthur Wormington, private secretary to His Majesty – Oh, Richard – I think I'm going to faint.

(She collapses into his arms.)

RC: Here, lie on the sofa, and I'll undo something for you.

MARJORIE: No, no, there's no time for that. I'm too excited. Oh, Richard! The King, dining here! It must be because of that chance meeting at the garden party. You remember – you weren't there.

RC: How can I remember if I wasn't there?

MARJORIE: I mean, I told you about it. I met him – and now he wants to dine here! And all because I offered him a pressed tongue sandwich.

RC: Are you sure that's all you offered him?

MARJORIE: Don't be silly, Richard. Now we must prepare. It must be kept a secret from the neighbours. Remember, he will be incognito the whole time.

RC: From what I hear, he always is these days. Can't do his liver any good. I'll ring for Hudson.

(He goes to bell-rope. As he is about to pull the rope, Hudson (RB) enters. RC doesn't hear him and pulls the bell.)

RB: *(immediately)* You rang, sir?

RC: *(turning round quickly)* Ah, Hudson. That was quick.

RB: I came in just before you rang, sir.

RC: That's what I mean. Your mistress wants a word with you.

RB: *(alarmed)* What, you mean she's here, now? In the house? Oh, my goodness!

RC: *(explains)* Lady Bellamy. *(Indicating his wife.)*

RB: *(relieved)* Oh, I see, sir. Sorry. Milady?

MARJORIE: We are expecting a very distinguished visitor for dinner on Friday, Hudson.

RB: *(to RC)* Would it be a fellow MP, sir?

RC: No, no – someone of far greater stature than me.

RB: Oh, really? I wonder whoever that could be?

MARJORIE: His Majesty, King Edward.

RB: The Seventh?

MARJORIE: Naturally. Edward the Sixth died in 1553.

RC: Did he, by jove? That's something else they didn't teach us at Eton. Just a minute, that can't be right. That would make this one over three hundred years old.

MARJORIE: No, silly – there have been others in between.

RB: Excuse me, milady – perhaps while you're sorting that out, I could go and inform the staff. *(He starts to go, then remembers)* Oh, milady, the reason I came in, in the first place, was to ask whether I could use the morning room this afternoon for my evening classes.

RC: What?

RB: Only we're all working this evening, and so I thought I'd have them this afternoon, and the morning room is ideal.

RC: Hang on a minute, I'm confused. You're not asking for the whole day off, are you?

RB: Oh no, sir. I'm working this morning and this evening. It's just this afternoon I want off, for the evening classes.

RC: In the morning room.

RB: Yes, sir.

RC: Alright then, Hudson – just try to put in an appearance from time to time.

RB: Certainly, sir, milady. Will that be all?

RC: Yes, thank you, Hudson. Nice to have passed the time of day with you. *(RB exits. To Marjorie)* What are these evening classes, anyway?

MARJORIE: He gives the maids lessons in deportment and physical fitness. He likes to show them a few wrinkles.

RC: I'm sure he does. Still, the King's visit should give the maids something to occupy them. I bet he can't wait to tell them the news.

Cut to: close-up of a maid, scrubbing a floor. She suddenly reacts violently to an attack from behind.

KITCHEN MAID: Ooh!

(We pull back a little as RB bends down and says in her ear)

RB: The King's coming to dinner!

MAID: Ooh!

Cut to: another maid.

Back view on her on a pair of steps, dusting the picture rail with a short feather duster. Close-up of her face. Suddenly she reacts in the same way.

PARLOUR MAID: Ooh!

(We pull back a little. RB is there. He too has a small feather duster, as the maid found out. He steps up and whispers in her ear)

RB: The King's coming to dinner!

PARLOUR MAID: Ooh!

Cut to: door with "servants bathroom no. 1" painted on it in gold lettering. Pull back to reveal RB, peering through keyhole. Sounds of water running and maid's voice, singing. RB enters quickly, clouds of steam emerge, sound of a slap.

HOUSEMAID: *(off)* Ow! Coo, that didn't half hurt, that did.

RB: *(off)* The King's coming to dinner!

HOUSEMAID: *(off)* Ooh!

RB appears again, wiping his soapy hands on his apron. He goes to next door, which says "servants bathroom no. 2" on it. He opens it, clouds of steam emerge. Sound of a loud slap, as before. Then a loud splash. RB reappears with a bucket over his head. He removes it. He is drenched. We cut inside. In the bath is a surly-looking gardener, gnarled, with a filthy old hat on, smoking a filthy old pipe and scrubbing his back at the same time. We fade out.

Fade in – close-up of desk calendar – "Friday May 21st". The great day. RC is in a brocade dressing gown and is speaking, or rather shouting, into the telephone.

RC: Hullo! Hullo in there! Is anybody in there? Hullo, mother. MOTHER! *(Marjorie enters)* Mother, if you're in there, answer me. *(Putting it down in disgust)* Dashed new-fangled things. Spend a fortune having the thing installed and then it doesn't work. Just can't make mother hear at all.

MARJORIE: Mother's not on the telephone.

RC: That's no excuse. *(Then realising)* What?

MARJORIE: Listen, I've something much more important to talk about. I've just been having a word with Rose, the head housemaid. She's very distressed, Richard.

RC: I absolutely deny it. Her whole story is a tissue of lies. I was at an all-night sitting. What did she say?

MARJORIE: She merely told me that Hudson, the butler, is missing.

RC: Oh, that's different.

MARJORIE: Have you got a guilty conscience, Richard?

RC: Certainly not. You can't afford one if you're an MP. Did you say Hudson is missing?

MARJORIE: He hasn't been seen since this morning. Apparently a man in a bowler hat called at the front door and, after a hurried consultation, left again – followed, five minutes afterwards, by Hudson. One of the maids saw him later this morning with a large bag in Burlington Arcade.

RC: Did the maid recognise her?

MARJORIE: Recognise who?

RC: The large bag he was with. It wasn't Gerty from the Gaiety, was it? I know he's been hanging round the stage door after her, ever since he saw her as Dick in the Panto.

MARJORIE: I don't know what you're talking about. All I know is that the King is coming to dinner tonight, and we are without a butler!

RC: Good grief! What are we going to do?

MARJORIE: You will have to be the butler, Richard.

RC: Me? I couldn't. I've never buttled in my life. I wouldn't know how to begin.

MARJORIE: Look, His Majesty doesn't know you – and I'm not having a strange butler in the house tonight. We've got six hours to prepare.

RC: No, it's impossible – my tailcoat is at the cleaners.

MARJORIE: Then you'll have to wear Hudson's. Richard – I'm determined.

Close-up of RC's resigned face.

Mix to: the house in Belgrave Square. A policeman saunters past. A nursemaid goes in the opposite direction, pushing a pram. The policeman stops and turns. We hear the faintest sound of a carriage and pair approaching. A close-up of the policeman as we hear the carriage stop. Footsteps approach. A look of recognition and a salute from the policeman. Then a close-up of the front door. The shadow of the King's top hat and cloak falls on the door. A walking stick comes into shot, presses the doorbell (they did have electric bells in those days!) after a moment, RC comes to the door, wearing gold-rimmed spectacles like Hudson's. He bows slightly.

RC: Good evening your, er, Lord, sir, Mr Windsor.

The King's top hat is handed over to RC. He goes to take it – we see a very large, long black coat-sleeve with no hand in sight. Eventually the hand arrives out of the sleeve and takes the hat.

Cut to: the dinner in progress.

The table is set very elaborately – for two. The King (RB) sits on the right of Lady Marjorie. RC is at the sideboard. Three maids hover about, assisting. As we cut, the King is roaring with laughter. He is obviously getting on very well with Lady Bellamy.

RC: Soup, milady?

MARJORIE: Thank you, Hudson.

RC places plates before them, then prepares to ladle out soup from a tureen held by a maid. To do so, he has to roll up his sleeves like a magician. He glares at his wife.

KING: He's going to do a conjuring trick! Can you pull a rabbit out of the soup?

RC: Why not? That's what went into it. That and a few other things.

KING: Such as what?

RC: Such as this sleeve, for instance. Feel that, it's soaked. Would milady mind very much if I removed my coat to serve the soup?

MARJORIE: You will do no such thing, Hudson. Where's your decorum?

RC: Could be anywhere under this lot.

MARJORIE: Kindly serve the soup, Hudson, and don't be impertinent.

RC: Very well, milady.

He ladles one dollop into each plate, ungraciously.

MARJORIE: *(her hand on his)* More wine, Teddy?

KING: Thank you – delightful. Where do you get it?

MARJORIE: My husband gets it specially. *(Looking into his eyes.)*

KING: Where from?

MARJORIE: Downstairs.

RC: *(to himself)* You'll get it specially upstairs if you carry on like this, my girl.

MAID: *(surprised, but interested)* Were you talking to me, sir?

RC: Shut up. *(Coming back to them, loudly)* More soup?

He ladles some into Marjorie's plate.

MARJORIE: No, thank you, Hudson.

RC: Oh.

He picks up her plate and pours it straight back into the ladle, then pours the ladleful into the King's plate and puts the plate back in front of the King.

KING: Please – no more.

MARJORIE: Oh, but I insist – it's oyster soup. *(With a wink)* A little more, Hudson.

She picks up the King's plate, holds it out.

KING: *(knowingly)* Oh, I see. You think I will be needing it later.

He leans over to whisper in her ear. She reacts, giggling, and moves the plate out of range just as RC pours a ladleful out, his eyes on her the whole time. The consequence is that the hot soup lands not in the bowl, but in the King's lap.

RB: *(leaping up in pain)* Ow! Och hoots, Sir Richard, you've scalded me – Ooh – oh, I'll never be able to wear a sporran again!

RC and Marjorie stare at him.

RC: Just a minute. Good grief – Hudson!

MARJORIE: What on earth does this mean?

RB: I'm sorry, milady, to deceive you. It was with the best intentions. *(Taking off his false beard.)*

MARJORIE: But why?

RB: The King's secretary called this morning and cancelled the visit – and I just hadn't the heart to tell you.

RC: Good gracious – you did it all – out of loyalty?

RB: Yes, sir. Oh milady, will you ever forgive me?

MARJORIE: Of course, Hudson – come upstairs and I'll see how badly you're hurt.

RB: Oh, it's nothing, milady.

MARJORIE: Nonetheless, it might need a poultice.

RC: Now, just a minute … you're not taking him upstairs – not after the way you've been carrying on.

MARJORIE: Then he must remove his trousers here. Come along, Hudson.

She starts to get his trousers off. Hudson resists feebly.

RC: Now look here ...

He starts to take his coat off. The maid enters, stares at Hudson's long johns.

PARLOUR MAID: *(flustered)* Milady – quick – can I have a word with you?

MARJORIE: What is it, Rose?

Before she can answer, King Edward VII walks in.

MARJORIE: Your Majesty!

Everyone bows and/or curtsies low.

OPEN WINDOW

Signature tune and caption: "Open Window," followed by a second caption: "A programme in which minority groups tell the world about their problem. This programme has been made entirely by amateur talent from within the groups, and the BBC takes no responsibility for it (and neither does ITV). This programme was originally made in black and white, but will be shown in colour."

(All the above over a picture of an open window – camera zooms slowly in on it.)

Cut to: another picture. Flat countryside. Caption over – "this week – flat is horrible".

(RB in garden, talking to camera.)

RB: I find digging in my garden is a bit of therapy and helps me to gain strength to carry on expressing my beliefs to a thoroughly sceptical and pig-headed world. *(Caption over – "Flat Earth Society".)* Because being in a minority can be very depressing, when people just won't believe you or take any notice of you. *(Shouts at barking dog)* GET DOWN, SALLY! Even when you have irrefutable evidence that the world is flat when your wife has actually fallen off it. My wife actually fell off it. I very nearly did myself, I only just managed to stop myself – GET DOWN, SALLY, DAMN YOU! When you have actually experienced it, then it's no good saying the earth is round, because it isn't, any more than a ten pence piece is round. It's not, it's flat. So I ...

(Dog leaps on him, he falls out of frame.)

Interior – house.

Cut to: RC, at piano, in the middle of a song. He is singing flat – "Drink to me only with thine eyes". He has long, straight hair over his ears. As he finishes the song, the caption appears over: "The Flat Singer's Society".

RC: *(speaking to camera)* I have sung flat all my life. I love music and wished to make it my profession, but my father is a piano tuner and has turned me out of the house, with the advice "Get it up or give it up". But music is my life; I've got all of Rod McKinar's records, which proves that it's not that I don't appreciate good music, because I don't. It's just my flat voice. I just can't get it up as high as the others. That is why I try to look like a musician, and wear my hair long, to try to hide the fact that I have no ear.

Exterior – garden: a girl with flat chest.

GIRL: You may think, to look at me that I haven't a thing to worry about, but I have. Well, two things, like, really. *(caption: "Flat Chest Society")* My bosoms. I've tried everything. I've tried that bust-developing cream, but it tastes horrible. I've tried stuffing a couple of lemons up inside my sweater, but boys only squeeze them and I get covered in juice without really enjoying it. Everything's been getting on top of me lately. It's horrible being flat. A man likes something comfortable to lie his head on. He doesn't want a walnut in his ear. The only benefit I've ever derived from being flat was that I made a black bikini out of two eye patches I got on the National Health. But people on the beach called me the Lone Ranger.

Exterior – street.

RB walks along in shopping area, flat-footed, with passers-by behaving as they would normally, looking at camera, etc.

RB'S VOICE-OVER: People laugh at me in the street when I go to work and I say to them, it's all *(Caption: "Flat Feet Society")* very well for you to laugh but it's not much fun when your feet are flaming flat. Doctors say they can't do nothing about it. The medical term for it is "flat feet" and that's it, ain't it? *(Cut to close-up – RB on park bench)* That's what I'm up against. My instep's level with me sole. One is supposed to be lower than the other, but it isn't. It's level. Which means that there's more to get dragged through the mud. What I feel is that I have missed out. There's lots of things I can't do, like, ballet dancing – *(pause)* things like that. The ballet *(pause)*, and I think the Government oughter do something about it.

Exterior – street.

RC at window of large car, in bowler hat, etc.

RC: My society is growing all the time. A lot of people have joined over the past year. *(Caption: "Flat Broke Society")* Everything's gone, as far as I'm concerned. This isn't my car. The chauffeur bought it off me last year when things got difficult. He very kindly gives me a lift to work every day. Sweet of him, isn't it? *(Cut to chauffeur, smiling)* No, I can't afford a big car like this. I've got a very small one. I just take it out on Saturday mornings, just to give it an airing. *(He gets out of car)* This is not my suit – I got it at a jumble sale. Thirty-eight pounds. My wife found it, didn't you, dear? *(Cut to close-up – wife's face, nodding and smiling.)* The trousers are very good *(cut to trousers and shoes)* but the sleeves are too long. *(Cut to RC showing sleeves)* However, my wife likes it, and it will do for now – until the time we can both afford to have one.

Widen to reveal the trousers are on the wife – with a bra. RC has long suit jacket only, with suspenders and socks. They turn and walk away.

Cut to: a front room, in fairly awful taste.

RC as husband in seedy, straight-haired wig, moustache and side-burns. RB as his wife.

RC: *(voice-over)* Of course it's a problem. It's a big problem. Well, you can see for yourself. It's obvious what a big problem I've got. *(By now we can see RB as wife.)* It's very difficult living in a tiny flat, with a woman as big as this. *(Caption: "Flat-Dwellers Society")* It was different when we first met. I was living in two rooms overlooking the Cromwell Road.

RB: I had a flat behind.

RC: 'Course, now it's all changed. And it's a very difficult thing to come to grips with. The kitchen is tiny with a sliding door. If she bends over the sink, she's liable to sit on the gas stove; and the whole flat smells of fried bacon. It's a big problem.

RB: I have to put tin foil in my knickers.

RC: The bedroom is very pokey. *(RB agrees, muttering)* Just room for the bed. If she's in bed first I have to climb over her, and that's no fun, is it, when you're tired. I rang up the Council to see if they could help; they suggested spiked boots. Silly. *(Cuckoo noise.)* I think everybody in flats has got a problem. I've got a big one; let's hope Mrs Thatcher gets in. I'll present her with it. And that's that. *(Sound fades. RC goes on talking.)*

RB: *(commentator voice-over)* All the people you have just seen are members of flat societies of one sort or another. I think you'll agree that, as they put it, "Flat is Horrible". We hope this programme has brought to light their private problems. Everyone has got one – but each one is different.

Cut to: a series of actual clips from the previous interviews.

FLAT SINGER: *(RC)* I just can't get it up as high as the others …

FLAT EARTH: *(RB)* My wife actually fell off it …

FLAT CHEST: *(girl)* Everything has been getting on top of me lately …

FLAT BROKE: *(RC)* I've got a very small one – I just take it out on Saturday mornings – just to give it an airing.

FLAT FEET: *(RB)* One is supposed to be lower than the other, but it isn't – it's level. Which means that there is more to get dragged through the mud.

FLAT DWELLERS: *(RC, RB)* I've certainly got a big one – let's hope Mrs Thatcher gets in. I'll present her with it.

FLAT DWELLERS: *(RB)* ... a flat behind.

FLAT FEET: *(RB)* ... that's what I'm up against.

FLAT CHEST: *(girl)* ... It's horrible.

FLAT EARTH: *(RB)* ... It's flat.

FLAT DWELLERS: *(RC)* ... And that's that.

Freeze frame on this, Caption over: "Flat is Horrible. The end".

I MARRIED A POLTERGEIST

An Edwardian "semi" in the provinces. outside, on the front door, hangs a funeral wreath. Noise of a party is heard.

Cut to: inside the room, sandwiches disappearing off a plate, as hands grab them. Loud party chatter. Two ladies in black, with lots of make-up, gossip in a corner.

AGNES: Certainly a good do, isn't it?

MAVIS: Lovely. Who did the food? Did his sister do it?

AGNES: He hasn't got a sister.

MAVIS: Who's that over there then?

AGNES: That was her sister.

MAVIS: Oh, poor thing. *(Looks round)* He seems to be enjoying it, anyway.

(Points discreetly to RB as Jim, stuffing his face.)

AGNES: If you were asked to pick out the bereaved husband, you'd hardly pick him, would you?

MAVIS: He's not sorry. He was glad to see the back of her.

AGNES: Well, he was certainly never too pleased with the front of her.

Cut to: RB eating. Cut to: RC, as Harold, approaching RB through the chattering guests. He reaches RB.

RB: Hello, Harold. Sandwich?

RC: Hello, Jim. No thanks. Just wanted to express my condolences.

RB: *(quietly)* Needn't bother, Harold. I'm not going to miss her. I couldn't have stood much more of her.

RC: I know that. Everybody guessed it, of course. But I know it.

RB: What?

RC: Being psychic, as you know.

RB: Oh, yes?

RC: Someone has dropped a vol-au-vent on the floor.

RB: Gosh, do you know that because you're psychic?

RC: No, because I'm standing in it.

RB: Oh dear. Oh well, it's alright, it's not the front room carpet. She was terrible about that, Jennifer. Her mother bought it for her. Great big, ugly, blotchy-purple thing.

RC: Her mother?

RB: No, the carpet. I had to take off my shoes before I was allowed on it. And her mother used to sit there, with that smug expression on her face. I used to long to jump all over it with big muddy boots on.

RC: Her mother's face?

RB: Absolutely. And the carpet. And Jennifer. It was her mother who instituted the kitchen blackboard. Jennifer used to write the day's orders on it in chalk. Jobs for me to do, messages if she wasn't speaking to me, that sort of stuff. Big black thing hanging there, spoiled the look of the kitchen.

RC: I'm still getting these mental pictures of her mother.

RB: Quite. She literally led me a dog's life, Jennifer. She used to take me for walks, I had to fetch her slippers, she even made me sit up and beg for my food. So then, when I heard she was having an affair with the postman, I did what anyone in my position would have done. I bit him in the leg.

RC: Well, you're free of her now, Jim. Do what you like, go where you please. You didn't kill her, by any chance, did you?

RB: 'Course not. Being psychic, you should know that.

RC: Oh, we don't know everything. Otherwise, for instance, I wouldn't have to ask you where your lavatory was when I needed it, which I do now.

RB: Oh, sorry – through there, just on the left.

RC: Ta.

(He goes.)

(A large, bosomy, middle-aged woman approaches RB, with a smile.)

WOMAN: Hello, Jim. Do you think I look good in black?

RB: You'd look better out of it.

WOMAN: Jim, really! That's not like you!

RB: No. Well, I'm not like me. Never have been, really.

(She reacts, and goes.)

Cut to: the front door. (The guests are leaving, RB seeing them off. RC among them. RB closes the door and leans against it.)

RB: *(sighs)* Alone at last!

(Suddenly, a vase smashes against the wall beside his head. He looks around, shocked. Then he quickly looks into the room where the party was. No one. Looks into the front room – silent and empty – the purple carpet presiding over the heavy old furniture. He looks into the kitchen. No one. Zoom in on the blackboard. Written on it is the single word: "Jennifer".)

(RB rubs it out with the yellow duster which hangs there for this purpose. He leaves the kitchen, starts to go upstairs. A crash in the kitchen. He rushes back. On the floor is a broken dish. Tilt up to

reveal the blackboard. On it, the words: "Leave this blackboard alone".)

RB: *(recoils, then angrily)* Shan't! Shan't! *(Grabs the duster and rubs out letters).* I've had enough of you, Jennifer. You're not ruling me any more. I've finished with you.

(The board in close-up. Writing appears – the words: "Oh no".)

Cut to: RB, watching, then back to the board. It now says: "Oh no, you haven't".

RB: Oh yes I have, Jennifer – you and your rotten mother.

(He leaves the kitchen, goes into the hallway, to the phone and dials.)

RB: Harold? Jim. Listen, can I see you in the pub? It's urgent. Yes, I know you've just got back, but you'll have to come out again. Something's happened. Couldn't tell you at the funeral, 'cos it hadn't happened at the funeral. Five minutes? Right. Bye.

(He returns to the kitchen. A cup smashes near his head. The blackboard says: "Go to bed. You're drunk".)

RB: No, I'm not, but I will be shortly. I'm going to the pub!

(He turns to go and a saucepan hits him on the back of the head.)

The pub. Two drinks put down on a table. Widen to reveal RC, still in black tie and armband.

RC: Thanks. Where are the nuts?

RB: Did you ask for nuts?

RC: No – I just had a feeling that you would bring some.

RB: A psychic feeling?

RC: No, just a greedy feeling.

RB: Well, what am I going to do, Harold?

(He reseats himself, moving away the glasses from their previous rounds.)

RC: You've heard of the astral body?

RB: What's that, like the Psychical Research Society?

RC: Your astral body is what some people believe rises from your own body when you're asleep, and floats about. Haven't you ever felt, in dreams, that you seem to be floating above yourself, looking down at yourself? And your real self is below, looking up at yourself looking down at yourself. Have you felt that ever?

RB: Yes, I have.

RC: Well, that's your astral body. Either that, or the drink.

RB: So you mean ...

RC: Yes. Jennifer's astral body is rising from the grave and floating about your kitchen, throwing things at you. She has become a poltergeist.

RB: But what can I do?

RC: Stay out of the kitchen. She will eventually run out of crockery.

RB: Then what?

RC: She'll start on the bedroom.

RB: Good grief.

RC: You'll just have to hope that she gets tired of it.

RB: Not Jennifer. She's relentless.

RC: Well, unless you can stop her astral body rising from the grave, you're lumbered. Just buy yourself a tin helmet and don't bend down in the bath. *(Picks up new glass)* Cheers!

(RB's face, brooding on this)

RB: Cheers.

The kitchen: day.

(All quiet. RB returning from the pub, opens door, looks in. We see a jug rise from a shelf and hurtle out of frame. It crashes near RB. The blackboard says: "Where have you been?" RB hurriedly shuts the

door and, as the crashes continue within, looks into the front room, at the big old pieces of furniture. He nods to himself.)

Outside the house: night.

(RB is loading the front room furniture onto an open truck ("Acme Rent-a-van". He is almost finished. He staggers out with half a table and throws it onto the truck. He gets into the cab and starts the engine.)

(Now a montage – RB arriving at the cemetery, taking things off the truck, staggering under the load of a corner cupboard across the graveyard, and the ever-increasing pile of furniture on the grave. An owl watches this macabre spectacle. Eventually, a close-up as RB throws the last object onto the pile.)

RB: Now, get out of that, you old bat. And I don't give a hoot!

(The owl looks disapproving, and does give a hoot.)

RB: *(looking up)* Well, you can please yourself.

Cut to: inside the house, the same night.

(RB enters front door. He looks into now-empty front room. Only the carpet is there, in all its patterned monstrosity. He looks into the kitchen. All quiet. The blackboard is empty. He closes door and stands in the hall. He nods in satisfaction and goes quietly upstairs.)

Exterior house: day.

(RB in raincoat, leaves for the office. Day turns to night in the same shot. RB returns from work with newspaper. He enters the front door.)

The kitchen: night.

(RB sitting with tea, scones and jam, contentedly munching. Suddenly, a whoosh and a loud bang. RB reacts. Another whoosh and several bangs, coming from outside. RB grabs newspaper. Zoom in on the date – November 5th. RB looks up in consternation.)

A bonfire – it is the pile of furniture. (Skinheads and other hooligans dance around it, laughing and drinking from cans. Others let off fire-crackers.)

(RB's little car approaches the camera and he gets out. The flickering firelight is reflected in his glasses. His expression is gloomy.)

The kitchen.

(RB enters. All quiet. The blackboard says: "Try to cremate me, would you?" and all hell breaks loose. RB tries to dodge the flying crockery. We see many objects lifted up as if by invisible hands, crashing round RB's head. He tries to leave the kitchen, but a narrow broom cupboard falls across the door, so that it cannot be opened.)

(He moves around the kitchen. Overhead cupboards open. A whole pile of spice bottles bounce on his head, one by one. An enormous jar of brown rice tips, spilling the contents on him, as further pieces of crockery burst round him.)

(A bag of flour falls and bursts on his head. He grabs a big saucepan and puts it over his head. A broom flies out of the cupboard and hits the saucepan with a clang. He comes out, looking dazed, and collapses on the floor. Above, on the work surface, a bottle of milk tips over. A close-up as the milk pours over RB's head. Chaos around him as we mix to: the pub.)

A caption: "Six weeks later".

(RC and RB are sitting at their usual table. RC drinks. We see that RB has a few cuts and bruises still showing.)

RB: Well, when I finally got out of there, I thought what a good idea! So I had the body exhumed and cremated!

RC: Has it worked?

RB: Like a charm. And guess what I did with the ashes?

RC: You sprinkled them all over the front room carpet!

RB: How did you know?

RC: I'm psychic – remember?

(Their laughter takes on an echo-like quality as we mix to: the front room. There, on the carpet, lies an upturned urn. Trailing from it, the spilled ash. We pan along a thin line of ash – and we find it forms itself into the words: "I will be back". The laughter distorts into an unintelligible shriek.)

COLDITZ

Caption – as in the original series, with theme music.

Scene 1: The yard of a castle.

As many extras as we can spare (or stock library film of yard from the original). Two men are throwing a ball to each other, others are crowded in a circle, talking. Close-up of a man looking up as the sound of a lorry is heard. The lorry arriving. It stops – four guards get out of the back escorting RC as the RAF air gunner (as played by David McCallum in the series) with pencil moustache and ruffled hair.

RC: So this is Colditz. They'll never keep me in here!

(Close-up as he looks up at the castle. He is roughly pushed in the back by one of the guards. They march him away – overlaid is the sound of heavy marching feet in echo. They pass the group seated in a circle and march round a corner, out of sight.)

(Cut to: round the corner, the guards come into view. RC, however, isn't with them. They realise this and Captain Helmut cries "halt". They run back round the corner. The group is seated there, still chatting. The Germans look suspiciously at them, then a guard points out of shot. We cut to RC walking away in the middle distance. He has his trousers rolled up, his jacket tied round his waist like a skirt, his scarf tied round his head and he carries a bucket and broom. He looks from the back like an old charwoman, but we know it's him. The guards run after him and grab him.)

RC: Just testing you.

(As he starts to remove his scarf, we cut to: studio.)

Scene 2: The prisoners' dormitory or rather, a corner of it, next to the latrines (as per original set for Colditz).

Two-tier wooden bunks, etc. On one of these lies Chapman, a pris-
oner, tall, thin. Perhaps two others, non-speaking, also two chaps
throwing a ball to each other.

(RC is brought in by a guard. Chapman gets up to greet him.)

CHAPMAN: Hello, there.

RC: My name's Carter. George Carter. *(Shaking hands)* How are you.

CHAP: I'm Dicky.

RC: I don't feel so good myself. How long have you been here?

CHAP: Four years.

RC: Four years, cooped up here? No wonder you're feeling dicky.
Haven't you tried to escape?

CHAP: My name's Dicky.

RC: Oh, I see.

CHAP: And don't think you're going to escape from here. The place
is impregnable.

RC: Don't you believe it, chum. That's what they said about Doreen
Phipps. How wrong they were.

CHAP: Were they?

RC: Well, I'm paying her thirty bob a week. Judge for yourself. *(He*
moves around, sizing the place up.) No, we'll soon be out of here.

CHAP: You'd better have a word with Captain Whitmore.

RC: Where is he?

CHAP: I'm not sure, I ...

(There is a banging from inside one of the latrines.)

RB: *(inside the loo)* Anybody there? I'm stuck. The door's jammed.
Hello. *(etc. as he bangs on the door.)*

CHAP: That's him. *(Calling)* Coming.

(They eventually succeed in prising open the latrine door. RB comes
out, dressed as an army captain.)

RB: How do you do – Whitmore. I'm the escape officer.

RC: Carter, sir.

(RC salutes. RB salutes back – he has an oil can stuck on his little finger.)

RB: Sorry about the oil can. Can't get my finger out. Got it stuck, trying to oil my bed springs.

RC: Really, sir? Is this a mixed dormitory then?

RB: Oh yes, rather. Officers and men.

RC: Oh, I see. You had me going there for a minute. I thought perhaps I wouldn't bother to escape, after all.

RB: Ah. Well, I'm sorry to disappoint you, but the only woman on the camp is the Matron.

RC: What's she like?

CHAP: Blonde. And big with it.

RC: I like big women.

RB: Luckily for you, she's a vegetarian.

RC: Why?

RB: She'd have you for breakfast.

RC: Oh. I see. Right, that does it. I'm getting out of here.

RB: Now listen, Carter. Sit down. It's not as easy as all that. We have a code of conduct here. Of course you want to escape. Everybody does. But it has to be organised. You need papers. Money. Clothing. A cover story. And that means none of this "go it alone" stuff. We've built up a specialist team to deal with every aspect, and each escape has to be planned. Planned down to the very last detail, do you understand?

(The door is opened by a guard. RB tries to make a dash for it.)

HELMUT: *(entering)* Get back! *(RB is dragged back by guards and flung onto one of the bunks.)* Flight Lieutenant Carter!

RC: Yes?

HELMUT: Hauptmann Ulrich wishes to speak with you. He is second in command. Quickly, please! You will come now.

RC: Alright, keep your hair on, Fritzy.

HELMUT: *(removes hat – he is bald)* I have no hair. And I have no time to waste.

(Hits RC with hat.)

RC: *(going)* Touchy lot, aren't they?

Scene 3: Hauptmann Ulrich's office.

RB as Hauptmann Ulrich, seated at desk. We hear feet approaching, a knock on the door.

RB: Kommen zie herein!

(RC enters with helmut and guards.)

RB: Ah Carter, sit down please.

RC: *(looks around)* There's no chair.

RB: *(quietly)* Well, stand then. We don't run this place for your comfort, Carter. *(RB takes file from drawer of desk.)* I just wish to make a few things clear to you before you begin your stay here at

Colditz. This is a top security prison and there is no escape. You are now in the hands of experienced prison officers. If you try to escape, here is a list of the men you have to deal with. *(Reads)* Hauptmann Leitz, Sturmbannfuhrer Schmelling, Standartenfuhrer Hessler, Unterwebel Blateau and Uppengruppenferanstarter ge-grossler Pintwinkler. Do you understand all this?

RC: Yes – luckily my father kept a delicatessen.

RB: Really?

RC: Yes – that was before he went into show business.

RB: Show business? What did he do?

RC: He was an escapologist.

RB: So! It runs in the family, eh? *(Looking at file)* I see that he was in the first war.

RC: Yes.

RB: Did he stay in the army after the war?

RC: No, he couldn't get out quick enough.

RB: "He then continued with his act – being dropped into the Thames in a padlocked trunk."

RC: Yes, it killed him.

RB: Why?

RC: He couldn't get out quick enough.

RB: I see. Well, my dear Flight Lieutenant *(getting up and moving across the room)* I hope you won't entertain any thoughts of following in your father's footsteps. *(Close-up)* Because I can assure you, escape is impossible. *(Looks around)* Carter? *(Cut to: long shot – RC is out of sight. RB looks under desk.)* Come out, Carter!

(RC crawls out.)

RB: I promise you, you will never manage it. Now *(goes to other side of desk, takes out papers)* here is your prison number and the address to which letters should be sent ... *(He again looks up. No one is in sight again. He walks over to large cupboard)* ... and they will then be forwarded to your family via the Red Cross. *(He opens the cupboard. RC is standing in it.)* Understand?

RC: Yes, perfectly. *(Stepping out of cupboard)* You realise, of course, that it is every officer's duty to try to escape?

RB: Of course I realise it, Flight Lieutenant. *(Goes to desk, picks up the file.)* It's just that I thought I might save you a lot of wasted time and energy. *(Long shot – no one there again)* I mean, after all *(goes to filing cabinet)* there are many more profitable ways of passing the time, don't you agree?

(He opens the top drawer of the steel filing cabinet. RC's head appears to come out with it.)

RC: I suppose you're right.

Scene 4: The dormitory.

RB as Whitmore, with Chapman, sit on bottom bunk. Two other prisoners are throwing a ball to each other.

CHAP: Sshh! I think he's coming back.

RB: Is that you, Carter? How's it going?

RC: *(emerging from under bed)* Pretty good. Another couple of feet.

(He hands RB two socks full of earth.)

RB: Oh, thanks. How much further to go?

RC: I've just told you, two more feet.

RB: Oh, I see – I thought you meant *(indicating socks)*. Here you are, Chapman.

(Gives socks to Chapman, who empties the earth into the drawer of his locker.)

CHAP: Isn't it someone else's turn to provide the socks? *(As he puts sock on his foot)* What about you, Whitmore?

RB: I've got a potato in mine.

CHAP: I shall be able to grow them in mine if this goes on.

(Approaching footsteps, marching. They halt. The door opens and in comes the matron. A large, curvy blonde, all knickers and knockers, as they say, but a wonderful actress.)

RB: Morning, matron.

MATRON: Good morning, Vitmore, Chepman. I am happy to inform you that the RAF have dropped a load of Red Cross parcels for you.

RB: Marvellous!

MATRON: Unfortunately, when they hit the ground they were flattened completely. Only one survived.

RB: How?

MATRON: I was sunbathing on the roof and it landed right on top of me. It bounced.

RB: It would.

MATRON: Bring it in, please.

(A guard brings in the box.)

RB: *(opening it)* Oh well, that explains it. It's a load of balls.

(He takes out a rubber ball. The matron eyes him, and exits briskly.)

RC: Right, lads, this is it. I'm going to make my final bid for freedom. If I'm not back in three hours, come through the tunnel and investigate.

CHAP: Good luck, Carter. Drop us a postcard!

RC: I'll do better than that. As soon as I get to France, I'll send you a letter. Bye, skipper.

(RB and RC shake hands. RC goes under the bed.)

RB: Well, now all we have to do is wait.

Cut to: clock on locker. Cross-fade to three hours later. Caption over: "3 hours later".

RB: Well, it's three hours later. I'm going through to investigate.

(He crawls under the bed. A close-up of Chapman, listening to marching feet as they pass the door.)

Scene 5: A close-up of a cupboard.

One door opens, RB crawls out, dusty. He stands up and stares.

RB: Good lord!

Cut to: RC and matron on top of bed, suspenders in evidence. We are in matron's bedroom.

RB: What are you doing?

RC: You've got to take it where you can get it.

RB: You never told me the tunnel came out in matron's room.

RC: Pure coincidence. Bit of luck though, wasn't it?

Scene 6: The dormitory – night.

RB and RC in same clothes, but blackened faces, à la commandos. Chapman is with them.

RC: This time it's got to work.

RB: Don't see why it shouldn't. We've got papers, money. Once we get over that wall, we stand a damn good chance.

CHAP: Got the sheets tied together?

RC: Only two. Most of the chaps have been damn mean about parting with their sheets. Selfish baskets. You were the only one who volunteered.

CHAP: That's alright.

RB: Just two sheets, eh? How high's the wall?

CHAP: Eighty feet.

RB: Hmm. Just have to drop the last bit. Right, come on then. *(To Chapman)* Bye, Chapman, old sport. See you after the war. *(Opens door.)* All clear.

RC: Cheerio, Dicky. And thanks again for the sheets.

(He goes.)

CHAPMAN: Bye. *(Closes the door and goes to the bunk bed.)* Who needs sheets? *(Calling under bed)* Coming, matron!

(He begins to climb under the bed.)

Scene 7: The escape.

This should be a montage – night shots of the castle, close-ups of RC and RB with blackened faces, scurrying here and there, climbing, listening, etc. Lots of mood music and sound effects – marching feet, etc. Finally, a shot of dummies of RB and RC landing at the foot of a high wall. Then a closer shot of them.

RC: Well, we're over. You alright?

RB: Fine. I suggest we stay put under the shadow of the wall until morning.

RC: Good idea. *(He puts a blanket round their knees as they huddle together for warmth.)* Goodnight, Whitmore.

RB: Night, old boy.

(They close their eyes.)

Cut to: early morning. Sunlight.

(They are still asleep against the wall. Shouting can be heard in the distance. A shadow looms over them suddenly. It wears a peaked cap.)

VOICE: *(off)*: Good morning, gentlemen. So you got over the wall, did you? *(They start to stir and open their eyes.)* You will be sorry, I can assure you.

(They stare up in dismay. Cut to: big close-up of man with big cap on.)

MAN: Velcome to Butlitz.

(*Now, at last, a shot of the scene. It is Butlins holiday camp at Bognor Regis. The man wears a striped blazer, white trousers and a coloured peak cap. Holiday-makers stroll about. We zoom in dramatically to the barbed wire on the top of the fence. We freeze-frame and superimpose the word: "Butlitz" in the same lettering as the opening titles. Music crashes in – slow fade.*)

QUIET WEDDING

A church. The bridegroom waits. Organ music playing. The vicar (RB) approaches the groom (RC) and speaks in a whisper.

RB: Good morning.

RC: Good morning, Reverend.

RB: Nervous?

RC: Yes, I am rather. (*Sheepishly*) I've had hiccups all morning.

RB: Oh dear – well, there's no need to be – although it's a rather solemn service, it is nevertheless a happy one, and a joyful occasion.

RC: Oh yes.

RB: You must forgive me if I sound a bit nasal.

RC: Oh – we've all got colds as well, haven't we, dad? Mum's chest is bad – must be something going round.

RB: No, mine's actually hay fever – always get it at Harvest Festival time – it's all the flowers.

RC: Oh yes – Leticia gets that.

RB: Leticia?

RC: Leticia, my – my intended.

RB: Oh, the bride.

RC: Yes – I was going to say wife, but that's not till tonight. That's not till after the service, I mean.

RB: Quite. Ha ha. Not straight after the service, I hope? *(Smiling)*

RC: No, no. Anyway, she's had it for a week.

RB: What?

RC: Hay fever.

RB: Oh, quite.

(The organist starts to play "Here Comes the Bride")

RB: Ah. Here she comes. Takes your places, please.

(The bride approaches, and stops. The organ finishes playing. Silence.)

(Girl, looking at RC, sneezes.)

(RC, looking at girl, hiccups.)

RB: Dearly beloved, we are gathered here in the face of the congregation, to join together this man and this woman in holy matrimony. Which is an honourable estate, and therefore not to be taken in hand inadvisedly, lightly or wantonly, but reverently, discreetly, advisedly and soberly, duly considering the causes for which matrimony was ordained. Aaahchoo!

RC: Hic!

RB: Therefore if any man ...

BRIDE: Zsst!

RB: ... if any man can show any Aaaahchoo! any just cause why they m-m-m-mmahay not lawfully be joined together let him speak now or foo-forever hold his peace. Aaaahchoo!

BRIDE: Zsst!

RC: Hic!

(A silence, broken only by mum's chest wheezing heavily.)

RB: Hah-hah-Harold Frederick, wilt thou take this woman to be thy lawful wedded wife?

RC: Hic!

RB: Wilt thou love her, comfort her, honour and keep her, in sickness and in her-heahealth, as long as ye both shall live?

RC: Hic! I will. Hic!

RB: Aaaahchoo!

RC: Hic.

BRIDE: Zsst!

DAD: *(into hankie)* Honk!

RB: Leticshoo! Leticshoo! Leticia Muriel–

BRIDE: Zsst!

RB: Wilt thou have this man to thy wedded husband.

RC: Hic!

DAD: Honk!

RB: Aaaahchoo! Wilt thou love, honour and keep him, in sickness and in Haychow! And forsaking all others keep ye only unto him as long as ye both shall lachoo!

BRIDE: I whizzt!

RC: Hic!

RB: Who giveth this woman to be married to this man?

DAD: Honk!

(Steps forward.)

RB: Aaaahchoo!

(The sneeze blows off dad's toupee. He ignores it.)

RB: *(putting on the ring)* I, Harold Frederick ...

RC: I, Hic Harold Frederick hic...

RB: Take thee, Leticshashoo!

RC: Take thee, Lettic-isha.

RB: To my wedded wife.

RC: To my wedded hic wife hic!

RB: *(desperately)* To have and to hold from this day forward, for better for worse, for richer for poorer as long as we both shall live, Aaaahchoo!

RC: I diccoo.

RB: For as much as Harold Frederick and Aaahchoo Muriel have consented together, by the giving and receiving of a ring, I pronounce that they be man and wahey! together. You may kiss the bride.

RC: But we didn't finish the Hic!

RB: Kiss the bride – please!

BRIDE: Come on, Harold.

(They kiss – RC hics and the bride sneezes during the kiss.)

DAD: Honk!

RB: I'm sorry I had to cut it short, but the hayayaay …

RC: But – Hic! – if we haven't had the full service, we're not properly married.

RB: Well, you'll just have to come next month and we'll fi-fi – finish it off.

RC: But what about the Hic! honeymoon?

RB: I should go ahead – at least it will cure your hiccups. Aaaahchoow!

(A pile of apples collapses behind him as the wedding party hurries out.)

CHEERS

A cocktail bar with glass doors leading to a terrace behind it. A crowd of well-dressed people, all chattering loudly in a tight group. RB emerges from the middle.

RB: Righto everyone – I think I've got the order – you all go and wait on the terrace, I'll get the waiter to bring the drinks out.

(He approaches the bar.)

BARMAN: Good evening, sir, what would you like?

RB: A large gin and tonic to start with. Very large.

BARMAN: Sir. *(He goes into action.)* Ice and lemon?

RB: If there's room in the glass, yes.

BARMAN: And what else, sir?

RB: Well now, I've only just met these people, don't know them at all. Friends of the wife, you know. So now, let's see. The lady in the sack dress wants an enormous brandy. The young man with the flat head wants a rum and Coke. Andy, the tall chap – he's Scottish; he wants a pink gin with lemon. The girl with the boobs wants a White Lady. My wife will have a Scotch on the rocks. The woman with bare arms behind her wants half a bottle of the house wine. And the old man with the shifty eyes wants a rough cider. *(RB drinks his gin.)* But before that, I'll have another large gin.

BARMAN: Very good, sir.

RB: Right, so that's an enormous brandy and a rum and Coke, a pink gin, a White Scotch, a wine and a cider and lemon on the rocks.

BARMAN: Pardon, sir?

RB: The lady in the sack dress, brandy. The flat head, rum and Coke. The Scotsman behind, a white gin. The lady with the pink boobs, a cider and … just a minute.

(He dashes out to the group, who can all be seen chattering at him for a few seconds. He returns to the bar.)

RB: *(indicating glass)* Is that mine?

BARMAN: Yes, sir.

RB: Good. *(Drinks it.)* Same again, please.

BARMAN: Yes, sir.

RB: Now, I've got it. One brandy, one rum and lemon, a pink thing, a white lady with double boobs, rough rocks, wine on the house and a big bottle.

BARMAN: Pardon, sir?

RB: Don't worry, it's all under control. The lady in the sack wants a tall Scotch. The bare lady with the behind wants a rum and Coke. My wife will have an old man on the rocks, and the girl with the shifty boobs wants a big bottle of brandy on the house. The young man with the flat wife wants an enormous wine ... the white lady with the pink ... just a minute. *(He goes to the group and returns, as above.)* Is this mine?

BARMAN: Yes, sir.

RB: Good. *(He downs it in one.)* Same again, please. Now then. Are you listening? Simple. I'll have a gin and tonic.

BARMAN: *(placing it down in front of him)* There it is, sir.

RB: Either one?

BARMAN: Yes, sir.

(RB manages to pick it up.)

RB: Have a beer.

BARMAN: No, thank you, sir.

RB: Right. *(Thumping counter)* Now, I do exactly what I'm knowing. Here goes. The randy girl with the big bottle wants a rough Scotsman. The tall lemon wants a double Coke on the rocks. The bare woman with the boobs like the side of a house wants a pink old man; the enormous man with the flat gin wants my wife with a beer behind.

And the white lady wants a sack of Coke. Simple enough. What are you having?

BARMAN: Look, sir–

RB: Look. Ready? This is it. Cancel all previous orders. Just give me a sack of Coke, two large rocks, two pink boobs, an enormous lemon and a large bare lady of the house.

BARMAN: Right, sir. I'm glad we finally got it sorted out.

(He deposits on the bar a small sack of coke, two rocks, a pair of pink model boobs and an enormous lemon. A large (almost) bare showgirl comes from behind the bar where she has been hiding and she and RB walk off towards the group, carrying the props.)

BAR ROOM SKETCH

A corner of a reasonably trendy bar.

(RB sits on a stool, finishing a drink. The girl behind the bar, very attractive, slightly barmaid-ish, lots of eyelashes. RB hands her his empty glass. He is a middle-aged lounge lizard and is about to try and "pull" the barmaid.)

RB: Same again, my dear.

GIRL: Large gin and tonic?

(She starts to pour it.)

RB: You're new here, aren't you?

GIRL: No. I've been here two years.

RB: Oh. Must be me then. That's why I've never seen you here before – I've never been here before.

(He laughs like the twit he is.)

GIRL: *(smiling)* That would account for it.

(RC enters and sits on stool next to RB.)

RB: Two years, eh? You must like it. The work, I mean.

GIRL: You meet a lot of people.

RB: Yes, of course you do. You must be a pretty good judge of a person, aren't you?

RC: Tomato juice, please.

GIRL: Small one, sir?

RC: Er – yes, why not.

RB: Yes – you're a pretty good judge alright. Pay well here, do they?

GIRL: Alright.

RB: I should think a pretty girl like you must be worth her weight in gold to a place like this.

GIRL: Flattery will get you nowhere.

RB: No, I mean it – you're a very pretty girl.

RC: Very.

(RB looks at him. RC eats a crisp from the bowl. RB looks back at the girl.)

RB: Very attractive. You must have been told that before.

GIRL: *(flirting)* Once or twice, yes.

RB: Do you think you're attractive?

GIRL: I'm too tall.

RB: I like tall girls.

RC: So do I.

RB: *(turning to RC)* Did you say something?

RC: Who me? No.

RB: The taller the better.

RC: Quite.

RB: What?

RC: Pardon?

(RB glares at RC. The girl tries to smooth things over.)

GIRL: You – er – you local?

RB: Me – good heavens, no. Just travelling through. Staying at the Plough. Ever been there?

GIRL: Mm. Nice bedrooms.

RB: *(surprised at this move)* Oh? Really? You know the bedrooms at the Plough, do you? You interest me enormously.

RC: And me not quite so enormously.

RB: Look, old chap, I'm trying to have a private conversation with this young lady. Now drink up and puddle off, will you?

RC: *(to girl)* Tomato juice, please.

(The girl glares at him, takes his glass, starts to pour another.)

RB: Ignore him, perhaps he'll go away. Listen, my dear, what time do you finish here tonight?

GIRL: Half-past ten. Why?

RB: I was just thinking. Would you like a drink?

GIRL: No, I don't think so.

RC: Go on, have one.

(RB ignores him.)

RB: Why not? Don't you drink?

GIRL: Oh, yes, I like a vodka – trouble is, two of them and I'm anybody's.

RB: Well, just have one.

RC: A double.

(RB controls himself with difficulty.)

RB: Look, please don't think I'm trying to get you drunk. I didn't mean that at all.

GIRL: You sure?

RB: No, really, honestly, I didn't.

RC: I did.

RB: *(desperate)* It's just that I find you very attractive indeed. Beautiful.

RC: Fantastic.

RB: And I'd love to take you out for a meal.

RC: Me too.

RB: Because you're friendly, and charming, and you've got such terrific ...

RC: Knockers.

(RB grabs RC and frogmarches him out. A crash off. RB marches back, dusting his jacket. RC marches back behind him. RB goes to bar, not seeing RC. They both sit.)

RB: *(to girl)* I'm sorry about all that – if you feel like a meal afterwards, ring me at the Plough. Here's my card.

(He turns and leaves, without seeing RC.)

RC: And if you do go out for a meal, don't be late home, Lillian, 'cos we've got to get up early tomorrow. Your mother's coming over.

(He sips his tomato juice.)

A CLINIC IN LIMERICK

A notice reads: "Limerick clinic. Consultant: R. Kelly, MD, assistant J. Long PhD. Please hang up your coat for ear, nose and throat. For a blister, see sister".

(A dizzy nurse sits at table. Patient enters, bent double.)

NURSE: Good day, sir. Have you an appointment?

PATIENT: I was just bending down and this joint went at the back of my thigh. I was just passing by ...

NURSE: Step through here and I'll rub on some ointment.

PATIENT: No, I'll just wait and see Doctor Smithers.

NURSE: I'm afraid he is no longer with us.

PATIENT: Oh, a new one, eh? Nice?

NURSE: Well, his hands are like ice. And while you're undressing, he dithers.

PATIENT: I've begun to feel weak at the knees.

DOCTOR: *(over the intercom)* Will you send in the next patient, please?

NURSE: In you go. Be a man! *(As the patient goes to the door)* I'll just switch off that fan – when you're stripped, there's a terrible breeze.

(They both pass through into the consulting-room.)

DOCTOR: Lord save us – he hops like a rabbit. *(He gets up, goes to the patient and holds his own arm outstretched.)* Grab my arm. *(The patient attempts to.)* Come on, man! I said, grab it.

(The patient tries – the doctor pushes him in the back, trying to straighten him out.)

DOCTOR: Well. We'd best oil the springs. Come on, take off your things.

(The nurse removes her uniform in one zipping movement.)

DOCTOR: Not you, nurse!

NURSE: I'm sorry – just habit.

(She picks up her uniform and goes out.)

DOCTOR: My name's Doctor Kelly – sit down. Oh, you can't – never mind, Mr …

PATIENT: Crown.

DOCTOR: Just go round by the screen.

(They go behind a screen – patient cannot be seen because he is bent over, but doctor can.)

DOCTOR: Now then, what's to be seen? Had your holidays yet? Aren't you brown! Oh, my gosh – hold your breath – grit your teeth! Your braces are caught underneath. Well, you are in a state – we were almost too late. If they'd snapped, you'd have needed a wreath. Now, there's one way to make you unbend–

(He brandishes a large pair of scissors, then disappears behind screen. A loud "twang" and the patient straightens up in agony.)

PATIENT: Ow, my … *(twang!)*

DOCTOR: There, you're cured, my friend. I'm a Limerick man; I make sure, if I can, that you get the joke right in the end!

THE REGIMENT

The living room of the colonel's residence – a stone's-throw from the barracks at Rawlpore, India. Time: 1894.

The room is overdressed, oppressive, above all, a feeling of heat. Sunblinds, etc., insect noises. The distant cries of a sergeant-major, and men drilling, marching feet.

(On the chaise longue, dressed from head to toe in white, lies the colonel's lady. She reclines, fanning herself languidly. She is beautiful, thirty and very hot. Next to her, in a wider chair, sits the colonel (RB). He is whiskered, dressed in full uniform, sixty and sweating profusely. After a moment or two he speaks.)

COLONEL: *(mopping his forehead)* Gad! The heat!

EDITH: It's the hot season.

COL: Yes – that's what does it. Phew! I hope it's not curry again tonight.

EDITH: It always is.

COL: The only thing they can make in this God-forsaken country. *(Pause.)* Would you like whisky?

EDITH: Fire water.

COL: Yes, quite. Tea?

EDITH: It takes two hours to get cool enough to drink.

COL: Fancy a game of cards?

EDITH: No – it's too hot for that.

COL: There must be some little thing I can tempt you with.

EDITH: It's too hot for that as well.

COL: True. Yes, thinking about it, I think you're right. Still, it's nice thinking about it. I think I'll have a gin. *(Rings handbell on table.)* Gad, the heat! Look at all this mess *(indicating drinking glasses on table)*. Damn filthy swine of a house boy. Mahmud! Where the devil are you?

(Enter an Indian house boy dressed in as little as possible within the conventions of the period.)

COL: Now look here, you damned beggar, Colonel-massa want all-same great big gin-tinkle, all-same full up top big big overflowing very little tonic water. You all-same lazybones, no sit about on big fat verandah, clear up all-same glasses in all-same living-hut or big Colonel-massa will all-same give you sack and big bag to put it in, understand? You all-same out on your big, fat, all-same ear! Savvy?

HOUSE BOY: *(shrugging)* It's all the same to me, dear.

(He minces out.)

COL: We must be nearer the border than I thought! Damned cheeky swine! Thank God, Corporal Bligh is starting work here this afternoon. He should be here by now.

EDITH: Corporal Bligh?

COL: My batman. You remember him.

EDITH: Of course I do, George. I'm hardly likely to forget him. He undresses you every night in the bedroom.

COL: Oh, of course. Damned good batman, Bligh. Dashed keen.

(Door opens and Corporal Bligh (RC) enters. Efficient, respectful and breezy. The perfect gentleman's gentleman. He carries the glass of gin for the colonel.)

BLIGH: Good afternoon, sir – madam. Your gin, Colonel.

COL: Bligh! Good lad – you've arrived already. Splendid.

BLIGH: Yessir. Thought I'd pop over a bit early. Bit warmish today, sir.

COL: Warmish! I don't think I can stand it much longer. Gad! What must it be like for the lads on parade.

BLIGH: They'll stick it, sir. It's the honour of the regiment, sir.

COL: The regiment. Yes. I must get out there, inspect them. Least I can do. *(Drinks gin.)* Where's my helmet? *(Picks up pith helmet.)* Gad, this thing weighs a ton – and it's too small *(which it is)*. Can't something be done about it?

BLIGH: We could try taking the pith out of it, sir.

COL: *(after reacting slowly to this)* Most of the chaps do that already.

(He exits.)

(Bligh goes behind the chaise longue.)

BLIGH: Everything to your satisfaction, madam?

(Edith immediately grabs him and pulls him over the back of the chaise lounge. He rolls on top of her. They finish up on the chaise, sitting, in an embrace.)

EDITH: You know everything is NOT to my satisfaction, Corporal. Ever since that first accidental brush in the bedroom. It's all your fault, you wonderful creature.

BLIGH: That first accidental brush in the bedroom, as you put it, was not my fault, madam. I happened to be using the brush, but it was you who turned round quickly. There was little I could do.

EDITH: And you did it beautifully.

BLIGH: Well, that's as may be.

EDITH: There was no maybe about it. Kiss me.

BLIGH: But supposing the colonel comes back and catches us?

EDITH: Let him.

BLIGH: But the honour of the regiment!

EDITH: Damn the honour of the regiment! What about my honour?

BLIGH: Ah, well, if you're going to start living in the past.

EDITH: *(she reacts)* It's the future I'm concerned with. The immediate future. Tonight?

BLIGH: Tonight? Where?

EDITH: In the clearing where we met that evening. I'll never forget that first moment when you came up behind me and grabbed me by the azaleas. Look at me! I'm trembling in your arms – my lips are burning, I've got pins and needles all up my back.

BLIGH: That's not passion, it's prickly heat. You ought to be lying down.

EDITH: That's what I keep telling you!

BLIGH: Look, madam, if you think I'm making love to you in broad daylight, you're mistaken.

EDITH: Let's go down into the cellar. *(She goes to the cellar door, opens it and looks down.)* It's not broad daylight down there.

BLIGH: I'm sorry, but I'm not sinking to those sort of depths.

EDITH: It's quite a shallow cellar.

BLIGH: Nevertheless, I'm afraid it's beneath me. Gad, if only you weren't so beautiful, if only it weren't so hot.

Cut to: a parade ground, backed by low, wooden army huts. A thin, red line of soldiers standing to attention, the colonel inspecting them. He stands at one end of the line with sergeant major. He starts to walk along the line, slowly looking them up and down. A shot of the men's sweating faces as we pan them. Back to colonel – he stops, looks down. We track along the men's feet, stop at one who is standing in a pool of liquid.

COL: *(staring at man)* Do you want to go somewhere?

SOLDIER: Yes, sir. Anywhere.

COL: What? *(To sergeant)* Is he all right?

SERGEANT: He sweats rather a lot, sir.

COL: Oh, I see. Alright, men. In view of the extreme heat, you may all undo the top button of your tunic!

(The men begin to do this, carefully. Close-up of one man. As he undoes the button, steam pours out from his tunic. We see others steaming, then cut to a long shot – we see steam rising all around the little group. The colonel and the sergeant exchange a look and mop their brows.)

Cut to: the living room.

(Edith, now without her dress, in white corset, bloomers above the knee, black stockings, bare shoulders, is smouldering on the sofa. Bligh stands by the door.)

BLIGH: Look, I've got to go. I've got to starch the colonel's front for tonight.

EDITH: Oh, very well. Go. But don't expect me to be any different when we next meet. I shall still want you, desperately ...

(During the following dialogue the colonel enters. The door hides Bligh from his sight, opening onto him. He takes off his hat, is about to hang it on the peg near the door, but stops to listen to Edith's speech. Bligh creeps round the door, takes the hat from the colonel, who still doesn't realise he's there, and goes out, quietly shutting the door.)

EDITH: I shall always want you. You did something to me that no one else has ever done. Not so violently, at any rate. You awakened something in me – something that had been lying dormant since I was a young, frightened girl at her first hunt ball. There's been a lot of hunt balls since then, but never any quite like the first. And so it was with you – I've never known anything that has moved me so much – or so often.

COL: *(now on his own by the door)* What the devil are you on about, old thing?

(Edith turns and reacts – how much has he heard, and where is Bligh?)

EDITH: Oh – I didn't hear you come in.

COL: Never moved you so much or so often? Sounds like an advert for Pickfords.

(He realises as he goes to hang his hat that it's already on the peg.)

EDITH: I'm sorry, I was rambling. I think I'm out of my mind.

COL: Nonsense. Talking of being out of things, what happened to your dress?

EDITH: I took it off. It's this accursed heat.

COL: I know. That's what drives a man mad. The heat. Like that chap who disappeared last month – Captain Wilcox. The Professor, they called him. Mad as a hatter, through the heat.

EDITH: What happened to him?

COL: Just vanished overnight. Took two hundred feet of water pipes with him. Pinched them from stores. Mind you, he was always inventing things. He invented a thing called the smelephone.

EDITH: The what?

COL: The smelephone. It was like a telephone, only when it rang you could smell it. He said it was for the benefit of the deaf. Just shows how mad he was. When they answered the phone they couldn't hear what the person was saying anyway.

EDITH: I know how he felt. George – we must leave here at once.

COL: What?

EDITH: We must leave the camp. I can't stay here a moment longer. Now. We must go now!

COL: But we can't, old thing – we're halfway through the bridge tournament. I haven't paid my mess bill, or anything. And there's another reason as well.

EDITH: What?

COL: I'm the Commanding Officer.

EDITH: You won't be for long if I speak my mind.

COL: What the devil do you mean?

EDITH: I'm having an affair with Corporal Bligh.

COL: *(shouting)* Corporal BLIGH?

(Bligh enters.)

BLIGH: You called, sir?

COL: I want a word with you, sir!

BLIGH: Is it about your stiff front, Colonel?

COL: No, it's not about my stiff front, Corporal Bligh. Is it true, about you and Edith here?

BLIGH: Well, perhaps. I suppose you could think that. Is what true, sir?

COL: That you had an affair with her. Is it all true? That you've caressed her, touched her, fondled her, kissed her?

BLIGH: Well – only bits, sir.

COL: Which bits? Point them out!

EDITH: I can't stay here a moment longer – I must get out of this stifling atmosphere.

(She picks up a small parasol and makes for the door.)

COL: Come back, woman – you've got nothing on!

EDITH: I don't care!

(She exits.)

COL: I'm going to fight you, sir. *(He starts to take off his coat.)* For the honour of the regiment. I may be twice as old as you, but what I give away in age, I make up for in weight.

BLIGH: At least.

COL: Come on, put 'em up.

(He adopts a fighting attitude.)

BLIGH: *(takes off coat)* Very well, Colonel – but only for the regiment.

Cut to: the parade ground, as before.

(The line of men see Edith approaching in corset and bloomers with parasol. The men all start to steam again. Then one faints. They all

faint as she approaches, except one big, grizzled, tough lump of British beef, who stands to attention. The sergeant is next to him. Edith passes them, then–)

SERGEANT: Why didn't you faint, Higgins?

HIGGINS: *(gruffly)* I'm not interested in women, Sarge.

(He spits on the ground.)

SERGEANT: Oh? And what are you interested in?

HIGGINS: Give us a kiss and I'll tell yer.

(He smiles winsomely at the sergeant.)

Cut to: the living room.

(The colonel and Bligh, still with their jackets off, are enjoying a whisky and soda together.)

COL: Much more sensible, deciding not to fight. Too damn hot for anything like that. No damn woman is worth it.

BLIGH: I'm glad I managed to make you see reason, Colonel.

COL: Quite, quite. So, you were fly-weight boxing champ of the Army, were you?

BLIGH: A few years ago now, sir. Lot of water flowed under the bridge since then.

COL: I wish some of it would flow through here. Gad, it's stifling. Just the sort of weather for a native uprising, this.

BLIGH: I doubt it, sir – too lazy, I ...

(A distant banging is heard. A sort of booming thud. The men look at each other.)

COL: What did I tell you? It's started. Gunfire.

BLIGH: That's not guns, colonel. That sounds as if it's coming from the cellar.

COL: *(listening at cellar door)* You're right! *(Picks up large Indian club as weapon.)* Stay here – I'll take a look.

(He goes.)

(Edith bursts in, sees Bligh.)

EDITH: Are you alone?

BLIGH: The colonel's in the cellar.

EDITH: The drunkard. Harry, forgive me. I'm sorry, but it would never have worked. Our positions are so very different.

BLIGH: Well, there's not much I can say to that, is there?

EDITH: It was just the heat. *(Despairingly)* This infernal, eternal heat! Will it never end?

(The cellar door opens – the colonel emerges with a mad-eyed, bearded, straggly-haired man in filthy, tattered captain's uniform. He is on the verge of collapse. He carries a piece of iron piping.)

COL: You remember the Professor, who disappeared with the water pipes?

WILCOX: I knew I could do it! It was all in my head.

BLIGH: Captain Wilcox!

COL: He's been down there for a month. No wonder we've been so damned hot. Damn fool's gone and invented central heating!

(Edith faints, as the professor dances about, half collapsing, and colonel and Bligh restrain him as the music swells up.)

THAT'S WHAT I SAID

(RC and girl sitting up at L-shaped bar. RB enters. Large-bosomed barmaid approaches him. She wears a very low-cut sweater.)

RB: *(to barmaid)* Good evening. Tickle your botty with a feather tonight.

BARMAID: I beg your pardon?

RB: Particularly grotty weather tonight.

BARMAID: Oh. Yes, isn't it.

RB: That sweater looks a little risky.

BARMAID: Pardon?

RB: I said, I'd better have a little whisky.

BARMAID: Oh. I thought you said something about my sweater.

RB: No, no – that's very nice.

BARMAID: Thank you.

RB: Mustn't get the hiccups or they'll fall out.

BARMAID: What did you say?

RB: I said, I've just heard the cricket score, they're all out.

(RB moves over to RC and girl, who had her arm round RC's neck.)

RB: Who's this silly ass with the ugly daughter?

RC: I beg your pardon?

RB: I said, I wonder if you'd pass the jug of water.

RC: Oh.

(He does so.)

RB: Thanks awfully, you dozy fish-face.

RC: Pardon?

RB: I said, thanks – awfully cosy, this place.

RC: You know, if you don't mind my saying so, you seem to sound as if you're saying things other than what you say you are saying, if you understand me.

RB: *(indicating his large moustache)* Oh dear – I'm afraid it's this moustache, it sort of muffles the sound. My wife likes it so, otherwise I'd shave it off, and drown it in the sink.

GIRL: Otherwise you'd what?

RB: Shave it off – I'm sounding indistinct.

GIRL: Oh, quite.

RB: You're a nice girl – do you drop 'em, for a friend?

GIRL: What?!

RB: I said, have you dropped in on your friend?

GIRL: Oh, no, he's my boss. He's an accountant.

RB: Oh, I see. My name's Gollinson, by the way. I sell long hooters to alligators.

RC: You what?

RB: I sell computers and calculators. So this is your secretary, eh?

RC: Yes – we're working late at the office.

RB: Ah! Going back for a tease and a cuddle.

RC: Yes, we're going back because the VAT's in a muddle. Miss Jones is new – I had to sack my last girl.

RB: Why, did she ignore your advances?

RC: That's it, yes. She was a big bore at dances.

RB: I bet this one's a right little goer.

RC: Yes, she does write a little slower, but I don't mind.

RB: I know the type – she's one of the "mad with desire" brigade.

RC: How funny you should know that!

RB: What?

RC: Her dad's in the fire brigade. Well, we must go. I want to look up your skirt and down your dress.

GIRL: Eh?

RC: I want to look up Lord Burton's town address.

GIRL: I think it's somewhere in my drawers.

RB: That sounds like an invitation. If I were you, I'd lurch through those doors and get her back to the office.

RC: I will. I'll search through her drawers and get her a bag of toffees.

(The girl exits with RC.)

BARMAID: Funny sort of chap.

RB: Yes. But let's talk about you. You'll never drown, with those water wings.

BARMAID: I beg your pardon?

RB: You should wear brown with those sort of things.

BARMAID: It's not really your moustache – you're actually saying those things on purpose, aren't you?

RB: Only trying to drum up a little trade, that's all.

BARMAID: What sort of trade?

RB: I sell deaf-aids.

PATIENTS, PATIENTS

A doctor's waiting room. Twelve patients sit round the walls. RB and RC sitting next to each other.

RC: Slow, isn't he?

RB: Who?

RC: The doctor. Slow.

RB: Difficult job.

RC: I know. But he's still damned slow. You've got to admit it. That last woman has been in there so long, I've forgotten who's next.

(A man emerges from the surgery door. A bell rings. All the patients get up and converge on the door. A man goes in eventually. The others sit down, grumbling.)

RC: That's why she was in there so long – she went in for a sex change. *(Bell rings.)* There you are, you see. Utter confusion. Nobody knows where they are. It's enough to make you sick.

RB: These people are sick.

RC: Listen, whose side are you on?

RB: Difficult job.

RC: Never mind "difficult job". It's a difficult job sitting here in confusion with a broken arm.

RB: Broken arm? Is that why your leg's in plaster?

RC: There you are, you see. Show you how confused I am. It's not that I've come about. Good God, no good coming to him with this leg. I'd have been here for months. Set that myself. The wife plastered it. She does all the decorating in our house. She's very keen. She wanted to give it a coat of green emulsion, but I wouldn't let her.

RB: I like it in white. Why are you here?

RC: Been getting pains in my back. Just there.

(He indicates, just above the waist.)

RB: Lumbar.

RC: It is – a dead lumbar. Interferes with all sort of activities.

RB: The lumbar region. Just there.

(Touches RC's back.)

RC: Ow! That's it. How come you know so much about it?

RB: I'm a doctor.

RC: You are? What are you doing here then?

RB: I'm not very well.

RC: Oh dear, I'm sorry to hear that. What's the trouble?

RB: Headaches, run down sort of thing. How long have you had this back trouble?

RC: Couple of months.

RB: *(gets out stethoscope from bag)* Look, lie down across these seats – excuse me, madam.

(Moves woman. RC lies down, RB examines him.)

WOMAN: *(to girl)* What are they doing?

GIRL: *(who has overheard)* He's a doctor.

WOMAN: Is he? Perhaps he'll sound my chest. *(She goes to RB, taking off her jumper.)* It's me chest, doctor – could you have a listen?

RB: Hang on a minute …

(The other patients all crowd round him, trying to ask for an examination – shouting and pushing.)

RC: Don't push!

RB: Get back, everyone.

RC: I was here first.

(They still clamour.)

RB: *(above the noise)* Listen, quiet everyone! Just take off your clothes and form an orderly queue – I'll see you as soon as I can.

(They all take off their clothes and stand around in their underwear, still chattering.)

RB: *(to girl who hasn't removed her clothes)* Hey you, come along – get those clothes off.

GIRL: Oh, me as well?

RB: Of course you as well.

(She does so.)

RB: Now, who's next? *(They all clamour.)* Quiet! Look, we're never going to get through this lot – I need some help.

VET: I'm a vet, can I help?

RB: Marvellous! *(To crowd)* Anyone with pains in their legs, over there with that gentleman.

(Indicates vet, some people go to him.)

VET: *(to middle-aged man)* What's your trouble?

MAN ONE: Hardpad.

VET: Oh, right.

(Takes pills from bag.)

(The girl is now with RB.)

RB: Now, why are you here?

GIRL: I'm waiting for my husband. He's in there.

(Indicates surgery.)

RB: Oh, sorry. You can put your clothes on again then.

GIRL: Oh, do I have to?

RB: Of course you don't, my dear young lady. *(He takes her to a chair and engages her in conversation.)* Next! *(They all clamour again.)* Quiet!

VET: *(shouting)* Could I have a second opinion over here?

RB: *(shouting back)* What's the trouble?

VET: This man's got a broken leg – do you think he ought to be shot?

RB: Certainly not.

VET: His wife's given the OK.

RB: Look, quiet everybody. Listen! Will you please form yourselves into couples and try to diagnose each other.

(They all start to examine each other and talk about their complaints. Some lie on the floor, the chairs, etc.)

RC: *(lying on his stomach, talking to girl, who is examining his back)* No, it's lower than that …

(Suddenly three policemen burst in.)

SERGEANT: Alright, this is a raid. You're all under arrest! Get your clothes on as fast as you can.

(Everybody does so. It is, of course, chaos.)

SERGEANT: Alright – quiet! *(They settle down.)* Now then. It's not really a raid, but we were in the caff next door, and we couldn't hear the juke box for the terrible row in here. Just keep quiet and behave yourselves – otherwise I'll nick the lot of you!

(The policemen exit. All is quiet. The nurse enters from the surgery, showing out the girl's husband.)

NURSE: *(in a whisper)* Next, please.

(RC gets up and starts to go in. The nurse then turns and whispers to the others.)

NURSE: Thank you for being so patient.

(RC turns, reacts to RB as he goes into surgery.)

DOCTOR SPOONER REVISITED

RB: *(as presenter)* Some time ago, we visited the abode of Dr William Spooner, the Oxford Don who, a hundred years ago, was confusing all and sundry with his unique habit of transposing the first letters of two adjacent words – hereafter known as "Spoonerisms". It was he who had proposed a toast to the queer old dean instead of the dear old queen. It was also he who shocked the wife of the new bursar of the college. What he meant to say was that, coming into contact with so many high-spirited young geniuses, she would be soon be as mad as a hatter, of course. Instead of this he said, she would soon be had as a matter of course. And so, in a special reconstruction, we return once again to the peaceful confines of Dr Spooner's house in Oxford ...

(Mix to: a Victorian vicarage – the garden room, with french windows to the garden. Mrs Spooner sits in a wicker chair, sewing. Enter RB as Dr Spooner with basket with flowers in it.)

MRS S: Good morning, William.

RB: Ah, good ray, Dosey. I mean, good day, Rosie.

MRS S: You were up early, dear. Where have you been?

RB: I've been rolling the strose bushes – strolling in the rose bushes. They love so smelly this morning.

MRS S: You do adore your garden, don't you?

RB: Indoo I deed – I mean indood I dee. Nothing makes me gappier than a spot of hardening. But I fear I have neglected it of late – and there is so much to do at this time of year. It's the rutting season for tea-cosies, you know.

MRS S: The rutting season? For tea-cosies?

RB: No, no, my dear – the cutting season for tea-roses. I declare, you're getting as mad as me!

MRS S: Is that what you intend to do today, my love?

RB: No, the roses must wait. The first thing I have to do is to spray my flies against greenbeans. And while I'm at it, I think I'll black my dooberries as well.

MRS S: Oh, that reminds me, I need some vegetables for dinner. Would you mind me a farrow?

RB: Mia Farrow? What has she got to do with it?

MRS S: I'm sorry, dear, I mean, could you find me a marrow?

RB: Oh, I see – a mere tip of the slung. Alas, my dear, I cannot. The garden gate must have been left unlocked. Someone has nip-toed in and tipped my barrow in the mud.

MRS S: You mean tip-toed in and nipped your marrow in the bud?

RB: I couldn't have bet it putter myself; I'll wager it was that villainous landlord of the Wig and Pistle.

MRS S: What, little Billy Humphries?

RB: Exactly. Little Hilly Bumphries. He's jealous of my prowess in the Shower Flow.

MRS S: My name is Rose, dear.

RB: No, the shower flow. The annual shower flow.

MRS S: Oh, I see.

RB: Don't you remember? Last year he sabotaged my peas. He covered them with creosote, and left the sore little pods to die.

MRS S: The sore little pods? Oh, the poor little–

RB: Exactly.

MRS S: William, are you sure it's him? Perhaps it was the bees.

RB: Bees can't open a garden gate.

MRS S: But how do you know the gate was open?

RB: I saw next door's dog loo-ing things on the dawn.

MRS S: Their pet poodle?

RB: Yes, their pod pettle.

MRS S: Pretty Polly?

RB: Yes, prilly potty. That villain! He'll pay for this. I've a good mind to creep over there and put dertiliser on his failures.

MRS S: William, dearest, don't get so upset. I will help you with the garden when I get time. At the moment we both have other duties – our students, remember?

RB: Good heavens. Took at the line! I mean like at the tomb! I've hissed a mystery lecture.

MRS S: And I have a Divinity class waiting. Let us hurry, dear William, and not keep them waiting any longer. *(She takes his arm.)* Dearest! You are my William – the sweetest sweet William that ever grew.

RB: And you are my Rose – the ricest nose I ever picked.

MRS S: But you know – you're much too gashionate to be a pardener.

RB: And you're much too titty to be a preacher!

(They exit.)

The Two Ronnies: The Serials

One of the most popular elements of *The Two Ronnies* were the weekly cliff-hanger serials. Throughout the show's 12-season run, these serials were penned by Gerald Wiley (with one exception, the fondly recalled *Phantom Raspberry Blower of Old London Town*, which was co-credited to Spike Milligan. This was, in fact, adapted and expanded on by Ronnie from an original half hour by Milligan that had made up one of the *Six Dates with Barker* series back in 1971). For various unfathomable reasons, the scripts for these serials have been lost. However, three still remain – *Done to Death* and *Death Can Be Fatal* (both featuring the Barker/Corbett alter-egos of Piggy Malone and Charley Farley) and one of the most popular of all the serials, the futuristic gender-bending *The Worm That Turned*, which of course featured the late Diana Dors as the Commander.

ᴏᴏ

DONE TO DEATH

EPISODE ONE

VOICE-OVER: Our story starts on the morning of the 1st of April – an apt date, you may think, for the strange charade that was about to unfold itself. Then again, perhaps you may not think that. It's up to you. What you think is your own affair. The fact remains that Piggy Malone, private eye and secret eater, was on his way to his office situated in the heart of unfashionable Neasden, over a greengrocers shop in the Harrow Road.

(Over this, shots of large calendar with date – April 1st – people and traffic in Harrow Road. Then RB walking through crowds, eating a ham sandwich.)

VOICE-OVER: He entered the door at the side of the shop, pausing only to acknowledge the cheery smile of the proprietor. *(Terrible ugly scowl from greengrocer. As RB passes, he throws fruit at him.)* And mounted the stairs, two at a time. He was in no particular hurry, but it saved wear and tear on the carpet. *(Close-up on RB's feet)* He opened the first door on the right and strode in – a mistake he often made. *(Still close-up on feet. We see man's legs with trousers round his ankles.)*

MAN'S VOICE: *(gruff)* Oi! I'm in here!

MALONE'S VOICE: Sorry.

(Door closes, feet continue along corridor to another door.)

VOICE-OVER: Waiting for him on that spring morning, as usual, was Malone's trusty assistant, Charley Farley, a failed undergraduate who occasionally rode to hounds, and invariably walked to work.

(RC as Charley, with newspaper. Enter RB.)

VOICE-OVER: Without a word, Charley handed Malone the morning paper.

CHARLEY: Here you are.

VOICE-OVER: Silently, Malone took it.

MALONE: Thanks very much.

(He looks at headline – his eyes widen.)

VOICE-OVER: There, in the paper, was the first in what was to be a long list of surprises ...

(Dramatic musical sting – then: close-up of newspaper – the headline says "Woman found on Heath". Next to it is (quite by chance) a picture of Mr Heath. Widen a little to show that Mr Heath's photo has another headline underneath "Prime Minister at London Airport".)

MALONE: *(sits and reads)* A woman's body was found this morning on Hampstead Heath, strangled with her own garter. The body is estimated to be about 31 – the legs about 28 1/2, and the bust about

44. The police were able to identify the body by a coat of arms tattooed on the lady's back – a unicorn rampant, and the family motto "Ready when you are". She was the wealthy Lady Brimstone, of Brimstone Grange, Surrey – widow of Lord Arthur Brimstone, the Treacle millionaire. Well?

CHARLEY: Sounds like a case for us, Chief.

MALONE: You reckon?

CHARLEY: Certainly. I've looked up the family in *Burke Peerage* – there's a swarm of relatives, all penniless. Any one of them could have a motive. And if she's put all her money into treacle, it's not going to be easy to get hold of.

(Miss Whizzer, a small, bouncy, scatterbrained secretary, enters. She brings coffee in paper cups.)

MALONE: Quite. And they'll all be up there, ready to contest the will.

(As Miss Whizzer bends over desk to give RC his coffee, RB notices her back view – she is facing towards the camera.)

MALONE: You've forgotten again, Miss Whizzer.

MISS WHIZZER: *(putting her hand behind her)* Oh, sorry, Mr Malone. I got up in such a hurry this morning.

MALONE: That's all right. Bring me a buttered bun, would you?

MISS WHIZZ: Righto.

(She bounces out.)

MALONE: Brimstone Grange, eh? Sounds inviting. A trip to the country.

CHARLEY: Yes – you've looked a bit peeky lately – a change of beer will do you the world of good.

MALONE: Anything we ought to finish off here first?

CHARLEY: Nothing that can't wait. Business hasn't exactly been brisk. *(Looking at file marked "outstanding")* Couple of lost pension books; oh, and the Mrs Thompson poisoning case.

MALONE: What, the window-box affair?

CHARLEY: Yes – while she was leaning out of the window talking to a neighbour at the front, someone crept round the back and sprayed her prize begonia.

MALONE: And it went yellow?

CHARLEY: That's it.

MALONE: We can't waste time on trivialities. Drop her a card and tell her to put the whole thing into the hands of a solicitor. We've got a murder to solve. Strangled with her own garter, eh?

CHARLEY: We're taking the case then?

MALONE: Yes.

CHARLEY: I'll go and get the tandem round the front then.

MALONE: It's not much to go on, Charley.

CHARLEY: No. P'raps we'd better go by train, eh?

MALONE: Go and pack – ride the tandem down to Brimstone Grange – I'll phone and say we're coming, then follow by train. We should be just in time to catch the funeral!

Cut to: Brimstone Grange.

(RB and RC ride up on tandem. They dismount, hear laughter, rather raucous, from about twenty people, obviously a party going on.)

CHARLEY: Sounds as if the funeral's in full swing.

MALONE: Better take a look.

(They enter the house through the front door. We see a large table, with about fifteen or twenty people sitting at it, all eating, drinking and making merry. We see shots of various guests and relatives – mostly played by RC or RB.)

VOICE-OVER: And so it was that Piggy Malone and his intrepid assistant, Charley Farley, came face to face with the Brimstone family, surely the most bizarre funeral feast the fat detective had ever clapped eyes on. At this moment in time they were just faces – but faces he would grow to know and hate before many days had passed.

(Shot of RC as bearded old professor, with two white mice in a cage, feeding them with a pipette.)

VOICE-OVER: There was Professor Amos Brimstone, the rightful heir – 72 years old, eminent gynaecologist and tug-of-war champion of the thirties, who at the moment was trying to get his pet mice drunk. *(Camera pans to RB as the Dowager Lady Brimstone.)* Next to him, the Dowager Lady Agatha Brimstone – ex Gaiety Girl, reputed to have been kissed on the lips at Balmoral by Edward VII, and in many other places as well.

(Reaction shot of the detectives. Then shot of RC as the young rip, with his bride – a sweet and innocent type.)

VOICE-OVER: Further along the table, young Billy Brimstone, with his brand new blushing bride, Brenda, was busily trying to brief her about the birds and the bees before bedtime.

(RB as northern tycoon joins RC and bride, raises his glass to them. Shot of RB and RC as detectives.)

CHARLEY: Is this a funeral – or a wedding?

MALONE: Bit of both, by the look of it.

VOICE-OVER: As indeed it was. Uncle Jo Brimstone, the bankrupt tycoon, who, at this moment, toasted the bride and groom, had decided to combine the two occasions in order to save time and money. It was he himself who had designed the unusual cake.

(A shot of bride and groom cutting the cake – it is black and white – half and half.)

VOICE-OVER: Two other pairs of eyes watched the proceedings with mixed feelings. *(Cut to RB as German, RC as frail old lady.)* Nellie Trembler, the Dowager's lady companion, and Otto Van Danzer – a permanent guest in the house ever since he had been flown over from Frankfurt in 1954 by the late Lord Brimstone to act as military adviser in the grouse-shooting season. It was no secret that Otto was madly in love with Brenda, Billy's bride.

(Shot of RC kissing Brenda. Shot of Otto crushing a meringue with his bare hands.)

VOICE-OVER: There remained but three people in the room worthy of a more than cursory glance before the drama is allowed to unfold itself – and they were gathered at the far end of the table, drinking heavily.

(Shot of RC as doctor, Blanche, a voluptuous femme fatale, dressed in low-cut black dress, and a tough-looking evil butler.)

VOICE-OVER: Pike, the sinister butler, Doctor Grist, the family physician, an eccentric, who had often been found in bed with his patients, and wore his stethoscope always – even in the bath, and last, but by no means least, the well-endowed Blanche Brimstone, sister of the deceased, who they said was like Mount Everest, she had been conquered few times, and then only by men willing to suffer great personal hardship, working in groups of three or four.

(Reaction shot of detectives, ogling Blanche.)

VOICE-OVER: Meanwhile, in another part of the grounds, the gardeners went about their duties. No one knew their names, but they worked with a relentless enthusiasm. At present, they were in the vegetable garden, engaged in moving a hole from one end to the other.

(RC is taking the last spadeful of earth out of a hole and putting it onto a small pile. RB is just finishing taking earth off the same pile,

and putting it into a hole which is now almost filled in. They mutter to each other all the time in a rustic way. As soon as they are satisfied that RB's hole is full up, RC starts to dig a third hole in order to get earth to fill up the second hole.)

VOICE-OVER: They worked on, little knowing that disaster was about to descend once more upon the Brimstone household.

(Shots of them working – suddenly a prolonged distant scream – they look up, startled. We cut to a close-up of a knife in the old professor's back, and the scream, which continued through the cut, is now twenty times louder. Dramatic music as scream ends.)

(Shot of detectives – RB leaves shot, going towards where professor is lying face downwards on the table. RB lifts professor's head from out of the cream gateau into which he had fallen – cream and cherries all over his face – he is unrecognisable.)

MALONE: It's the Professor!

(He lowers his face into the gateau again.)

BLANCHE: *(slinking into shot, breathing heavily)* Is it murder?

CHARLEY: *(approaching the group)* Well, it's not arson, is it, dear?

MALONE: *(loudly)* I don't want anybody to leave this room! Oh. *(Shot of the room – they have all gone.)* Especially you, madam.

BLANCHE: I knew this would happen. Inspector – you are from Scotland Yard, aren't you?

MALONE: No, Neasden High Road, P G Malone.

BLANCHE: There's something I must show you. Come to my bedroom while we've got the chance.

MALONE: Oh, right.

BLANCHE: When you've seen it, you'll realise what I've been going through.

MALONE: I understand, madam. Charley, stay here and look after the body. *(Then quietly, in his ear)* If I'm not down in an hour, bring up a couple of pork pies, will you?

CHARLEY: I'll do better than that, Chief – I'll send the Army in!

(RB gives RC an old-fashioned look, and starts to move off with Blanche.)

VOICE-OVER: Questions tumbled over each other in Malone's seething brain. What did Blanche know of the murder? What was she going to show him in the bedroom? Had he got clean underwear on? Had he cancelled the milk? One thing was certain – there would be very little sleep for Malone that night.

(Shot of Blanche, smouldering – shot of RB, gulping. Shot of RC, tutting – body with knife in foreground. Move in on it.)

Caption: Next week – Episode Two "Viewing the Body".

EPISODE TWO

Titles, scenes from previous episode.

VOICE-OVER: The place Brimstone Grange, the date April 2nd, the day Wednesday. Piggy Malone, unsuccessful private eye and Cornish pasty expert, and his undaunted assistant, Charley Farley, a man who said little and knew less, found themselves in the middle of one of the most extraordinary murder mysteries since *The Mousetrap*, now in its 82nd year .... Mr Brimstone lay murdered, a knife in his back and his face in a trifle. The beautifully upholstered Blanche Brimstone had urged Malone to go to her bedroom, saying she had something vital to reveal to him, and Malone didn't need much urging – in fact he'd had the urge before she even asked him. Charley Farley was left alone with the body.

CHARLEY: Stone the crows.

(The door opens and the formidable Lady Brimstone lumbers in.)

LADY BRIMSTONE: That sounds like a very nasty habit, young man. Still, I don't suppose you mean it literally. Just an expression.

CHARLEY: Tell me, madam, what do you know of this murder?

LADY B: Only what you told me, Mr Farley.

CHARLEY: I've told you nothing.

LADY B: Then that's exactly how much I know about it, nothing.

CHARLEY: I see. Would you be prepared to answer a few questions?

LADY B: Certainly.

CHARLEY: Right. I'll try and think of some. Question one. Why did you return to the scene of the crime so suddenly?

LADY B: I didn't return to the scene of the crime, as you put it, I simply came back to get me handbag. And I resent that word, suddenly. With my legs, you don't do anything suddenly.

CHARLEY: I'll bear that in mind. Question three.

LADY B: What happened to question two?

CHARLEY: I'm coming to that. Question four, what have you got in your handbag that you don't wish me to see?

LADY B: Oh well, let me see now. There's a photo of me in bathing drawers.

CHARLEY: Anything else?

LADY B: I think I was wearing a picture hat and plimsolls at the time, I can't quite remember.

CHARLEY: I don't mean that. I mean, anything else in the handbag?

LADY B: No, no, absolutely nothing.

CHARLEY: Very well Lady Brimstone, if that's the way you wish to play it.

LADY B: How do you want me to play it, with a limp?

CHARLEY: Look, madam, I refuse to stand here and bandy legs with you. Now, one final question. Is there a bathroom on this floor?

LADY B: Just outside. Why?

CHARLEY: Don't be personal.

(He leaves room. Lady Brimstone takes out poison. Woman enters – she is Lady Brimstone's constant companion. A smaller-scale version, but equally ga-ga. Her name is Nelly Trembler.)

WOMAN: Has he gone, Jemima dear?

LADY B: Yes, yes. All's clear, he suspects nothing. Mind you, there was one nasty moment. He tried to get his hands on my Dorothy bag!

WOMAN: Ooh, disgusting, I don't know what the younger generation is coming to. Well, I've cut the cheese into little pieces and put it on little pieces of bread.

LADY B: Oh good. Then all we have to do is to put a little drop of arsenic on each one and that will be that.

WOMAN: Oh, I do hope we're doing right, dear.

LADY B: Of course we are. It serves them right for trying to kill other little creatures. One should live and let live.

WOMAN: Exactly, so let's put plenty of poison on to make absolutely sure.

LADY B: Yes, come along then, let's hurry, because there's a programme I want to see on television when we've finished.

WOMAN: Oh?

LADY B: It's all about two clergymen who don't wear any underclothes.

WOMAN: What's it called?

LADY B: The Nickerless Parsons Show.

(They exit.)

VOICE-OVER: And so they went, leaving the room empty and the television critic of *The Sunday Times* wondering whether to quote that last remark as the worst joke of the year. Meanwhile, in a large, comfortable bedroom, with a view of the rolling hills, a woman answering to roughly the same description was deeply engrossed with a fat detective, who couldn't keep his eyes off her bedroom biscuit tin. It was Blanche and she was about to give him a piece her mind, which was the last thing he wanted at that moment.

BLANCHE: Would you mind going behind the screen? I want to change my clothes.

PIGGY: Seems a funny arrangement. Why don't you go behind the screen?

BLANCHE: I'm too tall. I'll show over the top.

PIGGY: I'm as tall as you are.

BLANCHE: I know, but it doesn't matter if you show over the top. You're not changing your clothes.

PIGGY: Yes, that makes sense, yes. Quite.

(He goes behind screen and can see quite clearly over the top.)

PIGGY: Right, carry on.

BLANCHE: I'd rather you sat down.

PIGGY: Oh yes. *(He falls)* Is there a chair?

BLANCHE: Over there. *(He sits over there. He is now in full view.)*

PIGGY: Oh yes, thank you. No, that's not right, is it? Oh, just a minute, excuse me. *(He moves chair to behind the screen.)* Ha, that's better. Now do you mind if I ask you a few questions?

BLANCHE: *(cannot hear him behind the screen)* What did you say?

PIGGY: Pardon?

BLANCHE: I didn't hear what you said.

PIGGY: I said, do you mind if I ask you a few questions?

BLANCHE: Sit down!

PIGGY: Oh yes, very well. But I get the feeling you're trying to hide something.

BLANCHE: Yes, and I'm finding it extremely difficult with you bobbing up and down like a jack-in-a-box.

PIGGY: Talking of boxes, who's the local undertaker?

BLANCHE: A man called Grout. He and his wife run the business. They've got a daughter called Debbie.

PIGGY: Oh, thanks. Pretty?

BLANCHE: Very. Why do you ask?

PIGGY: Oh, I don't know. It's just nice to know where you ...

(Two hands appear from a panel in the wall behind and Piggy is strangled. Dramatic music. Piggy eventually breaks free.)

BLANCHE: *(oblivious)* What's that?

PIGGY: That was an attempt on my life, that's what that was, madam. Two hands grabbed me through a secret panel, wearing gardening gloves.

BLANCHE: Who would want to murder you? No, Mr Malone, that was meant for me.

PIGGY: Possibly. But if you'd been standing behind the screen here changing, you'd have been standing up, wouldn't you?

BLANCHE: So?

PIGGY: Do you mind coming here a minute? Ah ha. So if you had been standing here, you couldn't have been strangled. But you could have been – hmmm. Are any of the gardeners desperately in love with you?

BLANCHE: I've no idea, there are so many of them.

Cut to: the ground outside. Gardeners go about their work.

VOICE-OVER: There were indeed many gardeners employed at Brimstone Grange and even the smallest of them was no bigger than the rest. And underneath his smock beat a heart just as strong, just as lustful as any man in the district, and he loved the Lady Blanche. He would mutter her name to himself as he wheeled his wheelbarrow.

SMALL GARDENER: My Blanche, my Blanche.

VOICE-OVER: Sometimes, because he was an idiot, he would say–

SMALL GARDENER: Blancmange, blancmange.

Cut to: corridor in house.

VOICE-OVER: Only one other man in the household equalled his lust – Pike, the butler. He was a lustful and a stealthy man, in fact everything he ever did was either stealthy or lustful. At the moment he was being both as he approached the bedroom door, behind which Blanche and the overweight Malone were in conference. Blanche suddenly tired and, not quite knowing what to do next, lay on the bed and smoked. Malone, suddenly not tired and knowing exactly what to do next, stood by the door and steamed.

(Cut to: Pike outside the door. Charley creeps up on him.)

CHARLEY: *(catching him)* Looking for something? You're a bit of a snooper, aren't you, eh?

PIKE: Yes, sir. I do snoop a bit.

CHARLEY: Why, why do you snoop?

PIKE: Why, sir?

CHARLEY: Why do you do it, why do you snoop about?

PIKE: Well ...

CHARLEY: Go on, admit it. You like it, don't you, snooping about?

PIKE: Well ...

CHARLEY: Come on.

VOICE-OVER: It was indeed the Dowager Lady Brimstone and Nellie Trembler, her aged companion, who never went anywhere alone unless they were together. They had somehow managed to become imprisoned inside the same outside WC or, as Shakespeare once put it—

CHARLEY: It's the two old ladies locked in the lavatory. Don't go in there. I think it's a trap.

PIKE: No, sir, it's a lavatory. Mind you, it did give me a bit of a nip once. I was—

CHARLEY: Don't pull the chain.

(Lavatory explodes. The toilet seat ends up round RC's neck.)

VOICE-OVER: Once more the unknown killer had struck, this time killing two birds with one stone, and old birds at that. Where would he strike next? Was he a madman or simply a lunatic? Would Charley get to the murderer before the murderer got to Blanche?

Would Malone get to Blanche before Blanche got her clothes back on? One thing was certain, there would be very little sleep for anyone that night.

EPISODE THREE

Titles, various shots from previous episodes.

VOICE-OVER: Malone, the fat detective, and his tireless assistant, Charley Farley, were in a tight corner. Murders were coming at them thick and fast. First the lady on Hampstead Heath, then the professor. Now, two old ladies blown up in the lavatory. Who was next for the chop? Was it Malone himself?

(Shots of professor in trifle, explosion of loo, etc. From previous episode.)

PIGGY: *(looking up)* No, I'm the steak and kidney pie – he's the chop.

(Wider – we see that he and Charley are being served by the butler. They tuck into their food.)

CHARLEY: What news from the doctor? Have they found him?

PIGGY: Not yet. He was seen leaving the house about an hour ago. Probably on a call. What did you find out about the professor's death?

CHARLEY: Well, whoever stuck that knife in his back was a much-travelled man.

PIGGY: Why?

CHARLEY: It said British Railways on the handle.

PIGGY: But surely the doctor wouldn't use a British Railways knife? He'd use a scalpel.

CHARLEY: Yes – by God you need them with that railway food – I had a meal going up to Birmingham the other day …

PIGGY: To kill the professor with.

CHARLEY: What?

PIGGY: The scalpel.

CHARLEY: Oh, quite – he could have given the old ladies arsenic.

PIGGY: With the scalpel, you mean?

CHARLEY: In the bottle.

PIGGY: Nasty. *(They both start talking with their mouths full.)* So the doccah glut my flings round the cormarer in spike of habben at a grump plog.

CHARLEY: Yg. Wib urrw glower in grundeming from ve viggle.

VOICE-OVER: *(as they continue to converse unintelligibly)* The doctor obviously had a lot to answer for. And while the two detectives stuffed their faces, the doctor himself was going about his normal duties in the village.

Cut to: bedroom – double bed. (Two people, completely hidden under blankets. Doctor's black bag in foreground. A bit of movement under the blankets.)

DOC: *(under blankets)* Say ah!

GIRL'S VOICE: *(deep breath, then)* Ahhh!

DOC: Again.

GIRL: *(sighing)* Again.

DOC: I see.

(They emerge. He is dressed, she is not. Their heads appear over the blanket.)

DOC: Well, my dear, there's nothing I can do for you. What you need is a good chiropodist.

GIRL: Thank you, doctor.

DOC: Not at all. Yo can get up. Keep off fatty foods, cakes and sofas. I'll see you in a week. Or I may pop round tonight. *(Phone rings.)* Answer that, it might be the phone.

(He goes to get his bag.)

GIRL: *(answering phone)* Brimstone ninety-nine.

DOC: *(putting stethoscope to her bosom)* Again.

GIRL: Brimstone ninety-nine. Yes, he's here. *(Handing doctor the phone)* It's for you.

DOC: *(putting the phone into his bag)* Thanks. I'll answer it later. I must get back to the Grange. *(He cuts through telephone cord with scissors.)* I've a feeling that all is not well back there. Goodbye.

(As he goes, we hear a voice from the phone in the bag saying "Hello? Hello?")

VOICE-OVER: Did the doctor have some strange premonition that Malone wished to question him? If so, he was wrong. Malone and Charley weren't even within a mile of the Grange. They were on the golf course. *(Cut to: various pretty shots of golf course.)* Sherlock Holmes, when he wanted to think – or to relax – played the violin. The large, economy-sized Malone had tried this, but had been advised to give it up by a leading heart specialist, who lived next door to him. So he had taken up golf and now, whenever he had a tough assignment, he and Charley *(shot of Charley, lighting pipe, with a caddie next to him)* would play a few holes and talk their way through the case. In the strange half-world of murder and suspense which Malone inhabited, golf was the one thing that kept him from going mad.

(Shot of Malone in sand bunker going mad. Then relaxed, peaceful shot of Charley and caddie watching.)

VOICE-OVER: Charley, too, enjoyed the game and, although not in the same class as Malone, still contrived to give his overweight boss a run for his money.

(Charley addresses the ball on the fairway, swings. A perfect stroke. The ball goes straight towards the green. Reaction of RB – he swipes at ball in bunker, it flies out and lands in golf bag on caddie's back. The caddie does not realise. Malone says nothing as they all walk towards the green.)

VOICE-OVER: But the evil presence of the Grange was nevertheless still at hand. The gardeners, ever watchful, lurked behind every bush – silent, primitive and, by all accounts, for the most part, completely insane.

(Shots – sinister, not too comic – of gardeners, melting into the scenery, peering through bushes, etc.)

(Charley, about to play, looks behind him. Sees six or seven gardeners behind the trees. Charlie swings. As the ball is about to land, a gardener suddenly appears and holds out a shovel. The ball bounces off the shovel and the gardener disappears. Cut to another gardener with shovel. He again deflects the ball so that it now returns towards Charley. It lands at his feet. Close-up of RB, smiling. He takes another ball out of his pocket, drops it down his trouser-leg, onto ground. No one sees. He steps back and slices it into the woods. The screech of a crow being hit by a golf ball. Reaction RB.)

Cut to: a wide romantic shot of Blanche in a negligée, riding a magnificent horse in slow motion.

VOICE-OVER: But even as another crow fell victim to Malone's deadly inaccuracy, the beautifully busty bulk of Blanche Brimstone was approaching the two second-rate detectives with all the grace and erotic charm of a petrol advertisement.

Cut to: the green.

(The caddie puts down the bag and RB's original ball rolls out of it, rolls to within six inches of the hole. RC putts. Ball goes to within three inches of the hole and stops. Intercut with Blanche riding in slow motion – close-up of the two golf balls, then Blanche's boobs. RB looks at the golf balls, then kneels down and, using his golf club as a billiard cue, knocks his ball off RC's and into the hole. Blanche rides up. Dismounts.)

BLANCHE: *(bosom heaving)* Oh, I'm out of breath!

PIGGY: *(staring at bosom)* Yes, I know.

(Close-up of Piggy. He starts to breathe heavily. Intercut shots of Blanche, Piggy and bosom, all breathing heavily. Then the caddies. Then a group shot, all breathing heavily. Malone sits down; so does Charley. They are all now out of breath.)

PIGGY: If you've come to see the game, I'm afraid you've missed it.

CHARLEY: Pity. We could play another game.

PIGGY: What, for instance?

CHARLEY: I mean another game of golf.

BLANCHE: No, no. I'd love to, but I can't. It's the doctor at the Grange. Dr Grist. He's ill. Pike, the butler, found him half an hour ago.

PIGGY: Where?

BLANCHE: Just outside the garage. He was in a coma.

CHARLEY: I hate those rotten Italian cars.

PIGGY: He's fainted, you fool. Come on, we'd better get back. Where is he now?

BLANCHE: Pike said not to move him, but the ground seemed so damp. So I put him in my bedroom. I thought he'd be more comfortable in familiar surroundings. *(She leaves them and mounts her horse.)* You'll probably be there before me – this horse is so damned slow.

(She rides off in slow motion again.)

PIGGY: Come on!

(They leave.)

Cut to: a shot of their motorcycle combination. It is covered in gardeners. Like monkeys, they are climbing all over it, curiously peering in at it. There are about eight of them now. Suddenly one of them looks up, says "Sshh!" then listens, then makes a dash for it. They all scatter rapidly. When RB and RC arrive, they have disappeared. RB and RC leap onto the bike and sidecar, and roar away.

We intercut between the slow-motion Blanche and the speeded-up shot of the motorbike. Then cut to the house.

VOICE-OVER: But, in fact, it was the superbly streamlined Blanche who reached the house first. *(She rides up, now speeded up, rapidly dismounts and goes inside.)* Closely followed by an exhausted, overweight detective and a tired-out, tireless assistant.

(The motorbike – now in slow motion – arrives. They get off and float towards the door. Malone falls over, gets up again and enters the house.)

Cut to: the bedroom.

(The doctor is lying in bed, a wide grin on his face. Malone, Charley and Blanche are looking down at him.)

PIGGY: I don't like the look of him.

CHARLEY: No. Ugly, isn't he?

PIGGY: Charley – wait outside the door. Keep guard.

CHARLEY: Right.

(He leaves.)

PIGGY: Why is he smiling?

BLANCHE: I don't know – he was like that when I found him.

PIGGY: *(lifts bedclothes and looks inside)* Hello, what's that?

(Puts his hand under bedclothes.)

BLANCHE: What's what?

PIGGY: A note – pinned to his pyjama trousers. *(Reads)* "Don't weep for me – I died of love."

BLANCHE: So he's dead!

PIGGY: Certainly. *(Indicating the note)* He admits it. Was he a lonely man?

BLANCHE: Oh, no. He had loads of friends – mostly women.

PIGGY: So when he says he died of love, he doesn't mean not enough love.

BLANCHE: On the contrary. He probably means too much of it.

PIGGY: Lucky swine – no wonder he's smiling. *(Stares – then lifts bedclothes again.)* Just a minute. He's wearing my pyjamas!

BLANCHE: Yes.

PIGGY: Aha! Then how did that note get there? You must have pinned it there yourself.

BLANCHE: I ...

PIGGY: What really happened between you and the doctor? Did he really die of love, Mrs Brimstone?

BLANCHE: You really want to know? Very well – I'll show you!

Cut to outside the door. (RC listens.)

PIGGY: *(voice off)* Keep away from me!

(Then crashes, and yells, and groans and grunts – sounding like a cross between a fight and an orgy. RC reacts. He opens the door to look in – Blanche's negligée flies out and wraps itself round his head. The door is slammed shut again. He removes the negligée and we see that he has a bra on his head.)

Cut to: a shot of the house – twilight. The crashings and bashings can be heard over.

(A group of gardeners, muttering and chattering, are digging a hole. We zoom in as they move away – it is a grave.)

VOICE-OVER: Was Blanche the killer? Had Malone bitten off more than he could chew? What was worse – had he brought another pair of pyjamas? Or would Blanche creep into his bedroom and do for him what she had done for the doctor? One thing was certain – there would be very little sleep for Malone that night.

(A long shot of the house – the gardeners wander towards it. The crashings continue.)

Caption: Next week – Episode Four "Blood will Out."

EPISODE FOUR

Titles, shots from previous episodes.

VOICE-OVER: Once again, our podgy and intrepid hero, Piggy Malone, and his slightly more tepid assistant, Charley Farley, had managed to be in the right place at the wrong time, and another murder had been committed behind their backs.

(Dissolve to dining room – RC and RB are having breakfast.)

VOICE-OVER: The latest victim, Dr Grist, had apparently died of an overdose of love, according to a note pinned to his pyjama trousers. Malone and Charley checked through the facts carefully next morning, while tucking into bacon and sausages, trying desperately to digest them.

PIGGY: Fact one, four people have been murdered since we got here four days ago.

CHARLEY: Right, chief.

(Writes on pad.)

PIGGY: Fact two. We haven't found any clues at all yet.

CHARLEY: Right.

(Writes on pad.)

PIGGY: Fact three. There are still five more people left.

CHARLEY: Right.

(Writes.)

PIGGY: Therefore – Question: Was I silly to get a weekly return? Would I have been better off with a monthly?

CHARLEY: That seems to me a pessimistic attitude, chief – sooner or later, we'll get him.

(Pike, the butler, enters with dishes.)

PIGGY: Or her.

CHARLEY: *(looks at pike)* Her? *(Puzzled)*

PIGGY: *(quietly)* It could be a her.

CHARLEY: You mean he could be a woman in disguise?

(A shot of Pike, looking like Jerold Wells.)

PIGGY: Not him – the murderer. Could be a her. *(Calling)* Pike!

PIKE: *(jumps and drops something)* Yessir?

PIGGY: I'd like a word with you, my good man.

PIKE: *(approaches)* Yessir?

PIGGY: As you know, four people have been murdered in this vicinity recently.

PIKE: I had heard, sir.

PIGGY: Doesn't that strike you as odd?

PIKE: No, sir.

PIGGY: Oh it doesn't, eh?

PIKE: No, sir.

PIGGY: Come on, Pike, what are you trying to hide?

PIKE: It's a bit of bacon, sir *(produces it from behind his back)*. I didn't get no breakfast.

PIGGY: Listen, Pike. You were jealous of the Doctor. Admit it – wouldn't you have liked to get your hands on him?

PIKE: No, sir!

CHARLEY: What about Blanche? Miss Brimstone?

PIKE: Yes, I'd like to get my hands on her, sir.

PIGGY: No – he means she wanted to get her hands on him.

CHARLEY: And your hands would be on her as soon as her hands were on the money?

PIGGY: Isn't that right?

PIKE: I'm confused, sir. I don't know whose hands are on what now, sir.

PIGGY: Alright – you can go.

(Pike goes to the door.)

CHARLEY: Oh – one more thing, Pike.

PIKE: *(returning)* Yessir?

CHARLEY: Would it be possible to have another sausage?

PIKE: Oh, certainly, sir. *(He gets the dish from the side table.)* I'll say one thing, sir. *(He looks around furtively, then whispers)* Old Jack knows.

PIGGY: What's that?

PIKE: It's a sausage, sir.

PIGGY: No, what did you say?

CHARLEY: He said "Old Jack knows". Who's old Jack?

PIGGY: Come on, Pike. Tell us.

PIKE: *(at the door)* That's more than my job's worth.

PIGGY: *(a thought strikes him)* What is your job worth?

PIKE: £2500 a year, sir.

(He goes.)

PIGGY: Hey, that's not bad. *(He hurries to the door.)* Is that all found?

(At the door he bumps into Blanche in her negligée.)

BLANCHE: Good morning.

PIGGY: Oh, good morning, Miss Brimstone.

(He is affected, as usual, by her beauty.)

BLANCHE: I'm starving. How do the grapefruits look this morning?

PIGGY: *(eyeing her bosom)* Very nice indeed.

(She passes him and goes to side table.)

CHARLEY: Miss Brimstone – "Old Jack" mean anything to you?

BLANCHE: Old Jack? Yes, he lives all alone in the old fisherman's cottage on the cliffs.

CHARLEY: Really? Alone, eh? Odd.

BLANCHE: What's odd about it?

CHARLEY: Why would he want to live in an old fisherman's cottage?

BLANCHE: He's an old fisherman. I'll take you to see him if you like – I quite fancy a day on the beach.

VOICE-OVER: This chance remark from the beautifully proportioned Blanche, which seems insignificant at the time, was to mean even less in the ensuing pattern of events.

Cut to: a cliff path. A signpost saying "Old Jack's cottage" pointing one way; another sign saying "to the beach" pointing down another path.

(RB, RC and Blanche enter and look at the sign.)

VOICE-OVER: Piggy Malone, unable to resist the idea of Blanche in a bikini, had decided to give Charlie the important task of questioning Old Jack, while he himself remained on the beach to keep an eye on, as he put it, "our principal witness".

(RC says farewell and leaves in the direction of Old Jack's cottage. RB and Blanche run off towards the beach. We pan down signpost. At the bottom is a pot of paint and a brush. A hand wearing a gardener's glove comes in and takes the pot out of shot.)

Cut to: them dashing down to the beach (speeded up), disappearing behind two adjacent rocks and hurling their clothes up into the air. Then cut to Blanche in bikini (slow motion again) as she floats in all her glory towards the sea. Cut to: RB comes out from behind his rock (speeded up), runs towards the sea, takes a flying leap. Cut to: him landing on his stomach in one inch of water. A pained expression.

VOICE-OVER: Meanwhile, Charley Farley, a man who had once played wing three-quarters for the England team, found himself in the unlikely situation of introducing himself to a man he had never met.

Cut to RC and Old Jack (RB), a man who is all hair, except for his eyes, dressed as a fisherman. He sits in an old armchair. RC is on a stool, a cassette tape recorder and microphone at the ready.

CHARLEY: Now then, Jack, I want you to tell me, in your own words, what you know of the murders.

JACK: Er–

CHARLEY: Hang on, just a minute. I'll just check if we're recording. *(Into mic)* Hello testing 1 2 3 4 5 4 3 2 1 Hello, hello, 2 4 6 8 Mary at the cottage gate 1 2 3 4 Mary at the cottage door. If he hollers let him go, England! Bom bom bom England! Bom Bom Bom. Right, we'll just see if that's recorded all right.

(Presses button, listens, nothing.)

Cut to: the beach.

Shot of Blanche with saucy yachting cap on, about to look through a telescope. Shot of Malone looking at a lifebuoy on a hook. He removes it and throws it into the sea. It sinks immediately. He looks puzzled. Blanche looks through telescope – her point of view, panning round countryside. Suddenly, we pan onto a group of gardeners, all creeping about as usual in a sinister fashion. Suddenly an enormous monster crawls into the picture. It looks like a horror film animated model of an insect. Blanche is horrified. Malone grabs the telescope – sees that there is a fly on the lens. Flicks it off. They laugh and run into the water.

Cut back to Old Jack's cottage. RC now has the back of the tape recorder off.

CHARLEY: It's brand new, this is. It should work – it fell off the back of a lorry. Now, let's be logical. Tape recorder. Battery or mains? Not plugged into mains. Therefore should work off batteries. Not working. Why not? Answer. No batteries in it. *(Looks inside.)* Correct. Sorry, Jack, shan't be a minute. I'll have to plug it into the mains. That wall light will do. *(Cut to shot of unlit gas light.)* Oh, you've got gas lighting. Ah. Well, that won't work. You probably need a special adapter for that.

Cut to the beach.

(RB and Blanche splashing water at each other. Intercut between the two – three playful splashes, then close-up on RB as about four gallons of water hit him, knocking him backwards. Cut to Blanche, giggling. Cut to RB getting up, running after Blanche. They disappear into a solitary beach hut. RB shuts the door – the hut completely collapses.)

Cut to the top of a telegraph pole (RC attaching a wire to one of the terminals).

CHARLEY: That should do it.

(He climbs down out of frame.)

Cut to the beach.

(RB is now buried up to his neck in sand. Blanche is draping seaweed around his head. Close-up of RB – he suddenly looks alarmed. Cut to wide shot just in time to see the waves break over his head as the tide comes in. Blanche giggles as she runs away up the cliff path. Final long shot – the tide coming in.)

Cut to Old Jack's cottage (RC with tape recorder).

CHARLEY: Right, Jack. It's finally working. Now tell me all you know.

JACK: Er – ar oi in er oh ha ha wor oi ee oh ugger amar er oi oh ar an all eh her ag roit of …

Close-up RC. (He looks at camera – raises his eyes to heaven in despair.)

Cut to the house.

(Blanche, still in bikini, carrying her dress, strolls up to the door. As she approaches, Pike rushes round the corner.)

PIKE: Miss Blanche! Quick! Come round to the vegetable garden.

BLANCHE: I've told you, Pike, it's all over between us.

PIKE: No, no, not that, Miss Blanche – the gardeners! Oh, it's terrible! Terrible!

(RC arrives on the scene and joins them. He carries a stuffed fish in a glass case.)

BLANCHE: What's that?

CHARLEY: Old Jack gave it to me. What's happened?

PIKE: Oh, it's terrible!

BLANCHE: Come on!

(They all run round the corner to the vegetable garden. We see a pair of gardener's legs sticking out of the soil. They react in horror. We cut to their point of view – wider. There are about eight or nine pairs of legs sticking out of the ground in rows, like plants.)

CHARLEY: All murdered. Buried alive.

(A close-up of Blanche, looking guilty.)

VOICE-OVER: Only Blanche knew the answer to that question.

(Cut to Malone's head, half submerged in waves. A seagull perches on his head.)

VOICE-OVER: Had she deliberately left him there to die? What was the significance of the seagull? Would Malone get the message? The fish that Old Jack had given to Charley – was it a red herring? *(A close-up of the fish held by RC. It winks.)* Only one thing was certain – there would be very little sleep for anyone that night.

A long shot of the gardeners' feet.

Caption: Next week – "Dead Men's Shoes"

EPISODE FIVE

Titles.

VOICE-OVER: The latest disaster to hit Brimstone Grange, scene of many a gory murder in the past week, was the mass murder of the gardeners – buried in their own vegetable patch. Neither Piggy Malone, our fat hero, or the undaunted Charley Farley, his assistant, had been at the scene of the crime.

Cut to Blanche.

(Surveying the scene of horror, she faints gracefully.)

VOICE-OVER: It was too much for the hot-blooded but highly strung Blanche. She collapsed on the ground in a dead faint.

(Malone, now completely dressed, rushes in, takes in the scene, talks rapidly with RC.)

VOICE-OVER: Malone and Charley knew there was only one thing to do – get back to the house as quickly as possible.

(Malone tries to pick up Blanche. RC eventually helps him. Malone carries her off on his own. He staggers, falls, and they both lie there on the ground. RC rushes up. He tries to pick up Blanche, half gets her up then falls backwards, her on top. She recovers, looks resigned, then she picks up Malone and gives him a fireman's lift. Wide shot to show she is also dragging RC by his coat. She strides out towards the house like a true amazon.)

Cut to Blanche's bedroom.

(All three are lying on their backs on Blanche's bed. Blanche has now changed into a tight-fitting cat-suit.)

VOICE-OVER: Three hours later, they were still no nearer to solving the mystery. Malone had suggested that they all relax and make their minds a blank – a method he had used with some success ever since his early school days – and in this, they had found the beautifully built Blanche more than co-operative.

Close-up of Blanche.

BLANCHE: Whose turn is it?

CHARLEY: I think it's Malone's – but he's asleep.

BLANCHE: *(turns to Malone. He sleeps.)* Then it's your turn again. If you like.

CHARLEY: Would you like?

BLANCHE: I don't mind – if you think it helps.

CHARLEY: *(thoughtfully)* I think it does.

BLANCHE: *(looking at him)* Fine. OK?

CHARLEY: OK. I spy, with my little eye, something beginning with "T".

BLANCHE: *(suddenly getting up)* Otto!

CHARLEY: No. That begins with "O". These begin with "T".

BLANCHE: It must be Otto! The murderer!

CHARLEY: What makes you say that?

BLANCHE: Look, Charley, there's only him left. And Pike the butler.

CHARLEY: How about young Billy Brimstone and his brand-new blushing bride, Brenda? They're still alive and kicking.

BLANCHE: How do you know?

CHARLEY: They're in the room next to mine.

(He waves his arm across her, indicating his room. He accidentally brushes against her.)

BLANCHE: That's my point.

CHARLEY: Oh, sorry.

BLANCHE: No, I mean that's exactly what I mean. Otto is insanely jealous of Billy. He's always been in love with Brenda – everybody knows that.

CHARLEY: I didn't.

BLANCHE: No, I mean everybody who is anybody. I think we should keep a very close eye on Herr Otto Van Danzer! Remember – he's a crack shot!

Cut to: a row of eight bottles on a wall. (They shatter, one by one, until only one is left.)

Cut to: Otto with a peashooter. (He shoots another pea. The last bottle falls. He looks satisfied. He sees something and suddenly looks insanely jealous.)

Cut to: RC as Billy and his bride Brenda are walking towards the woods. (They carry a picnic basket and travelling rug. Otto ducks down from sight as he follows the happy pair. He carries a shotgun – close-up – dramatic music.)

VOICE-OVER: And so it was that on that gloomy (or bright) afternoon a strange game of chess was to play itself out – and the overweight detective and his fearful assistant, Charley, were to find themselves mere pawns in a deadly battle for survival.

Cut to RB and RC: standing by a cottage watching Otto following Billy and Brenda. (They creep after him. A milkman sees the detectives creeping about. He looks puzzled. Otto creeps through the undergrowth.)

(RB and RC creep through the bushes. They creep into frame, stop by a tree and creep out again. The milkman creeps into frame then and follows them out.)

(Billy and Brenda are walking along. They see another couple coming towards them. They smile. As the other couple pass, Billy and Brenda turn to look at them, turn, look surprised, giggle. We see retreating couple – she has her dress tucked in her knickers and he has his shirt tails hanging out.)

(We see Otto approaching a low wire fence with a notice near it. It says "Cattle, control-electrified fence". Otto starts to put one leg over it. Close-up of his riding boots. As the leg comes down the other side, the wheels of his spurs go whizzing round with a loud electrical buzzing, and a yell of pain comes from Otto. He leaps off quickly.)

(Billy and Brenda are setting up their picnic. Billy is blowing up two large plastic chairs. Brenda kisses him. As she does so, we hear a strange squeaking noise as the air escapes from the blow-up armchair. He then has to start blowing it up all over again.)

(Otto watches from behind a tree. Piggy and Charley watch from the long grass nearby.)

(The milkman watches from inside a bush. A rather bedraggled housewife comes into his shot.)

HOUSEWIFE: *(whispering)* You didn't give me my change!

MILKMAN: Oh, sorry, madam. *(Gives her change. She crawls out of shot.)*

(The picnic – Billy and Brenda, with cups of tea and plenty of dainty sandwiches, are about to sit on their blow-up armchairs. They do so.

Two loud pops. The chairs deflate rapidly.)

Cut to: Otto, gleeful, pea shooter in hand.

Close-up of Billy eating. (A gypsy violin is heard. Widen to include Brenda. They look at each other lovingly. We cut wider still and see Otto dressed as a gypsy violinist, approaching. He walks round them, serenading them in the usual manner. They take very little interest in him, then Billy notices his spurs and leaps up.)

BILLY: Stop! You're an impostor! You're Otto Van Danzer – I recognised your spurs.

OTTO: So! You have discovered my secret. *(Makes a grab for Brenda.)* I'm taking your pretty young wife with me. I warn you, if you try to follow me, she will die.

BILLY: You – you German pig!

(Sits on ground.)

OTTO: *(dropping Brenda immediately)* You dare to call me names? I demand satisfaction.

(He throws down his glove. It lands in a large gateau. RC picks it up, slaps RB's face with it, leaving a lot of jam on the face.)

(We see the detectives watching, as is the milkman. Billy and Otto go off for the duel.)

VOICE-OVER: So Otto Van Danzer, a recognised crack-shot, was to fight a duel with young Billy Brimstone, a man whose inaccuracy was well known. Even at his London club he had never once got his umbrella into the stand at the first attempt.

(We see Brenda clearing up the picnic, tearful. She throws sandwiches into the bushes. We see Malone rummaging around, finding a sandwich and eating it. Over this, two pistol shots. He stops munching. He and Charley run off in the direction of the shots.)

(Another clearing: Malone, Charley, the milkman and Brenda all appear from the bushes. They look horrified. Billy lies dead on the ground. Otto appears to be standing to attention, gun in hand. Blanche also now appears from the bushes with a bunch of primroses.

She gasps, runs forward to Otto and touches him. He falls forward, revealing a noticeboard against which he was propped up. It reads "Please do not throw stones at this notice".)

VOICE-OVER: What did it mean? Had they really killed each other? Or was that strange noticeboard merely part of the killer's fiendish sense of humour? And what was Blanche doing in the woods? Had she gone there simply to pick her nosegay? *(Shot of Malone and Charley approaching Blanche.)* Malone intended to find out. One thing was certain – there would be very little sleep for Malone that night.

Caption: next week – Episode Six "No Flowers by Request".

EPISODE SIX

Titles, shots from previous episodes.

VOICE-OVER: The latest victims, done to death in the continuing gory story of Brimstone Grange, were none other than young Billy Brimstone, who had been married for only a fortnight – what the Sunday papers would describe as a two-week bridegroom – and Otto Van Danzer, oily German crack-shot, asnd hitherto chief suspect in this bizarre affair. Piggy Malone, second-rate private eye and inveterate glutton, and his more fastidious but equally pathetic assistant, Charley Farley, had witnessed the whole affair and spent a long time at police headquarters, helping the police with their enquiries.

(Mix to police car arriving at Brimstone Grange. Piggy and Charley get out, with sacks over their heads. They bid a muffled "cheerio" to the police driver.)

POLICEMAN: Oh! Er – could we have our sacks back, please. They're my mum's ones she keeps for the onions.

PIGGY: Oh yes, certainly.

CHARLEY: Sorry.

(They hand back the sacks. A third person has got out of the car with a sack on. The policeman spots this.)

POLICEMAN: No, you don't get out here, Mrs Parsons – we're not at your house yet.

MRS P: Oh.

(She is helped back into the car. It drives off. Piggy and Charley wave it off.)

PIGGY: Come on – let's go in.

CHARLEY: Wait, chief – you realise there's only Miss Blanche left? And Pike, the butler?

PIGGY: *(dramatic)* You mean ...

CHARLEY: *(dramatic)* Exactly!

PIGGY: What?

CHARLEY: What?

PIGGY: What do you mean?

CHARLEY: How do you mean?

PIGGY: You said "Exactly".

CHARLEY: I meant "exactly what you were going to say".

PIGGY: I wasn't going to say anything.

CHARLEY: Oh. Well, what I was going to say was, the murderer must be Pike, the butler.

PIGGY: Or Blanche.

CHARLEY: Exactly.

PIGGY: I suggest we approach them both with caution.

CHARLEY: Right.

(They stealthily open the door.)

Cut to: inside house.

(Dramatic suspense music, played mostly on violins, sawing away as the two detectives creep round the house. We cut to a shot of them spotting something. Their eyes widen. Cut to what they see.)

(A curtained alcove. We see the toes of three pairs of feet protruding from beneath the curtain. One moves slightly. Charley grabs a heavy brass ornament to use as a club, as Malone cautiously approaches. His point of view as we move in – a sort of "Psycho" feeling – the violins screeching away. Malone's hand comes into shot, grabs the curtain. He pulls it aside. The camera does a fast pan down to three violinists, scraping away like mad. They are sitting on chairs. They stop, raggedly, as they are discovered.)

PIGGY: What the devil are you doing here?

1ST VIOLIN: Oh, er – we're rehearsing. For the musical evening tonight.

CHARLEY: Musical evening? What musical evening?

1ST VIOLIN: Miss Blanche always has a musical evening on the first Thursday of the month. She loves anything musical.

CHARLEY: Does she, indeed. I must show her my cigarette box.

(Blanche enters, in a ravishing evening gown.)

BLANCHE: Ah, gentlemen – you're back.

PIGGY: Is it true, madam, that you are holding a concert here tonight?

BLANCHE: Yes – but never mind that now. Come to my bedroom. I've got something to show you that will make you go hot and cold.

(She goes.)

(The two men look at each other. Then both make a rush for it through the door.)

Cut to: close-up of letter. (Piggy is reading it. They are all in Blanche's bedroom.)

PIGGY: *(reading aloud)* "I am out to get you. I will kill you like I killed all the others. You will die a horrible death, I promise you. Very best wishes, Anonymous" … Do you know this man?

BLANCHE: It can only be from Pike. He's the only one left.

PIGGY: And yourself, of course, madam.

BLANCHE: But I wouldn't threaten my own life!

CHARLEY: No, chief, stands to reason. Otherwise, if she continued to ignore the note, she'd be forced to kill herself.

PIGGY: Exactly! She could commit suicide and make it look like murder! That would incriminate Pike and she would get away scot-free!

BLANCHE: Except I'd be dead.

PIGGY: True. I see. Right – anybody else got any ideas?

CHARLEY: Where is Pike?

BLANCHE: I haven't seen him all day. You don't think he's hiding somewhere, do you?

CHARLEY: Wherever he is, whatever he's doing, Miss Blanche, one thing is certain. From now on, neither of us must leave your side for a moment. Ever.

Cut immediately to a shower curtain, with water spraying onto it. We pull back as we hear all three of them singing "Raindrops Keep Falling on My Head" and giggling and splashing about, all very happy. We can vaguely see three shapes.

BLANCHE'S VOICE: Well, what shall we all do today? Any ideas?

PIGGY'S VOICE: Could all go to the pictures.

BLANCHE'S VOICE: Oh yes – what's on at the local, anyone know?

CHARLEY'S VOICE: The Hitchcock picture – you know – *Psycho*.

(Suddenly, the camera, which has been slowly moving round the room, picks up someone's head coming into view. Shock stuff. It is in silhouette – rather heavy. Cut to reverse angle – it is a stuffed gorilla, on which are draped the three bathers' clothes. It looks very unfrightening, from the front.)

VOICE-OVER: The two detectives worked tirelessly to safeguard the life of the splendidly proportioned Blanche. And it was here that Charley Farley, failed undergraduate, was to shine – bringing his keen mind to bear on the problem of a foolproof warning system. Malone was content merely to look in occasionally, and receive a progress report.

(We see Charley working at a table with drawings, ruler, etc. Blanche joins him, looking over his shoulder. Then a shot of Malone approaching Blanche's bedroom.)

Cut inside. (He opens the door. A bag of flour bursts over his head.) Cut to Charley, pleased.

CHARLEY: Well, that works alright.

PIGGY: Yes, it's very good.

CHARLEY: Ah!

PIGGY: Exactly. Where's the string?

(Charley hands him the string, then various shots of them both winding string round table legs, under chairs, etc. Music. General documentary feel.)

PIGGY: That's more like it.

(He is surrounded by string.)

CHARLEY: Yes. Now, how are you going to get out?

PIGGY: Er. Don't worry, I'll go through this door and come round.

(He goes out of the door.)

Cut to Charley, waiting. (He looks thoughtful. The door opens, Piggy enters and is hit by the flour again.)

PIGGY: Hm.

(Mix to: even more strings everywhere. Piggy by the door, Charley by the other door.)

CHARLEY: Right. That's definitely got everything wired up. OK. Go out and try it, chief.

PIGGY: No, no, no, you go out and try it. Go on.

CHARLEY: Oh. Alright.

(He exits. Shot of Piggy by the main door, waiting. Shot of Charley entering other door. Shot of Piggy, being hit by the flour again.)

PIGGY: Hm.

(Fade out – fade in. All the strings are gone, the room is free of flour. RB and RC sit either side of the door, with a poker.)

CHARLEY: I suppose this is simpler.

PIGGY: Definitely. Mind you, it means we've got to sit up all night.

CHARLEY: I'm ready to do anything to protect Miss Blanche. Where is she, by the way?

PIGGY: She's er – *(looking concerned)* The last time I …

(They both look at each other in alarm, then rush out of the door.)

(The corridor outside Blanche's bedroom – Piggy and Charley rush out and bump into Pike, who is outside the door.)

PIGGY: Ah – where is Miss Blanche, my good man?

PIKE: I'm not sure, sir.

PIGGY: Then search for her, man! Her life has been threatened.

PIKE: Yes, sir.

(He hurries off, round a corner. The two detectives walk down the corridor. A couple of paces, then RC stops RB.)

CHARLEY: Hang on, chief.

PIGGY: What?

CHARLEY: That was Pike!

PIGGY: Good God! After him!

(They rush back, look round the corner. Cut to their point of view: an empty corridor.)

CHARLEY: Disappeared. I suggest we search for Miss Blanche, chief. We must get to her before he does!

(Cut to the grounds. RC and RB walking, looking.)

VOICE-OVER: It was three hours later when they finally found her.

Cut to a lawn and some bushes. We see a pair of female legs, naked, lying behind a bush. Reaction of RC and RB. They rush forward. Cut to reverse-angle Blanche, in brief shorts, lying on tummy behind the bush, on the lawn, reading.

BLANCHE: Hello, boys.

CHARLEY: Oh, Miss Blanche! I'm so glad we've found you. I've been so worried – when I saw your legs lying on the grass, I didn't know where to put myself!

BLANCHE: Naughty boy!

PIGGY: I don't want to alarm you, madam, but Pike is back.

BLANCHE: I know. I've seen him. I think he's quite harmless.

PIGGY: You may do, but I'd still like to have a word with him.

BLANCHE: *(getting up)* Well, let's all go and look for him.

PIGGY: Any idea where we should look?

BLANCHE: Well, where would you expect a butler to be? I should think he's probably hanging around the kitchen.

Cut immediately to Pike, a rope round his neck, hanging in the kitchen. A stool overturned, Pike's legs hanging down in foreground of shot.

Cut to dining room. (Blanche, RB and RC enter.)

PIGGY: I suggest you get him in here at once.

BLANCHE: Very well – I'll ring for him.

(She pulls bell rope.)

Cut to kitchen – the legs dangling as before. They rise up, out of frame. Cut back to Blanche – she lets go of rope. Cut back to kitchen – the legs drop back into frame.

VOICE-OVER: So the butler didn't do it, after all. And if he didn't, then who was the mysterious killer who lurked unseen in the dim corridors of Brimstone Grange?

Cut back to dining room. They wait. Then close-ups of Blanche, Charley and Piggy.

VOICE-OVER: Piggy Malone and Charley Farley had already agreed to sleep in Blanche's bedroom to protect her. Or was it to protect each other?

One thing was certain – there would be very little sleep for anyone that night.

Caption: Next week – "Two Flies in Her Parlour"

EPISODE SEVEN

Titles, shots from previous episodes.

VOICE-OVER: The trail of death and destruction that had dogged the footsteps of our overweight hero, Piggy Malone, and his much maligned assistant, Charley Farley, continued relentlessly. The beautiful Blanche Brimstone, who was admired throughout the country and whose puppies had won prizes at Crufts, was now the only surviving member of the household. The latest victim of the killer was Pike, the butler ... *(cut to Pike's legs hanging in the kitchen)* ... who had been discovered in the kitchen, hanging from the bell rope. *(Cut to dining room. They ring for him. Cut to kitchen. His legs go up on the rope.)* Piggy Malone eventually located the body and returned to the dining room, where Blanche and Charley waited anxiously.

Cut to the dining room. Blanche and Charley in a passionate clinch on the sofa as Piggy enters. Cut to after Piggy has broken the news.

BLANCHE: He was obviously preparing dinner when it happened. The rest of the staff left days ago. It's terrible. Terrible! What are we going to do?

CHARLEY: Well, we could eat out.

PIGGY: Yes, that's true.

BLANCHE: No, no – don't worry – I'll prepare dinner. You stay here and rest. You must be worn out, poor things.

(She exits.)

CHARLEY: Do you think we should let her go on her own, chief?

PIGGY: We'll have to risk it, Charley. I'm starving. Anyway, I want to talk to you. Why would anyone want to kill Pike? Surely he wouldn't inherit the money?

CHARLEY: Could be another motive entirely, chief? *(Picks up brief-case.)* I've taken the liberty of making out one of my charts. *(He removes a large piece of paper from the briefcase. It is folded many times.)* This shows all the suspects, with cross-references to all their motives, and opportunities to commit all the various crimes.

(He unfolds it – it gets bigger and bigger – RB helps him. Eventually they fix it to the wall. It is 12 feet by 6' 9".)

CHARLEY: You'll notice I've used code words so nobody can understand it, chief, should it fall into the wrong hands.

PIGGY: Good work. I presume you can understand it, can you?

CHARLEY: Oh, yes. It's all in my head. Now with this column, we have the various methods of death that could be used: Balloons, Trouble and Strife, Glug glug glug, Gardens of Babylon, etc.; then on this column …

PIGGY: Hang on. What do all those mean?

CHARLEY: Oh, sorry – Balloons, that means blown up. I mean, a balloon is blown up, isn't it? Then Trouble and Strife – that's knife. Glug glug glug – that's drowning. And Gardens of Babylon – hanging. Hanging Gardens of Babylon, see? It's all quite simple.

PIGGY: What's this – "potatoes"?

CHARLEY: Eh? Oh, that means nothing.

PIGGY: Nothing?

CHARLEY: That's just a space. If I've got any empty spaces, I just fill them up with potatoes.

PIGGY: Oh, I see. And you reckon this chart is going to show us who's been doing the murders?

CHARLEY: I think you'll find if we study it for long enough, yes. Sooner or later, the killer will emerge.

(A close-up of Charley as he says this. A tearing sound. We cut to a wider shot of chart – Blanche has opened the door behind the chart and walked in, giving the effect of stepping through the chart. Dramatic music.)

BLANCHE: Dinner will be ready in fifteen minutes. I'm sorry – did I interrupt something?

PIGGY: No, madam – your entrance was very timely. Very timely indeed.

BLANCHE: Oh, good. Perhaps you'd like to open a bottle of wine.

(She goes again.)

PIGGY: Good God! Why didn't we think of that before? Blanche Brimstone! Of course!

CHARLEY: You mean – she committed these horrible crimes?

PIGGY: Why not?

CHARLEY: But what makes you think it's her?

PIGGY: Motive, opportunity – they're all there. But there's one reason that outweighs all the others, Charley.

CHARLEY: What's that?

PIGGY: She's the only one that's not dead.

CHARLEY: That's true. So. We've been fooled all the way along. Nothing but a big front.

PIGGY: Just a series of boobs.

CHARLEY: It sticks out a mile when you think about it.

PIGGY: I don't know how she keeps it up. Look, Charley, there's a couple of points I'd like to discuss.

CHARLEY: I thought we were discussing them.

PIGGY: No – what I mean is, dinner. You realise, of course, that it is in fifteen minutes?

CHARLEY: Good grief! And she's preparing it, with her own fair hands!

PIGGY: Ever heard of poison?

CHARLEY: Oh, my God! And we've got to eat it – otherwise she'll suspect something.

PIGGY: Exactly! I wonder what devilish concoction her warped mind is going to produce?

Cut to a plate of baked beans. (Blanche hands the plate to Piggy.)

BLANCHE: There we are, Mr Malone. Eat them all up, make you a big boy!

PIGGY: *(reluctantly)* No – that's far too many – you have those, I'll have yours.

(He gives her his beans. They are sitting in a line, on one side of the table. They all have a plate of beans in front of them.)

BLANCHE: Nonsense! I wouldn't hear of it.

(She returns Piggy's plate to him. While she is doing so, Charley steals hers and puts his plate in front of her.)

PIGGY: Please! I insist – they give me indigestion.

(He puts his plate in front of her, taking her plate, which was Charley's.)

BLANCHE: Oh, very well. *(Then, to Charley)* You like beans, do you, Charley?

CHARLEY: *(thinking he's got the unpoisoned plate)* Oh yes.

BLANCHE: Then you have this large helping.

(Swaps plates with Charley.)

CHARLEY: I say, chief.

PIGGY: Yes?

CHARLEY: I think you've got the plate that I started with.

PIGGY: Oh, really? Sorry.

(They swap quickly. They both look satisfied and laugh, uneasily – each thinking they've got Blanche's plate.)

BLANCHE: Well, let's eat – they'll be getting cold. *(They all tuck in, heartily.)* You know, isn't it silly? I've got my own plate back. I remember the little crack on the side.

(Reaction – mouths full, alarmed.)

BLANCHE: Come on, eat up. There's plenty more.

VOICE-OVER: And so our two pathetic heroes ate a frightening three-course meal of beans, beans, and more beans ... *(mix to the three of them with coffee cups)* ... they all retired to bed, with indigestion, whilst outside, fog began to build up in the channel.

(Shot of door marked "WC" – liner's fog horn sound over.)

(Cut to the bedroom. The two men, with their suitcases on Blanche's bed, unpacking.)

PIGGY: Well, I'm not sleeping with her.

CHARLEY: Well, I'm not. I'm having the camp bed.

PIGGY: Oh no, that's my camp bed. I'm having that. You'll have to go in with her.

CHARLEY: Look, it was me who took the trouble to lug the camp bed all the way up here. "Why take a camp bed to a large country mansion?" you said. "It's like taking coals to Newcastle," you said. Well, now your coal has come home to roost, so you can put that in your pipe and smoke it. You've burned your boats and I'm going to lie in it. So there.

(Blanche has entered, in a very feminine fluffy negligée.)

BLANCHE: What's going on, boys?

PIGGY: Oh, we were just arguing about who's going to sleep with you.

BLANCHE: Oh. Why not both of you? It's a very big bed – there's plenty of room for all of us. You did say you'd protect me!

CHARLEY: Oh, oh dear. I'm sorry, but I can't. I haven't brought any pyjamas. Look.

(Indicates his suitcase.)

PIGGY: What?

CHARLEY: You've got yours, I see, chief. It'll have to be you.

PIGGY: Now hang on–

BLANCHE: Don't worry – I know what we can do. Come with me, both of you.

(She ushers them into the bathroom. Piggy, with his pyjamas in hand, glares at Charley as they go through the door.)

BLANCHE'S VOICE: *(off)* Now, give me that. You take that, you have that – and I'll have this – there. There we are.

(Rustle of clothing throughout the speech, then Blanche emerges, dressed in Piggy's pyjama top only. It is big enough to cover what is necessary.)

BLANCHE: *(over her shoulder)* I like wearing men's pyjama tops. Don't you find it attractive, Charley?

CHARLEY: *(off)* It would be all the same if I did, wouldn't it? *(Cut to Charley, who enters, wearing Piggy's pyjama bottoms. They come all the way up to his neck. The drawstring is, in fact, tied round his neck. His arms are inside the legs.)* I couldn't do much about it in this lot.

BLANCHE: I think they look adorable, don't you, Mr Malone?

Cut to Malone, who is wearing Blanche's negligée.

PIGGY: Don't ask me. Look, I feel ridiculous in this.

BLANCHE: It's all in a good cause. Come on, into bed.

CHARLEY: Could someone give me a hand?

(They lift Charley into bed. Malone gets in, but Blanche hesitates.)

BLANCHE: I'll just clean my teeth. Shan't be a moment.

(She exits to adjoining bathroom.)

PIGGY: *(when she has gone)* Why have you got your hands inside the trousers? If she attacks you, you're defenceless.

CHARLEY: Oh no, I'm not. I'm holding a blunt instrument inside here.

PIGGY: What is it?

CHARLEY: A brass candlestick. Have you got the automatic?

PIGGY: Yes, it's tucked in my matching briefs. What do you reckon she's doing in there?

Cut to bathroom. A close-up – striped toothpaste going onto a toothbrush. Shot of Blanche, brushing her teeth. Cut back to bedroom.

PIGGY: We'd better put her in the middle, Charley.

CHARLEY: Right, chief – then we shall know where she is. Anyway, I'm not sleeping next to you. Not in that nightie.

PIGGY: Don't be so daft – I wouldn't ...

(There is a crash from the bathroom as if some jars or bottles have fallen into the washbasin.)

PIGGY: What's that?

(They both rush out of bed, RC still with his arms inside trousers. They exit into bathroom. We cut inside. They stare in horror at Blanche lying there, dead in the empty bath, her legs over the side. She clutches the tube of toothpaste. Dramatic music.)

Mix to the dining room.

(Both men are dressed again. RC sits in a high-backed chair, RB at dining table. They are both facing away from the door.)

PIGGY: Poisoned. No doubt about it. But how?

CHARLEY: Exactly.

PIGGY: We all ate the beans, then we all drank the coffee – and after that, no one ate or drank anything.

Cut to the door.

(The handle turns slowly. The door opens about two inches. Cut back to Malone, unaware of this.)

PIGGY: We all came to bed, then she went to clean her teeth and – my God! The toothpaste!

(A close-up of Malone as he realises. Then a voice, out of vision, says –)

PROFESSOR: Precisely. The poison was in the stripes.

Cut to the Professor, who died in the first episode. (He looks very much alive now and holds a pistol in his hand.)

PIGGY: *(staring)* Professor! But – but you're dead!

(Charley is hidden by the high-backed chair.)

PROFESSOR: It would appear not.

(Reaction on Charley – he cowers in his chair.)

VOICE-OVER: So the Professor had not died after all. Piggy Malone was stunned. Charley Farley's brain began to race – had the Professor seen him? Where had he left his blunt instrument? Why hadn't he followed his mother's advice and become a window dresser?

(A shot of the Professor sitting down opposite Malone at the dining table. The gun is still pointing at Malone.)

VOICE-OVER: One thing was certain – there would be very little sleep for anyone that night.

Caption: Next week – "The Final Act"

EPISODE EIGHT

Titles, shots from previous episodes.

VOICE-OVER: The final act in the terrifying saga of Brimstone Grange was about to unfold itself. Piggy Malone, a pitifully boring, over-fed private eye, and his equally pathetic, underweight assistant, Charley Farley, had at last come face to face with the homicidal maniac who had murdered ten people in six days – a new British all-comers record. The fiendish Professor Amos Brimstone held them at gunpoint while he indulged in an orgy of self-confession, a popular pastime among murderers the world over. There seems to be no escape ... One slim chance lay open to Charley ... *(Cut to wide shot wherein we see that Charley is hidden from view by the wing-back chair.)* ... it was just possible that the Professor hadn't seen him. It was a risk he had to take.

(Charley starts to slide out of his chair without being seen.)

Cut to the Professor and Piggy at the dining table.

PROFESSOR: Yes, I did it. I killed them all – partly for the money – but mainly, simply because I enjoyed it. I've always wanted to know what it felt like to kill someone. Now I know. It's a nice feeling, Malone.

PIGGY: You're off your bloody head. That gun's not loaded.

PROFESSOR: You think not?

(The pistol comes up into shot and fires past Piggy's ear. Cut to the other side of the wing chair – a bullet hole through the back of the chair. Piggy gets up, terrified that Charley has been shot. Charley isn't in the chair. Cut to Charley waving from under the table. Piggy sees him and pretends to be examining the bullet hole as he takes a visiting card out of his pocket and writes three words on it. As he returns to the table, he drops it near Charley, who picks it up and reads the words "Tie shoelaces together".)

PIGGY: That's a pretty nasty hole you've made in that armchair, Professor. If anyone had been sitting there, it could have been nasty.

PROFESSOR: But there wasn't, was there? Which reminds me – where's that obnoxious assistant of your's – Mr Farley? I thought he never left your side.

PIGGY: Well, he, er, he has to sometimes, doesn't he? He's only human. He'll be back in a minute. It never takes him very long.

(Cut to Charley tying the Professor's laces together, then cut back to Professor.)

PROFESSOR: Well, you may rest assured I will be ready for him, Mr Malone.

PIGGY: But the door's behind you, my dear Professor.

(Cut to Charley – he has finished the shoe laces. He pokes his head out from under the cloth and tugs at Piggy's trousers. Piggy looks down.)

CHARLEY: *(whispering)* OK.

PROFESSOR: *(alarmed)* What was that?

(He looks round at door.)

(Piggy, catching the Professor off guard, knocks the gun out of his hand. It slithers down the dining table and crashes off the end.)

PIGGY: *(triumphant)* Now, Professor – it's you against me. We'll just see who can run the fastest!

(Both men leap up. The Professor runs off out of door. Piggy minces after him with his shoe laces tied together.)

PIGGY: *(furious)* Not my shoelaces, you damn fool!

(Charley emerges from under table. They argue pathetically.)

Cut to a car driving away from the Grange at speed.

VOICE-OVER: And so the wily Professor escapes for the moment the clutches of the law. But Piggy and Charley were not beaten yet ...

(Mix to Piggy's London office. The two of them are on the phone. Miss Whizzer is pouring tea. Piggy is eating sandwiches.)

Back in London, they discovered that the mad Professor was on the board of a well-known chemical company. They accordingly made plans to waylay him when he attended the next board meeting, at the firm's head office in Southall the following Friday. *(Mix to very tall office block. Cut to sign – "Brimstone Chemicals ltd, 14th floor".)* They rendezvoused at the head office the day before, and finalised their scheme.

Cut to Piggy and Charley entering building, walking past sign, into lift and out. The number 14 is on a notice by the lift door.

PIGGY: Now, this is my scheme. We change all the numbers of the floors so that when he arrives and takes the lift to the 14th floor, he will get out and see it marked 15th. Now, he will simply walk down the stairs to the floor below, which is unoccupied. And we'll be waiting for him.

CHARLEY: But why change all the numbers on all the floors?

PIGGY: So that he's confused and will naturally get back into the lift and start again. That way we'll make sure he eventually gets out at the right floor. The right floor for us, that is.

CHARLEY: Exactly. It's a marvellous scheme, chief. However did you think it up?

PIGGY: It was in a film on telly last night. Right – we'd better get started.

(They each get out a screwdriver and start to remove the floor number board from the wall.)

VOICE-OVER: And so the trap was laid. Next morning, at precisely 10.57 a.m., the mad Professor, brutal killer of almost a dozen people, walked sedately to a board meeting of the Brimstone Chemical Company – completely unaware of the net that was closing inexorably around him.

Cut to the Professor walking in through the doors. He carries an umbrella. Cut to Charley, hiding behind something, watching.

VOICE-OVER: With split-second timing, Malone was about to take his place on the floor below. *(Shot of Malone, inside lift.)* Fate, however, was about to take a hand, in the shape of Dulcie Latimer – typist.

Cut to Piggy's point of view. Dulcie is bending down, lifting tray of coffees from floor, knickers in evidence. Malone stares.

DULCIE: Could you hold the lift, please. *(She straightens up and enters lift with tray.)* 17th, please.

(Malone looks annoyed, but presses button. Dulcie smiles at him, warmly.)

Cut to 17th floor – it says "15th". The lift door opens. Dulcie comes out, stares at notice.

DULCIE: This says 15th floor.

PIGGY: Ah – that's wrong. This is the top floor, 17th.

DULCIE: Oh. Could you open this door for me?

(Indicating office door.)

PIGGY: Er – all right. *(He leaps from the lift, opens the door, the lift doors close. He just fails to get back in.)* Damn.

DULCIE: Thanks.

(She goes.)

(Close-up of Piggy's annoyance. Shot of professor getting in lift.)

(Back to Piggy waiting by lift. Door open. He steps in as Professor steps out. They both do a take ... but the doors close before either of them can do anything about it. Close-up of Malone. He waits for doors to open. They do. He peers out. Umbrella comes into shot and hits him on the head. The Professor leaps upon him. They struggle as lift doors close on them.)

(Inside lift – they fight. The Professor swings at Piggy with the umbrella. Close-up of the umbrella hitting the floor indicator sign. It smashes. Another swipe at Piggy.)

Cut to a door opposite the lift. Sign on door says "Magnifique Model Agency Ltd". (Five girls in bikinis and heavy eye make-up come out and wait for the lift. It arrives. Doors open. Piggy and the Professor seem to be behaving quite normally as the girls get in.)

(Inside lift – the doors close. They are unable to fight. The lift stops.)

(Outside lift – the girls get out.)

(Inside lift – the doors close. RB and RC leap on each other once again.)

(Outside lift – floor number 6. A little old lady waits. Lift arrives. Doors open. RB and RC on floor of lift, fighting. Reaction of old lady.)

(Inside the lift – the old lady watches the doors close, unable to get in. RB and RC continue to roll around the floor. The doors open and close very quickly as a man bends down to pick up a large cardboard box. We just glimpse him before the doors shut. The men fight. Door opens. The little old lady belts the staggering Professor with her umbrella. Knocks him back into the lift again. The doors shut before she can get in. They fight.)

(Outside the lift – the man with the cardboard box is just putting it down. The lift doors open. He quickly picks it up and tries to get into the lift. The doors squeeze the box and lots of tins of peas fall out of the bottom of it.)

(Inside the lift – the doors close and the man has to remove the box. The men fight.)

(Outside the lift – close-up of the old lady, waiting. As the doors open, she leaps in on top of the fighting men.)

(Inside the lift – the doors close. The Professor lunges at Piggy with his umbrella like a sword. Piggy side-steps, umbrella point goes into wall panel, smashing it. Sparks everywhere, terrible whining lift noise. The men, and the old lady, all lurch and fall over.)

(Outside lift – floor number 3 – lift doors partly open and close once again, very quickly. This happens over several other floors – 15, then 2, then 11, then 1. When they reach number 17, this time the doors open fully and the two men and the old lady stagger out. The old lady staggers back in again and the doors close. Piggy recovers, grabs the umbrella and gets to his feet just as the Professor sits up.)

PIGGY: Have you had enough?

PROFESSOR: It was the lift that beat me – not you, my friend. I never could stand very high speeds. That's the trouble with the world today – speed, speed, speed. Well, thank heaven I shall soon be out of it.

PIGGY: What do you mean?

PROFESSOR: You don't think I'm going to let you take me alive, do you?

(He backs away towards a large window of frosted glass.)

PIGGY: What can you do? You have no weapon.

PROFESSOR: Haven't I? Haven't I? You notice that number near the lift?

PIGGY: What – 17?

PROFESSOR: Exactly. The 17th floor! Don't try and stop me, Malone. *(Shouting)* Goodbye, frail world!

(He takes a run towards the frosted window, screaming as he goes.)

Cut to the outside of the building, wide shot. A crash of glass as the professor flies out of the ground floor window. He lands in a flower bed.

Cut to Charley, now with two policemen.

CHARLEY: That's him. Come on, lads – let's move in.

(They start to move towards the flower bed – leaving the shot.)

Cut back to Piggy near lift. (The lift doors are open. He is sitting mopping his brow. Two girls from the typing pool approach him. They look at him.)

PIGGY: *(heroically)* Yes, I'm alright. Now.

1ST GIRL: Oh, right.

(The girls get in the lift.)

PIGGY: *(suddenly realising)* Don't go up in the lift! It's too fast!

(But too late, the doors are almost closed. Whip pan up and whoosh sound effect.)

Cut to outside the lift – sign says "top floor". (The doors open. The two girls look dizzy. They go to step out – pan down to their feet. Their knickers are around their ankles.)

Mix to Malone's London office. Close-up of large, jovial, loud, well-spoken gent who is talking to RB and RC.

GENT: But what I still don't understand is how the Professor managed to appear to be killed right at the beginning of the case and then to conceal himself in the house without being spotted by the servants.

PIGGY: Simple. He simply grew a beard, which made him look exactly like his elder brother. Then he invited him down for the weekend and killed him. Pushing his face into the trifle helped.

CHARLEY: And of course the fellow was deaf and dumb anyway, which made it a lot easier.

GENT: Well, I'm damned glad you've managed to clear it all up – it's been a messy business. A messy business. Well, I'd better get back to the yard. Lot to do this morning. *(Starts to take his coat off – revealing bib and brace overalls.)* All those apple boxes to shift. Can I leave my coat here, dear?

PIGGY: Yes, all right. *(Gent starts to go.)* Oh Daisy, just a minute.

GENT: What, love?

PIGGY: Would you put a couple of bunches of bananas aside?

GENT: Righto, dear. Well, off we go. Woman's work is never done.

(He camps off.)

VOICE-OVER: And so the saga of Brimstone Grange drew to a close. Piggy Malone and Charley Farley were once more about to sink back into obscurity. *(Miss Whizzer enters with visiting card – she hands it to Piggy.)* Once more it was to be the unending dreary day-to-day tasks of an unsuccessful private eye.

(Close-up of Piggy and Charley, looking at card. Cut to shot of two large-busted girls entering. One big, one small. The men get to their feet.)

VOICE-OVER: Or was it?

1ST GIRL: We work at the nudist camp, and we need protection ...

VOICE-OVER: One thing was certain – there would be very little sleep for anyone that night.

Songs

A PINT OF OLD AND FILTHY

In 1964 Ronnie Barker was filming the Galton and Simpson scripted movie, *The Bargee*, alongside Harry H. Corbett. As a way of passing the time between set-ups, he started writing parody lyrics of Edwardian music hall songs. He showed these lyrics to Galton and Simpson, who were impressed and amused. By the time he was a regular on *Frost on Sunday* Ronnie had penned several more songs and showed them to musical director Laurie Holloway, who suggested setting them to music and making an album out of them. The result was released in 1969 as *A Pint of Old and Filthy*. "The title indicates that some of them are old and some of them are filthy. Or both," explained Ronnie. "And I don't know how successful they were, but they were published and I enjoyed it very much."

NOT TOO TALL AND NOT TOO SHORT

VERSE ONE:
I haven't been out with a girl for years–
Now maybe you think I'm slow
No, that's not the reason: I'll tell you why–
I'm particular, you know.
Some girls are two a penny,
And others a halfpenny each.
I don't want them – the girl I seek
Must be a perfect peach.

CHORUS:
Not too tall and not too short,
Not too thick or thin;
She must come out where she should come out,
And go in where she should go in;
She mustn't have much too much behind,
Or much too little in front;
If ever I have a girl again,
That's the girl I want.

VERSE TWO:
I heard about a girl called May,
She sounded quite a catch.
"She's only five foot five," they said,
"With golden hair to match."
But when I met her in the woods
I knew I'd been sold a pup;
'Cos she was taller lying down
Than when she was standing up.

REPEAT CHORUS: Not too tall ... etc.

VERSE THREE:
Then I met Rachel Rosenbloom,
An Irish girl from Wales.
She had a face like a summer's morn,
And a shape like a bag of nails.
"Could I only see your face," I said,
"I never more would roam.
So bring your dear sweet face to me,
And leave your body at home."

REPEAT CHORUS: Not too tall ... etc.

VERSE FOUR:
At last I met my heart's desire,
A girl called Annie More.
She walked in beauty as the night,

With legs right down to the floor.
I pressed my suit, she creased her frock,
We had a splendid spree–
She was the girl I'd been looking for,
Now her husband is looking for me.

REPEAT CHORUS: Not too tall ... etc.

I BELIEVE IN DOING THINGS
IN MODERATION

VERSE:
I'd like to introduce myself to all you lovely men,
My name is Miss Golightly, and I'm on the loose again;
My engagement to the Duke of Diss was broken off in May,
And he sent me to the South of France for nine months holiday.
Now I'm back in circulation, I've rejoined the social whirl–
I'm really awfully popular, and have been since a girl,
But I do have certain standards, and I never let them drop–
I'm very good at most things, but I do know when to stop.

CHORUS ONE:
If I'm drinking at a party, then I stop when I'm half-tight–
I believe in doing things in moderation.
If I'm dining with a man, I only stop out half the night,
I believe in doing things in moderation.
I went out with a footballer – he really was sublime,
I said "Are you a half-back?" as I sipped his gin and lime,
He said "No, I'm centre-forward," so I stopped him at half-time,
I believe in doing things in moderation.

PATTER:
Oh, I've met some men in my time. I met one last week.

He was gorgeous. I said "Marry me!" He said "I can't, I'm not working at the moment." I said, "Never mind, I can always have you repaired!"

CHORUS TWO:
When cuddling with a motorist, I don't mind if he swerves,
I believe in doing things in moderation.
I tell him, "Take your time and please go easy round the curves,"
I believe in doing things in moderation.
The meanest man in London once lured me to his lair,
He asked for my hand in marriage, so I told him then and there–
I just held up two fingers and said, "That's all I can spare,"
'Cos I believe in doing things in moderation.

PATTER:
I was a nurse in the Boer War, you know – oh, those soldiers – they were always trying to get me into trouble. One night I was in the ward and this soldier whispered "Give us a kiss, nurse."

   And I said "Certainly not!" and he said, "Oh come on, one little kiss," and I said, "No! It's against the rules. Nurses must not kiss the patients – matron's orders. And if I hear another word out of you I shall get out of this bed and report you." I mean, you've got to draw the line somewhere, haven't you?

CHORUS THREE:
I met a charming golfer – oh, he's really awfully bright,
I believe in doing things in moderation.
He's teaching me the game – I played a round with him last night.
I believe in doing things in moderation.
"Now this one is a two-stroke hole," he said, which sounded fun.
"So just give me a chance and I will show you how it's done."
I finally gave him half-a-chance, and he got it in in one!
Oh I believe in doing things in moderation!

I GO OOMPAH

VERSE ONE (SPOKEN):
My father was in the Swiss navy,
Und he yodelled all day, on the deck.
Till one day he slipped, and fell off the ship
Und broke both his voice, und his neck.
In his will he had left me his "oompah",
A euphonium that I learned to play.
And now when folk ask what I do all day long,
I just show my euphonium and say:

CHORUS ONE:
Oompah ... Oompah,
I just sit alone and go oompah.
I find it enchanting, so good for the mind
It helps me to leave all my worries behind.
I go Oomph ... Oompah
It fills me with constant delight.
And when day is done, I find it such fun
To go oompah-pah all through the night.

VERSE TWO:
When I first tried to find rooms in London,
The landladies were a disgrace.
They just took one look at my oompah
And closed the door right in my face!
But one lady I called on was different,
She had not seen an oompah before.
She invited me into her parlour
And as soon as she'd closed the front door–

CHORUS TWO:
Oompah ... Oompah,
I gave her a bit of the oompah.

She found it enchanting, so good for the brain,
And each time I stopped she said, "Do it again!"
I went Oompah ... Oompah,
And now we've become man and wife,
And as long as I keep going oompah
She'll be happy the rest of her life!

THEY TELL ME THERE'S A LOT
OF IT ABOUT

VERSE ONE:
When I got home last Wednesday I was feeling rather queer,
A little out of sorts, you'll understand:
I found a little drinking-house, conveniently near,
And went in with my threepence in my hand.
The barmaid she was six foot two, and every inch a gent–
With a figure like a well-made double bed;
"What can I do for you?" she said, and on the counter leant–
And I stared into her feather-boa and said–

CHORUS:
They tell me there's a lot of it about,
They tell me there's a lot of it about–
Some get it here,
Some get it there,
Others seem to pick it up any old where;
It's definitely on the increase,
Of that there is no doubt;
It's not a thing that you can put your finger on,
But there's certainly a lot of it about.

VERSE TWO:
On looking round my property, imagine my dismay,
To find the fence all broken, by the door;

So I popped round to the carpenters to tell him, right away,
My perimeters had fallen to the floor.
He brought some wood, all full of holes – "They're knot-holes,"
     he explained –
"If they're not holes, what are they then?" I cried.
"Of course they're holes – they're knot-holes," he replied in
     accents strained,
"The hole's there, but the knot is not inside."

REPEAT CHORUS
Well! ... They tell me there's ... etc.

VERSE THREE:
In the old Egyptian desert, there's a frightful lot of sand,
And in crossing it, one's mouth gets awfully dry.
My camel got the hump one day, it got quite out of hand–
Just lolloped off, and left me there to die.
I strolled about for days and days, as thirsty as could be,
Till round the corner came an Arab bold.
I cried, "Water, water, water," as I clutched him round the knee,
And his answer made my fevered blood run cold.

REPEAT CHORUS:
Well! ... They tell me there's ... etc.

VERSE FOUR:
Two honeymooners, rather tired, preparing to retire,
Began to kiss and cuddle on the bed.
His love it was so ardent that the bedclothes caught on fire–
"Quick, dearest! Through the window – jump," he said.
Her nightie caught upon a nail, she nearly fell right through it,
She hung there, with her arms flung open wide:
The lady in the flat beneath said, "Kindly pass the cruet,"
And the firemen down below as one man cried–

REPEAT CHORUS:
Well! ... They tell me there's ... etc.

I CAN'T STAND BY AND WATCH OTHERS SUFFER

VERSE ONE:
I mingle a lot with society,
I'm well known by the gentry, you see–
I often go round to Quaglino's;
And he sometimes comes round to me.
I sat next to a beautiful lady
When I last went around there to sup;
She was wearing a frightfully low-cut gown–
You could see she was well brought up:
She began to converse rather freely,
Her one pleasure, she said, was to cook–
She described what she did with her dumplings
Till I didn't know which way to look.
Just then, an itinerant waiter
Dropped a large ice-cream right on her chest;
As it slid out of sight she cried, "Help me!"
"It's freezing! Oh quick! Do your best!"

CHORUS ONE:
Well, I can't stand by and just watch others suffer,
No, I have to go and try to make amends–
So I held her down by force,
And applied hot chocolate sauce,
And ever since we've both been bosom friends!

VERSE TWO:
One night at the club I'd been drinking
And was staggering home, about three–
Well, I'd missed all the cabs, and decided
It was their turn to try missing me.

As I zigzagged along the embankment
(As I said, I'd had several halves)
On the bridge stood the butcher's young daughter,
I could tell it was her by her calves.
She spoke in a disjointed fashion,
"All the lights have gone out of my life–
I know it's not meet, but there's so much at stake,
I shall chop out my heart with a knife!"
I murmured, "That's tripe – you're a chump, dear,"
(T'was the language she best understood)
She replied, "If I had but the guts, sir,
I'd throw myself into the flood!"
(She was Northern.)

CHORUS TWO:
Well, I can't stand by and just watch others suffer–
And other people's fear just makes me brave.
So like the dear kind soul I am
I threw her underneath a tram,
And saved her from a very watery grave.

VERSE THREE:
As I wandered through a cornfield last September
A couple sat beneath the harvest moon
And I saw the lady cuddling the fellow,
Persuading him to have a little spoon;
First he wouldn't, then he would, and then he didn't–
Then he tried to, and he couldn't, just the same.
Then he wondered if he should or if he shouldn't,
As he didn't even know the lady's name.
No, finally he decided that he oughtn't–
As he'd always wished he hadn't, once he had;
Then he asked her, "Is it really that important?"
And she said it was, which petrified the lad.
Well, she lay there on one elbow, so romantic,
And he stood there, undecided, on one leg;
In her eyes I saw a longing that was frantic
Like a cocker-spaniel, sitting up to beg.

CHORUS THREE:
Well, I can't stand by and just watch others suffer–
It makes me suffer so myself, you see:
So I pushed, and he fell over;
They were married in October,
And they've called the baby Cyril, after me!

OUR MARY ANN IS WITH A HAIRY MAN

VERSE ONE:
There's a girl down our street
Pretty as can be.
Mary Ann's her name and
She never smiles at me.
She likes men with whiskers,
And when she's about
With her latest fellow, why,
The kids all shout–

CHORUS:
Our Mary Ann is with a hairy man,
Our Mary Ann is with a hairy man,
Fetch dad quick,
And stop it if you can
'Cos a hairy man is dallying
With our Mary Ann.

VERSE TWO:
Once she went a-gathering
Watercress for tea,
Down by the brook she saw
A man behind a tree
She knew he was a Scotsman
Because his knees were bare.

But when she saw his sporran, why,
She went quite spare!

REPEAT CHORUS

VERSE THREE:
One day her uncle
Took her to the zoo.
She saw the lions and tigers
And the baby kangaroo
But then the big gorilla
Snarled at her with rage,
She gave a little giggle and
She jumped inside the cage!

REPEAT CHORUS

BLACK PUDDING MARCH

VERSE ONE:
A soldier lad was far from home, a-fighting at the wars
To win the day for dear old England's name.
They'd sent him off to Africa to battle with the Boers
To do his best, though he was not to blame.
He thought of his old mother, a sitting all alone
At supper and a lump came to his throat.
He took up pen and paper to send a letter home
And his eyes were filled with tears as he wrote:

CHORUS ONE:
Send me a lump of your old black pudding
That's the stuff that I love most
Send me a lump of your old black pudding
And a slab of dripping toast

We're fighting to make this old world good enough
For folk who really care
So send me a lump of your old black pudding
And I'll know that you're still there.

VERSE TWO:
A Scottish lad was over there and he was fighting too
And thinking of his homeland far away.
He thought of all the things his darling Maggie used to do
As they wandered through the heather on the brae
And then a dreadful longing seemed to fill his Scottish heart
As he pictured Maggie sitting by the fire
And he wrote these simple words to her:
"Although we're far apart
There's really only one thing I desire–"

CHORUS TWO:
Send me a lump of your dear old haggis
That is what I'm craving for the noo
If I could just get my hands on your dear old haggis
I would know that you're still true
I've never seen a haggis like my dear old Maggie's
And although I'm far from home
Just send me a lump of your dear old haggis
And I'll know you feel the same.

VERSE THREE:
An Irish boy lay wounded in the camp that very night
But the suffering and pain he bravely bore
And he watched the others writing
And he wished that he could write
To his Colleen back on dear old Erin's shore
But his wound would not permit it
So he just lay back and thought
Of the little patch of green that he called home
Of the humble little cottage and the girl for whom he thought
And his loving thoughts went winging o'er the foam

CHORUS THREE:
Send me a parcel of Irish stew, dear,
Wrap it up and send it piping hot.
If I could just dip bread in your Irish stew, dear,
Then I'd know you've not forgot.
There's nobody nearly as good as you, dear,
With yer taters and yer meat
So send me a parcel of Irish stew, dear,
And my life will be complete.

VERSE FOUR:
They're fighting to make this old world
Good enough to live in, side by side,
So with yer stew and yer haggis and yer old black pudding
You can keep them satisfied.

NOT ROUND HERE

VERSE ONE:
This village is a friendly place – I live with Mrs Meek,
And so do seven other men as well;
She keeps a little lodging house – I moved in Wednesday week –
And I'm very well looked after – you can tell.
There's nothing that I lack, except one thing; that is to say,
An object usually found beside the bed.
So to the nearest household stores I trotted, straight away,
But when I told them what it was, they said–

CHORUS ONE:
Oh, you won't get those round here!
No, you won't get those round here;
Well, there isn't any call for them – round here.
Why not just forget about them?
You're much better off without them!
No, you won't get no alarm-clocks, not round here!

VERSE TWO:

One sunny morning, Daisy Jones leapt gaily out of bed,
And went to spend a weekend on a yacht;
The sea-breeze blew her skirts about, and Daisy, blushing red,
Became aware of something she'd forgot–
A part of her apparel that she couldn't be without,
And still appear a lady, so to speak;
So to the nearest draper's shop she went, and blurted out
Her shy request, and heard the draper shriek–

CHORUS TWO:

Oh, you won't get those round here!
No, you won't get those round here;
Well, there isn't any call for them – round here.
Why not just forget about them?
You're much better off without them!
Not handkerchiefs with lace on, not round here!

VERSE THREE:

Young Archibald was getting wed to lovely Betty Blue,
The poor chap was so scared he could have died!
He trembled when he thought of all the things he'd have to do
On the day that Betty Blue became his bride.
Our hero's tum felt absolutely full of butterflies
As at the local chemist's shop he called:
He asked for what he wanted, with a glazed look in his eyes,
And the girl behind the counter loudly bawled–

CHORUS THREE:

Oh, you won't get those round here!
No, you won't get those round here;
Well, there isn't any call for them – round here.
Why not just forget about them?
You're much better off without them!
No! Not stone hot-water bottles! Not round here!

I PUT IT IN THE HANDS OF MY SOLICITOR

VERSE ONE:
I've always been a careful man – I don't go out in fog;
I don't believe in saying "Boo" to geese;
I don't converse with Irishmen, I never stroke a dog,
And I always raise my hat to the police.
And so when trouble comes my way, I do not fuss or shout,
I simply carry out this little plan;
I just put on my ta-ta, I go forth, and I seek out
The opinion of a proper legal man;

CHORUS ONE:
And I put it in the hands of my solicitor–
Yes, I put it in the hands of my solicitor.
So if trouble troubles you
You will know just what to do,
Simply put it in the hands of your solicitor.

VERSE TWO:
I ventured out one Friday morn when no one was about,
To buy a pound of apples, for a tart;
I was edging down the High Street, when I heard the butcher shout,
As round the corner rushed his horse and cart.
It hit a stone, the cart collapsed, the horse dropped to the ground,
And something nasty hit me in the eye;
It proved to be a piece of tripe, marked "one and eight a pound";
It was sticky; it was horrid; it was high.

CHORUS TWO:
So I put it in the hands of my solicitor
Yes, I put it in the hands of my solicitor–
And the butcher went to "Clink"

For creating such a stink,
When I put it in the hands of my solicitor.

VERSE THREE:
One day Miss Flo, a shapely lass, whilst on the river bank,
Removed her clothes and dived in, pleasure bent–
A passing navvy spied her skirt, and took it, for a prank.
And wrapped his dinner up in it, and went.
This thoughtless crime was soon revealed, poor Flo came to a stop
While still half-dressed – imagine her despair!
She had her blouse and feather-boa to cover up her top,
But she'd nothing left to cover her – elsewhere.

CHORUS THREE:
So she put it in the hands of her solicitor
(spoken) Yes, the whole thing.
She put it in the hands of her solicitor;
Having carefully weighed her case,
He then sued for loss of face!
When she put it in the hands of her solicitor.

ALL SORTS

VERSE ONE:
Off for a week at the seaside,
Oh, what a jolly affair!
Off for a pint, and a paddle–
All sorts of folk will be there.
Last year I stayed at Miss Knocker's;
Really, the food was a crime–
Sausages; all shapes and sizes,
That's what she served all the time:

CHORUS ONE:
There were small ones, tall ones, rolled up in a ball ones,

Long ones, strong ones, horrible and high,
Pale ones, frail ones, thereby hangs a tale ones,
Red ones, dead ones, and ones that wouldn't die.
Edible, treadable, some that were incredible,
Bashed ones, mashed ones, not a pretty sight;
Tangled, mangled, very nearly strangled,
Washed ones, squashed ones, you got 'em every night.

VERSE TWO:
Out for a blow in the evening,
Stroll down the prom after dark;
Down past the pier and the lighthouse,
Then take a turn round the park;
They say all the world loves a lover,
In the park that is certainly true–
They are so busy loving each other,
That you've hardly got room to get through!

CHORUS TWO:
There are slim ones, grim ones, pretty little prim ones,
Shy ones, sly ones, fancy ones and plain,
Rough ones, tough ones, cannot get enough ones,
Some who hadn't been before, and wouldn't come again.
Squat ones, hot ones, give me all you've got ones,
Game ones, tame ones, putting up a fight–
Vast ones, fast ones, try to make it last ones,
Everybody spooning on a moonlit night.

VERSE THREE:
Dow for a dip in the Briny!
Laughing and splashing about.
Watching the girls in the water,
Waiting for them to come out.
Stroll past the back of a beach hut,
Glimpsing the ladies behind;
All in their best bathing-dresses,
Each one a different kind:

CHORUS THREE:
There are green ones, lean ones, stringy runner-bean ones,
Black ones, slack ones, barrels and balloons–
Fat ones, flat ones, welcome-on-the-mat ones,
Tiny little orange ones, and big full moons;
Square ones, bare ones, toss-'em-in-the-air ones,
Bright ones, tight ones, lollipops and lumps;
Town ones, brown ones, wobbling up and down ones,
Dainty little spotted ones, and great big bumps.

CODA:
It takes all sorts to make a world
Or so they always say–
And down by the sea all sorts you'll see,
On a seaside holiday!

BILLY PRATT'S BANANAS

VERSE ONE:
Little Billy Pratt, what a funny fellah,
Sold bananas on the street, they were so big and yellah
They soon became quite famous and wherever people meet
They vowed they were the ripest and the best they'd ever ate,
And now throughout the land you'll find them near at hand
You'll see them in the Café Royale if you go there to sup,
Whenever men and women meet, they're always popping up,
You don't win silver cups no more at races and gym-kha-nas,
The prize is now a handful of young Billy Pratt's bananas.

VERSE TWO:
You'll find them in the nicest homes, at court they're "just the
    stuff".
They do say that his Majesty just can't get enough.
I know a wealthy widow in the better part of Ealing

And every time I visit her I get a lovely feeling.
I drink her fine old brandy and I smoke her fine Havanas
And all I give her in return are Billy Pratt's bananas.

VERSE THREE:
I took Mary Jane to church, it was a lovely wedding,
We'd been betrothed for fourteen years to save up for the bedding,
The folks all started throwing rice, which very nearly struck me.
One chap threw milk and sugar, and an Indian threw some
     chutney.
They wrote "Just Married" on my back, they played all sorts of
     tricks,
They nailed my topper to the floor, they filled our bags with
     bricks.
But still the worst was yet to come, I gave my bride a kiss
Then climbed the hill to Bedfordshire to start our wedded bliss.
"Oh Jack," she said as she undressed, "what's in your pyjamas?"
And I found out that it was one of little Billy Pratt's bananas.

BANG, CRASH, OOH, AH ...

VERSE ONE:
I live
Down in Peckham Rye
17 Canal Street
It's a proper "pals" street
We're all
Friendly as can be
One big happy family.
But the
People next to us
Had a little daughter
Proper little snorter.
She would

Fight with all the boys
My! You should have heard the noise
Every day you'd hear her in her old back yard
Knock the living daylights out of some young card ...

CHORUS:
Bash, Crash,
Ooh, Ah,
Whizz, bang, ding, dong. There they go again.
Grunts, groans, cries, moans.
Leave him alone, girl, do!

VERSE TWO:
That was
Twenty years ago
Now she's quite a big girl
Doesn't care a fig girl.
She got
Married last July
To a fellah six foot high.
But she
Hasn't changed a bit.
When they have row, why,
You should see the fur fly.
Poor chap
Doesn't stand a chance,
She's leading him a right old dance.
Every night she starts as soon as he comes in
Giving him a licking with the rolling-pin.

REPEAT CHORUS

VERSE THREE:
Mind you
I'll say this for her,
Though her temper's strong, it
Doesn't last for long, it
Soon e–

vaporates away,
Long before the break of day.
When they
Wander up to bed
She's apologising,
He's philosophising.
Then they
Start to bill and coo,
Just like married couples do.
But oh dear me, this doesn't mean we get a peaceful night—
The noise when they are making up is worse than when they fight!

REPEAT CHORUS.

NELL OF THE YUKON

My tale is a weird one – 'twas found, long ago, In a book on my
    Grandpappy's shelf;
So hush while I tell it, and don't make a sound,
'Cos I'd want to hear it myself.
It was writ in the days when the Yukon was rich,
And the miners got drunk every night.
It was writ all in red, by my old Uncle Jed,
'Cos he was the one as could write.
Now the story begins with a quarrel, one night,
Between Jed and his pretty wife, Nell;
She'd lost all his dough at the gambling saloon,
And one of her garters as well.
Now Nell was a gal with a wonderful shape;
She could hit a spitoon at ten paces;
When she went on the town, she wore a tight gown,
And was seen in all the right places.
Well, she'd come home that night, just a little bit tight,
And she threw off her clothes in disgust.
"What's the matter?" said Jed, and she drunkenly said

As she undid her corset, "You're bust!"
Now Jed knew what she meant, all his gold she had spent,
And he sat there awhile, making faces;
Then as she bent over to unlace her boots,
He gave her a belt, with his braces.
Nell gave a great jump, with her hand to her rump,
And a yell all Alaska could hear,
Then she made a quick run, and she snatched up Jed's gun,
And she poked it inside of Jed's ear.
"That's the finish," said Nell, "I've had all I can take,
Do you hear me? – Get out of my sight!"
Well, old Jed could hear – and the gun in his ear
Made him hear even better that night.
So he quitted the shack, and he never looked back,
And he set out to search for more gold:
But his luck it was out, and he wandered about
Till at last he was dying of cold.
So he dragged himself into a nearby saloon,
Which was known as the "Barrel of Glue".
It was one of those joints where the men are all men,
And most of the women are, too.
The place was a gambling hell, it was clear;
Every man jack was betting and boozing–
Three miners were winning a strip poker game,
And a girl with no clothes on was losing.
Jed sat down at a table and bought himself in
By producing his very last dollar;
And he started to deal with hope in his heart,
And three aces under his collar.
And he won thick and fast; when the evening was past,
He owned all the gold on the table–
As well as six mines, and a three-quarter share
In a Mexican showgirl called Mabel.
Then in walked Black Lou, with a sackful of gold,
And he challenged poor Jed, with a leer–
"One cut and one call, and the winner takes all,
And the loser must buy all the beer."
What could Jed do? He hated Black Lou,

As everyone did in those parts;
So Jed shuffled the cards, and both players cut,
And both players cut – Ace of Hearts!
Then up jumped Black Lou, and his face went bright blue,
(Which astonished a passing physician)
And he used a foul word that no one had heard
Since the time of the Great Exhibition.
"You cheated, you swine!" said Lou with a whine,
As he grabbed Uncle Jed round the neck;
And he started to squeeze, till Jed dropped to his knees,
And with one final wheeze, hit the deck.
The whole saloon froze as Black Lou drew his gun.
"Alright, stranger!" said he. "Have it your way."
When in rushed a woman – and as Lou turned round,
She spat straight in his eye, from the doorway.
It was Nell! There she stood, and she really looked good
As she grabbed Jed, and rushed him outside–
And they didn't stop running for seven long miles
Till they found themselves some place to hide.
'Twas a room booked by Nell in a sleazy hotel,
A dollar-a-night double-roomer.
It was built out of driftwood, and named "The Savoy"
By some guy with a quick sense of humour.
Well, they flopped on the bed – "Thank the Lord," said old Jed,
"My gambling days are behind me,
But I'm puzzled, dear Nell, and I want to hear tell,
How in hell's name you managed to find me?"
"I've been wandering too, all around, just like you,"
Said Nell, "and the thought makes me wince;
And the reason, my dear, was that whack on the rear –
I just ain't sat down, ever since."
And they lay there awhile, then Jed, with a smile
Said, "I'll never more leave this old town–
We'll find peace, you and I" – but he got no reply,
For young Nell was a-sleeping – face down.